PENGUIN BOOKS
FEELING YOU'RE BEHIND

Peter Nichols was born in Bristol in 1927 and, apart from two-and-a-half years in the RAF, lived there until his early twenties.

He is the author of over twenty television plays including *Walk on the Grass*, *Ben Spray*, *The Gorge*, *Hearts and Flowers* and *The Common*; of five feature films; and of the following stage plays: *A Day in the Death of Joe Egg*, *The National Health*, *Forget-me-not Lane*, *Chez Nous*, *The Freeway*, *Privates on Parade*, *Passion Play* and *Poppy*. These have won him four *Evening Standard* Drama Awards, the Society of West End Theatres' Best Comedy and Best British Musical Award and an Ivor Novello for the Best Musical. He has directed the Greenwich revival of *A Day in the Death of Joe Egg*, the Guthrie Theatre production of *The National Health* and the premiere of *Born in the Gardens* for the Bristol Old Vic.

Peter Nichols is married with three children, and lives in London and Shropshire.

PETER NICHOLS

FEELING YOU'RE BEHIND

Penguin Books

Penguin Books Ltd, Harmondsworth, Middlesex, England
Viking Penguin Inc., 40 West 23rd Street, New York, New York 10010, U.S.A.
Penguin Books Australia Ltd, Ringwood, Victoria, Australia
Penguin Books Canada Ltd, 2801 John Street, Markham, Ontario, Canada L3R 1B4
Penguin Books (N.Z.) Ltd, 182–190 Wairau Road, Auckland 10, New Zealand

First published by Weidenfeld & Nicolson 1984
Published in Penguin Books 1985

Made and printed in Great Britain by
Richard Clay (The Chaucer Press) Ltd, Bungay, Suffolk
Typeset in Century Schoolbook

To Violet my mother
Thelma my wife
and Peggy my agent

Contents

Illustrations

Part One Boy

There is no such thing as forgetting. The secret
inscriptions are waiting to be revealed when the
obscuring daylight shall have withdrawn.

Thomas de Quincey

1 Family Trees

No sooner had my car's engine died than the double garage doors were opened on to the pavement and the present owner of our family house appeared.

'Mind you don't park there,' – in an accent I knew to be Polish – 'I got to be bringing a car out here.'

It was clear that keeping a way out on to the avenue is still a full-time job, as it had been in his latter years for my father. The Pole was lying in wait for untidy parkers much as Dad had done when, in the late 1950s, technical college students had begun cramming the kerbs with their vans and motorbike combinations. A sad, symptomatic decline from the days when ours had been The Only Car In The Avenue.

The Pole retreated into the backyard, satisfied that his way was clear. I crossed York Avenue to photograph the house from the far side. He had added two dormer windows, boarded up the greenhouse where Dad died, and painted the external rendering *eau-de-Nil*, a shade Dad much admired – mostly for the chance it gave him to pass on another scrap of useless information.

'Waters of the Nile, boy –' (he was still calling me Boy in the mid-1960s, by which time I was myself the father of three children with another on the way).

One of his last domestic dreams was to paint the banisters *eau-de-Nil*, a gallon of which he had got dirt-cheap in a clearance sale. This was never realized. He had no sooner started than he tipped the whole pot down the stairs, staining the brown carpet for ever. His attempts at DIY always finished with my mother calling The Proper Man.

Focusing my Nikkormat, I saw that the word Palatine had been picked out in white, an act Dad would have approved. His letter headings always had it, above the address, in nearly illegible Gothic script. 'Notice that, boy? Not just the number and street but the *name* of the house. And – listen to this, Violet,' as my mother started talking across him, 'pay attention to the Old Man, you might learn something useful. What does Palatine mean?'

'Something to do with the Jews?'

'Go to the bottom of the class, Violet. What about Buzfuz? Don't make those idiotic faces when I'm speaking to you, boy. Palatine. I copied it from the dictionary . . . here. . . .'

And while he drew a torn-off fragment from his wallet, separating it from a wad of scraps and cuttings, I would writhe with rage and remind myself that a Jerry called Goethe had refused to believe he could be his father's son, consoled by the hope that a wandering nobleman had sired him during some rapacious Grand Tour. But such a fantasy was not for me. Dukes were corny and had no chins and talked funny and were never seen in north-east Bristol anyway. Film stars possibly? Cary Grant came back regularly to visit his birthplace and childhood streets not a mile away. Not very likely, though. I had my father's nose, jutting jaw and pillar-box mouth.

'Palatine! You listening, boy? A lord having sovereign power over a realm, province or dependancy of an Empire. In other words, a Big Cheese! The Master of the House, the great R.G.N., Richard George Nichols, the first and foremost! Pay attention, noodle, take your hands out of your pockets.'

The new snapshot I took that day shows that the laburnums have gone from either side the front door, where all my childhood their golden chains shone through the stained-glass of the lobby. The back garden is now bare, no trace remaining of the five apple trees that served me for the rigging of galleons, the oaks of Sherwood Forest, the bamboo of Tarzan's jungle – any landscape my dreams required. My earliest memory is of Eden. A girl cousin was lured into the lowest branches of a Bramley seedling and persuaded to show me hers if I showed her mine. It is a mystery why, without husbandry or blight prevention, without pruning by a Proper Man, several of these handicapped trees produced year after year prodigal harvests of eaters and cookers, later to be set out in rows on pages of the *Daily Herald* spread in one of our two attics. These lofts had no dormers then, only one glass tile each in the sloping ceiling. A fragrance of apples hung about the upper floors, prevailing over the lavender furniture-polish my mother applied to her walnut bedroom suite. Palatine is a corner house with windows on both the main Ashley Down Road and its tributary York Avenue and the front rooms enjoy sweeping, panoramic views of Muller's Orphanage. Or, my new photograph reminds me, *would* have enjoyed, had the windows not been – then, as now – festooned with yards of net. Wartime pictures show, behind the smiling figures of my mother and grandmother, the front bay-windows criss-crossed with strips of sticky paper against the blast of bombs that never fell.

4

The orphanages now house a technical college, massive roughstone mid-Victorian structures in the Georgian style, a monument to Georg Muller's belief in God as sufficient for all purposes, temporal and spiritual – grim blocks that frowned over my childhood, a Dotheboys Hall unchanged till the outbreak of the Second War. By pulling aside the net curtains, I could watch from the bedroom windows the orphan boys toiling like peasants on the vegetable plots, later a student car park. They lived in a world apart but always present, trespassing into *our* streets in neat grey-suited crocodiles, with cropped heads and eager smiles. The smiles were trying to say 'hullo', which was forbidden. To real children like us, they were only slightly better off than the outings of Mongols from asylums at nearby Fishponds, with their mad greetings that turned my bowels to water. When my brother Geoffrey and I were especially disobedient, my grandma would threaten us with: 'Little buggers! I'll get you put in the orphanage!' If this frightened Geoffrey, I would explain to him that not being orphans we weren't eligible and we'd play up our indulgent grandma all the more.

'You wicked devils, you'd like to see me in Fishponds!' she'd finally cry. Or sometimes Doctor Fox's, a madhouse of her childhood. She knew very well we wanted no such thing for she, my mother's mother, was my refuge when I felt confused by my parents' complexity. We always called her Nanny or Nan and I was amazed to learn from books later that toffs had nannies too. But, it turned out, toffs' nannies weren't their grandmas but paid servants who answered similar emotional needs.

Muller's must have been the first 'Home' in Ashley Down, but others had followed. The neighbourhood was full of them – Horfield Prison (where the last hanging took place in the 1960s); the Glosters' Barracks; and, at the other extreme, the asylums with their pastoral names left over from the great houses they had once been – Purdown, Glenside, Manor Park and Meadowsweet. R.G.N. noticed none of this – only the County Cricket Ground beyond Muller's, the Memorial Rugby Ground and, beside the gas works, Bristol Rovers' football stadium. He often said that he lived in a fine house in a beautiful part of the world. The more my mother implored him to move to a nice bungalow in Westbury-on-Trym, the more he praised Ashley Down.

'Where else on earth could you find the Australians playing Gloucestershire not a stone's throw from your house? Or catch the train to South Wales? Or within a short walk enjoy God's good air and the wonderful view from Horfield Common?'

'Or look out for the umpteenth time at that blooming orphan house?' Vi would ask.

5

'A darn sight preferable to looking out on a never-ending parade of funerals!' – a reference to one of the miserable Sundays we spent looking at houses for sale in genteel Falcondale Road. Their pebbledash and half-timbering appealed to all of us except my father.

'Mum, there's a lovely swing in the garden,' I shouted one such after-noon, thundering up the uncarpeted stairs to the bedroom where they stood locked in conflict.

'I thought you'd like that,' Violet said. 'You could play on it all day long. And did you notice the serving-hatch between the kitchen and the dining-room? No nasty steps to climb like we've got at home.'

'The garden's big enough to play French cricket,' I said, as much towards my father's back as to my mother. He stood in the bay window glowering at the street and spoke without turning.

'Violet –'

'Yes?'

'What's that building opposite?'

'Where?' my mother said, joining him. 'Oh. The public library. Nice and handy for Peter and Geoffrey when they do their exams.'

'In case it had escaped your notice, Vi, Yours Truly *buys* all the books these two noodles are ever liable to need for their exams. And what's wrong with the Grammar School Library? Don't walk away when I'm talking to you, Buzfuz! Stay where you are.'

'What for?'

'What for? What's "What for?" Looks to me as though you could read a few more books of the right kind. Until you learn not to end sentences with a preposition. It's not "What for?", it's "for what?"'

'Only someone who's never read a real book could think "What for" is a sentence.'

'Now, now, you're carrying on the right way to feel the back of my hand.'

'Oh, for goodness' sake, Dick,' said my mother, 'are we going to spend another Sunday afternoon arguing the point? I came out for a nice run away from gloomy old Ashley Down. I'm sick to death of the whole place. The house, the orphanage, the neighbours, the 21 bus-stop. I sometimes think if I see another 21 bus go past, I shall scream!'

During this I was exploring the bedroom floor, the modern bathroom with no sign of an exploding gas geyser, the lavatory without a chain, the room I would have to myself and the smaller one I'd make sure went to my younger brother.

'Well, it's beyond my comprehension', I could hear my father saying, 'how anyone in their right mind could find Ashley Down gloomy yet happily contemplate living opposite an endless stream of people bobbing in and out with handfuls of books! And, half a mo,' – throwing open the casement window, craning to look up the street – 'I thought so – another funeral! On its way to Canford Cemetery. That's the second in thirty minutes. Are you telling me you'd pay through the nose for a shoe-box like this with uninterrupted views of people being laid to rest? Well, Violet, I'm not. You'd go for a walk and every few yards you'd have to be paying your respects to another cortège. Your jolly old tit-fer would never touch your barnet.'

His use of rhyming slang and his London accent were signs of his Cockney origins. He spoke the language of the smoking-concert and music-hall. An umbrella was a gamp or brolly, a pub was a four-ale bar and hats were lids or tit-fers. Born and brought up in the East End of London, this was his native tongue. He didn't leave for the West Country until he was nearing forty. I never knew his parents but a lost photograph showed a grim woman seated on a farm-cart and a moustached man standing by, holding the bridle of a shire horse. This is the only evidence I've seen that they were country people. They are said to have come from the Sandringham Estate some time in the last century and settled in dockland Canning Town, where my father was born. His brothers were Rob and Bert, his sisters Bea, Hattie and Florrie. All these uncles and aunts I knew but several others died in infancy, including a pair of twins. He always referred to '*Brother* Bert' or '*Sister* Hats' as though they were members of an order and indeed there was something monastic about the family home at Stratford, where the bachelors Rob and Bert lived with the spinster Hattie till the last of them died in the 1970s. The father at the bridle had become a master butcher with his own business in Angel Lane, by R.G.N.'s account a brutal drunk who boxed his ears if he refused to fetch his porter from the four-ale bar.

'Which accounts for my partial deafness, boy. And that, together with my varicose veins, exempted me from service in the Great War.'

'Got something to thank him for, then.'

'Precious little. If you'd seen the effects of drink at first hand you wouldn't pine for The Good Old Days.'

'I don't.'

I didn't care one way or another about the days before I was born. They seemed, to a boy brought up in the age of cinema, to be entirely black and white and populated by posturing figures climbing public steps, puffing cigars, garrulous but silent. Films make those times *less* real. The earliest pictures of R.G.N. show him as an Edwardian masher, on the top step of a Brighton boarding-house called Sans Souci with fifty other lodgers; or with a tilted boater standing behind a laughing girl in a long white dress; or even earlier as a gauche youth with a racing cycle, wearing a high-necked sweater and long shorts, his bare legs already ominously veined, his facial expression very like my youngest daughter's who never met him but shares his passion for bikes; in another he is face-making with a monocle, and there are two of his spell in the army hospital, the bedclothes lifted on a frame to allow his post-operative scars to heal. Discharged from hospital and army, he was told to bandage his legs and was still doing it in his seventies. Every morning he'd sit on the Lloyd Loom wickerwork chair unrolling the strips of crêpe from his ankles up to his calves like puttees, fastening them with a safety-pin.

'Why d'you put that bandage round your leg?' asks the teenage boy in my play *Forget-me-not Lane*. He's afraid his father will find out that he chases girls and is trying to change the subject.

'You surely know already,' says the older man. 'My varicose veins?'

'No.'

'During the First World War, as I was due for military service. Months in hospital, a hundred stitches. That – together with the deafness caused by that clout across the ear – saved me from the trenches so I'm not sorry.'

'Your veins must be all right by now. Why d'you still wear it?'

'Nobody's ever told me to stop. Besides, it keeps my ankles cosy.'

Was this the only reason? Certainly he wore high boots or felt spats till the end of his travelling life, long after they had gone out of fashion. His brothers went to the war and served all through.

'You'd go over the top,' said Uncle Bert when I asked him about it, 'you'd look round for your mate and blimey! he was dead.'

He did that peculiar laugh, more like a bark, but I wanted some Robert Graves or Wilfred Owen recollections. I asked about the companionship.

'Well,' in that London growl, removing his pipe, 'I never thought much to that. A lot of working-men, in a manner of speaking, Peter, they're more or less scum.'

If the experience taught him anything, Bert didn't let on. Uncle Rob I could never imagine in the trenches. He was always at the grand piano which filled the tiny front parlour at Stratford. He worked in the office of a theatrical agent and liked to suggest a life apart – in the West End. 'Actresses,' said my mother when I asked what sort of thing. What could Rob have found to do in Flanders? How could he have mucked in? One night, God knows when, sitting in a hip-bath before the coal fire, he had glared angrily as his sister came in.

'Harriet,' he said, 'don't barge into the room when the old man is in the bath. You never know what he might be a-doing *of*.' Or so my father told me, relishing the wicked final preposition. They posed all the time, these men, thriving within the narrow limits they'd set themselves, building their characters from props and catch-phrases and unkind jokes. How did they really feel about That War? They had all survived and yet had nothing to say. Or couldn't speak. In a time of white feathers and 'What did you do in the war, Daddy?', how had mine felt about working in an office at the Co-op? He saw himself as a co-operator and all his life was loyal to The Movement, in the way a Salvationist might be to the army or in these days a Japanese to the family of Suzuki. The Co-operative Wholesale Society had its London headquarters at Silvertown and Dad's only experience of the war was seeing from a safe distance the great explosion at the munitions works which killed and wounded several hundred workers. His only attempt at literature (apart from some tirades against Masons) was his eye-witness account of the disaster, which ended with his reaching home, sitting at the kitchen table and 'bursting into a paroxysm of tears'. It's clear he wouldn't have stood up well under fire. He was often nervy in the air-raids of the next war, forever losing his gas-mask or warden's helmet. I felt safer when he was away. 'The Silvertown Explosion' has gone the way of the Sandringham snapshot. He was polishing it well into the 1960s and a threat to recite it was the quickest way to clear a room. I have inherited his fear of violence and my chronic pacifism has a lot to do with not wanting to be hurt.

When Bert came home from the trenches, Dad was able to get him a situation at Silvertown, pushing casks of pepper about in barrows, a job he kept till retirement, spending little, never improving the gaslit family house for which he still paid rent, investing his spare cash to leave to his nephews and nieces. I visited him in the terminal ward two days before he died. He seemed frightened and wet his pyjamas but couldn't speak. He'd left it too late.

Dad was the one who got away. There was a job 'on the road' and he took it, coming to Bristol in the mid-1920s. He'd signed the pledge with the Band of Hope and never let strong drink, tobacco smoke or foul language pass his lips. This was the man who, approaching forty, began his unsuitable career as a commercial traveller. Based in Bristol, he would cover the south-west, from Worcester to Penzance, Swansea to Reading, pressing C.W.S. goods on the managers of retail societies. He called himself not a grocery traveller but A Representative In Drysaltery. To us the words 'A Great Society' had no meaning beyond a Co-op at Shepton Mallet or Exeter. The Great Western Railway took him from one commercial hotel to another, Monday to Friday, week in, week out. And never anything wicked. He could have had a girl in every port, but once he'd met my mother I don't believe he wanted anyone else.

Violet Annie Ladysmith Poole was born, as her third Christian name nicely tells us, on 1 March 1900, the siege of the South African town having ended the day before. She liked to keep her age secret but, once my father knew her name, she had no chance.

'Have you met my good lady?' was his usual introduction, 'Violet Annie Ladysmith.'

'Dick!' she always said, though as time went on more earnestly, 'Why tell everyone *that*?'

It didn't occur to her to mention that he'd been born on April Fool's Day. Repartee is not her line. Her character hadn't been formed in the capital but in the gentler climate of Bath and Bristol. She could never cope with the cruel tongues of his family. For *Forget-me-not Lane* I borrowed her description of Dad's mother: 'All in black, with her hair strained back and her lips a thin white line. Don't tell me. No wonder his father drank. I remember the first time she saw you, in her home, straight out of Dickens. I was trying to bath you, in a tub on the table with the gaslight low to save money. She stood there criticizing. "You should wear glasses," she said when I nearly let you slip, "stop thinking about your looks and get some glasses." I finished up in tears, which is what she wanted. And I thought to myself "What have I come into?" In our family we were poor but happy. Mother enjoyed a drink, a laugh and a song.'

My maternal grandfather, a cabinet-maker, had carried a symbol of his trade in the procession that opened Clifton Suspension Bridge. Mum's father died of cancer when she was still a child and Nan had to work in a tailoring factory to provide for her and her two brothers. These uncles also survived That War, George a private in the infantry, Harold a Royal Air Force cadet.

'When George came on leave from the trenches,' my mother remembers, 'the mud caked up to his knees, Nan made him take off his uniform outside so as not to bring lice into the house.'

Wounded four times, he finally came home to find there was no work. He had been apprenticed to a German firm, which of course had gone. Within a year, he followed his brother to Canada. Since the Cabots colonized Newfoundland, Bristolians have been going west. My mother's uncles, aunts and cousins continued sending Christmas cards and food parcels from Australia, New Zealand, the States and particularly Canada. They went gold and opal mining, dammed lakes, built railways. Or so the story goes. Harold became, we were told, Chief Electrician for the Canadian Pacific, a claim we put to the test years later when he came visiting. His failure to wire up a three-pin plug embarrassed everyone but him. We should have left the myth unchallenged, a dream like Uncle Rob and the actresses. In Mother's family no uncle was a platform porter, he was the stationmaster at Waterloo; nobody had a boss, they had fifty men under them; male nurses were brain surgeons, privates got commissioned, barbers ran beauty parlours. Such claims, though, were never made for George, who was also the only member of either family to hold radical views. In Canada he married a left-wing journalist, became a Labour organizer and was victimized for unionizing a shop. He moved on and on across the country, settling at last in Calgary. Here he decided it was time to attend to his growing family, took a steady job and kept his nose clean. Not long after, he was killed by a truck. I never met him or his widow, but she wrote me the one truly interesting letter I've ever had from a relative, describing her feelings after his death as she went over his personal belongings.

Nan married again, but my mother never liked her stepfather and was suddenly isolated. Her girl-friends were married, her brothers gone, she was heading for thirty. R.G.N. must have seemed a snip. They met, as everyone seems to have done in the 1920s, at a dance.

'He was acting the goat and like a fool I laughed,' says the mother in *Forget-me-not Lane*. 'Well, before I knew it we were out there doing the fox-trot and the whole floor stopped to watch us. He was like a gazelle in those days with his patent pumps and his hair smarmed down.'

He was middle-aged, true, and funny about drink and tobacco or having a flutter on the Derby, but on the credit side he'd put by enough cash to buy a house outright, he was amusing, an amateur entertainer, he had a safe job with a good salary and he was full of beans. What did such a Big Cheese see in Violet Annie Ladysmith? She was pretty, that much is clear even through the sepia tints of studio portraits, or peering from under the brim of a cloche, pretty even in mortar-board and gown, displaying a scroll from the London Academy of Music. She was a Licentiate in singing and had diplomas for piano. Dad had already begun his record collection with Caruso, Kreisler and Galli-Curci. Perhaps he thought they shared a love of music but, though Mum sang pleasantly in the mezzo-soprano range, she was more interested in passing exams and performing than listening to the classics for hours on end. He probably saw Nan as a drawback. She hadn't had much education, came to grief on words like certificate and wasn't above taking a glass of porter in the four-ale bar. But she had a husband to look after and it wasn't likely they'd see much of her once they'd set up house. On the whole, Vi was quite a catch.

A month after their first fox-trot, he took her to see a business colleague who lived in Ashley Down, and Vi thought they were simply visiting, but next day he asked her what she thought of the house. It was all right, she said, a bit old-fashioned. That was the furniture, he told her, that could be changed. If she was prepared to marry him, he'd buy the place, cash down, but she'd have to be quick about it, the offer wouldn't last forever. There was no question of being swept off her feet. She prudently accepted. To the end of his life, driving past the church in City Road where they were married, he would raise his hat.

'Notice that, boy? Always show respect to those who've passed on, entered the Vale of Tears, had the jolly old ball and chain clapped on and committed themselves to a life sentence like lambs to the slaughter.'

Like many of his running jokes, it got less funny the more you heard it.

'You can have your blessed freedom any day you want it –' Mum would insist from the back seat.

'When I think of the girls I could have had, boy. Amy Biles – I wonder what Amy's doing now?'

'Drawing the old-age pension, I should think.'

'Hold your tongue, Capstan Connie, and if you're going to light up another fag, please open the window your side and let the smoke out.'

Brother Bert and Sister Hattie came down for the wedding and, apart from Nan, were the only guests. Hattie had eaten something she liked that didn't like her and belched loudly throughout. The Nichols family obviously disapproved. Their boys and girls were not expected to marry. Look at Sister Florrie – she'd gone off with a blind man who often ran berserk, chasing her with a carving knife and swearing he'd kill her if he could only find her. When my mother first visited the Stratford home some months later, Sister Hattie stared at her stomach and asked if she was expecting.

'Yes, as a matter of fact.'

'Disgusting!'

It can't have seemed a promising start, that wedding without wine, a deferred honeymoon, a sheltered girl leaving her mother to live with this middle-aged stranger.

By the time I was born, though, their new life had got momentum. The old furniture gave place to new Co-op three-piece suites; they ate Co-op groceries, spread Co-op jam on Co-op bread with Co-op knives, took delivery of Co-op coal, put out metal checks for milk from Co-op cows, and visited the Co-op depot on the Tramways Centre several times before choosing a cot and pram. Dad learnt to drive and, the Co-op not having developed a motor-car, bought a bull-nosed Morris Cowley with maroon bodywork and called it Joyce. Last year I saw a veteran exactly like it in a village street, same colour, same black seats, and my infancy came back like a rush of blood. In time the firm provided a navy blue Morris Twelve, streamlined, with a walnut dashboard. He now became, as he called himself in his letters to the papers, A Knight of the Road. His guilt pricked him whenever we took out the firm's car for 'pleasure' (a word he never used lightly) so Joyce was replaced by the Green Goddess, a secondhand Wolseley Fourteen saloon. What I wrote before wasn't strictly true – we had The Only *Two* Cars in the Avenue. He drove the Goddess till the early 1950s, as impeccably as he lived, then one night went into a bollard.

'I couldn't see it, boy. I said to your mother, "That's it, Vi, no more driving for me." Next day I gave the car to your brother, young what's-his-name.'

I hated that Wolseley as a boy. The smell of its leatherwork that made me sick, the rituals of getting it from the garage, opening two sets of double-doors, setting out the wedges of wood that let the wheels drop gently off the kerb without damaging the tyres, but most of all the painful squabbles that started whenever we went 'out for a run'.

` 'Now, hold your tongue!' he'd finally say from the driving seat, 'no more of your dashed impertinence. Look out of the window at God's green fields.'

This was a relief. I could stare into my head at visions of girls in bathing-suits and cami-knickers, their sensual lips imploring me to kiss them. Strings surged on the soundtrack, the camera came in for a close-up. Fade to black. Run it again. God's green fields were boring, unlike the moors with their wild ponies or the combes and gorges of the Mendips, where we chased girls in the bracken, or the beaches of Portishead, Clevedon and Weston-super-Mare, from which we could see across the Bristol Channel to South Wales. Villages depressed me – always grey and stony.

'Fancy living here,' my mother would say from the front seat – and I agreed. Everything old was dull – churches, cathedrals, graveyards, thatched cottages, colleges, banks, inns, almshouses. My spirits rose at the sight of the new factory estates on the road to Bath, functional glass and concrete structures housing Top Dog Brake Linings, Crittall's Metal Windows and Smith's Crisps. Filling-stations and petrol pumps, blocks of flats, outdoor pools, cinemas and road-houses raised my spirits. I warmed to the Bauhaus before I'd even heard the name.

But as yet I am still a baby in my grandmother's arms as she poses proudly with this parcel of white shawl among walls of trellis in our back garden. Half this space was soon to be taken to build the garage. Is it any wonder I've always hated cars? Even from the start, they nibbled away at paradise.

13

*   *   *

Lining up my Nikkormat for one last picture, it came to me that he had hated nature. Trees had always been anathema (another favourite word). He cut them down if they gave the least trouble. The image of Palatine in the viewfinder had reminded me of the missing hawthorns that shielded us from the orphanage and blossomed with red may throughout the springs of my infancy. I can see him oiling his saw.

'Your mother's complaining they keep out the sun,' approaching the culprits like a policeman. 'Added to which, passing urchins like nothing more than pulling the blossom off. I should say "pulling *off* the blossom". I've *seen* them, boy. Jumping up on our wall to do it, then when I knock on the window, they run off, dropping the may, giving me cheek. Then I have to go out and sweep the pavement.'

'What for?'

'What for? What's "what for?" To keep it clean, you great noodle. I detest an untidy footpath. Same with people who allow their dogs to foul the public way.'

In later years he wore a white coat to sweep the street, a grocer's overall he'd scrounged from the manager of some society. He posted his own notices too, telling the world in sloping copperplate that dog turds were a public nuisance.

I'm sure it was in some such way that the hawthorns went. Did he manage the saw, I wonder, or did my mother have to call The Proper Man?

Rain was beginning to fall now. I took the picture, put on the lens cap and went back to the Renault 18 automatic, where my wife and our friend Joe Melia were waiting.

Another memory came to mind. For some years during the 1960s, Thelma and I lived in a house of our own in another part of Bristol. Three of our children were born there. When we visited Palatine in our mini-van for Sunday dinners or teas, Abigail, Louise and Daniel lay sprawled on a mattress in the back. Come bedtime, we'd pack our gear – the carry-cot, baby-chairs, nappies, feed bottles, toys – with the kids in the back and seat ourselves in the front seat ready for Dick's inevitable good-bye.

'Which way you going, boy? Down the main road to Chesterfield, turning right into Cromwell Road and down to the Arches? In that case, I should pull across here, asking your good lady – what's her name? Stella? Bella? – to tell you if the way's clear . . .'

'Fine, Dad, thanks, we'll see you next week –'

'. . . taking care you pause at the main road to check the oncoming traffic then gently pull forward . . .'

By which time I had driven off.

I climbed into the Renault and stowed the camera. Thelma sat in front and Joe behind. We had come down the day before to record my choice of prose and verse for BBC West.

'Proustian, was it?' Joe asked, nodding at the house.

'Does it *look* Proustian?' I said, giving Palatine a last glance.

'It doesn't have to, does it?'

I started the motor.

'Shame you didn't have better light,' said Thelma.

'That wouldn't have been as true, would it?'

'Not according to you, though I remember a *lot* of sunshine.'

'You *imagine* a lot of sunshine.'

'*You* imagine a lot of rain.'

'It's more grand than I expected', said Joe, 'from the plays.'

'The Nicholses were *posh*,' said Thelma. 'Cars, radiograms, a phone.'

'It's much grander than the place where I was born,' said Joe.

'No use talking, Joe, he won't believe you. He likes to feel behind.'

'I can understand that,' said Joe.

'Well,' I said, 'is it back to London now?'

'It is,' said Thelma, 'and if I were you I should pull across the Avenue, pausing at the main road, turn right along Ashley Down, third to the right down to Muller Road, right again –'

'Alternatively I could do a three-point turn here, down York Avenue to Ashgrove, left and along that way –'

'This is fascinating,' said Joe. 'You'll be putting this in, of course?'

There was some mist on the M4 but it cleared up just outside Bristol and within two hours we were – what shall I call it? – home.

2 The Proper Man

Revisiting Palatine Lodge did little to break the dream in which I passed my early years. Are they largely lost because there was nothing to remember? The only material clues show me to have been much loved, and too much photographed – held, embraced, fondled, neatly dressed in woollen twin-sets, fat and pouting like Oliver Hardy. In one sepia portrait I hold a rubber ball between my podgy knees, looking surprised and resentful as though someone off-camera had just thrown it. In others I stand or sit without a stitch on, like an entry for the bouncing baby competition. These were the pictures Dad kept in his sideboard to trot out during my early teens to anyone who came to the house – uncles, colleagues, chimney-sweeps, religious maniacs – girls! In another I am in rubberized rompers on a donkey at the seaside; a row of bathing-huts behind, a sandcastle to the left with a paper Union Jack, half my mother caught at the edge wearing a broad hat and 1920s dress.

By the time my brother appears I have lost weight and am seen more in berets. Against a background of the pier at Weston-super-Mare, my first school cap appears. I am eight and Dad is paying for me to go to the Grammar School prep. This entitles me to wear the cap and blazer badge – a gold lion rampant on a blue ground. Face-making soon follows. I'm never photographed without acting the goat. Fifty years before, Dad had done the same with a monocle on the Isle of Wight. Like all photographs, they tell us more about the costumes and customs of the time than they do about ourselves. Of course that frowning boy later grew to be me, and Geoffrey, the dark-skinned toddler in the sailor-suit, is the grey-haired man of fifty we last saw playing jazz trumpet in the 100 Club. What puzzles me is that none of this objective evidence rings a bell in my head – neither the glossy snaps nor the revisited home nor talking to those who were there can conjure more than a few fragments. My early years are like a dream or tune that fades the more you try to recall it. Was it simply serene then, uneventful? No one's childhood is. Or perhaps staying in one place means there are no landmarks or milestones for memories to gather round. My London visits come back in glimpses or fragments – staying with Auntie Lil and another Uncle Bert in Manor Park, where the table-top in the scullery was taken off to reveal a bath, where the rest of the small terrace house was warm and friendly but the front parlour was cold and smelt of museum. Lil and Bert weren't relatives – she'd been my father's girl-friend in his London days.

'She kept him out of trouble,' my mother said mysteriously.

Lil had married Bert Orritt, who was for me Bob Cratchit reborn. My mother thought him a fusspot and a note in Dad's copperplate on the back of a snap of them reads 'Mrs Orritt and Husband *née* Lily'. They are at Eastbourne in 1924, perched on deckchairs provided by the photographic service. Behind them boats have been pulled up on to the shingle, other-wise the beach is empty. Bert wears a heavy suit with a waistcoat and watch-chain, high boots and woollen socks.

'Brilliant,' said my eighteen-year-old son when he saw this snap. 'Bril-liant clothes. Who was he?'

He was Lil's husband, he smoked sixty Players Navy Cut every day of his life, coughed over each one and died in the 1950s in an old folks' home, unable to keep up the rent on the house in Manor Park where I used to stay with them. Every morning he left at eight-thirty on the 15 bus for the printing office in The City where he earned his living as a low-grade clerk. Bert was never promoted, never got a rise and after a lifetime's service was given nothing but a cheap gold watch and the old-age pension. Lil died first – of bronchitis, they said, but it was Players Please and London fog. They wore their cigarettes like clothes, allowing the smoke to drift up their faces, squinting as their eyes watered. My mother loved her – she saw her as a refuge from the gaslit morgue at Stratford. Mum would come back almost in tears from Hattie's scathing tongue.

'Never mind, Vi,' and Lil would be pouring them each a glass of ruby port. 'Why don't we get the cards out and see what's in store?' They'd sit around the red plush tablecloth, Lil dealing, face askew as the smoke slid up her nose and into her eyes. If it wasn't cards it was tea-cups. After every cup she read the leaves, finding in these soggy outlines a promise of future thrills. Her prophecies ran to the usual pattern – sea voyages, visitors from faraway, births, deaths, sudden wealth....

'What's this? ... Oh, Violet!'

'What Lil? What can you see?'

'I can see a fortune.'

'For me? That's nice.'

'Wait a bit, dear, I'm not sure whether it *is* for you. Let me see what's over here. Oo-er!'

'What is it now, Lil?'

For some years I was mildly excited by her promise of 'bumping into a tall dark stranger', thinking she meant it literally: a collision with a huge negro. These sessions spoiled superstition for me. The women on my mother's side were haunted by crossed knives, spilt salt, broken mirrors and three-on-a-match, but to me their lives were all misfortune so why bother with details? It amazed me when I became an actor to find intelligent people insisting that if you mentioned 'Macbeth' you should go outside, shut the door, turn round three times, spit and knock to be let in.

'It's something to do,' said my mother, who never went to the seaside without a visit to the palmist.

The Orritts came with us to Scotland, and there we are to prove it in tartan berets, holding sprigs of heather with Loch Ness behind. From left to right, Bert, Lil, me, Dad, a tight distant group at the centre of a broad stretch of scenery, which means my mother was behind the Brownie.

'Come a bit closer, Vi, you'll never see us from back there.'

'If I come any closer I shan't get you all in. Now what do I press?'

'The jigger at the side, near your thumb –'

'All right, I've done it now.'

'Blow you, Vi, I was talking!'

He was often open-mouthed in her photographs, caught giving instructions.

I *do* remember seeing the Loch Ness Monster. We stayed in lodgings overlooking the water and during the night a dragon's head drifted by serenely, dipping to drink then rising again to look about.

'I expect that was a tree trunk floating down,' Mum said when I told her in the morning. She was probably stripping my wet bed at the time. At that age, of course, this was not yet a real embarrassment. It was at sixteen that the rubber sheet and morning apologies ruined any time I spent away from home. Enuresis, says the Medical Dictionary, from the Greek 'I make water', is a condition due either to faulty training (unlikely in my case) or psychological ill-health. 'Control is usually achieved in the second or third year but in some cases not until the fourth or even the fifth.' No mention of the seventeenth, when the prospect of army service stopped my bed-wetting suddenly and forever. It's the only evidence of real tension but so strong that it can't be ignored. What was the trauma so effectively erased from my conscious memory? Why did the plump child emerge from these hidden years as a myopic weed with jutting wrists? First there was the apple tree, my girl cousin, loving parents, unusually secure in a world-wide depression, an equally loving grandma. It should have been paradise but what brought on the Dark Age that followed? Was I literally spoilt? Or was it only my brother's birth? My mother did not have an easy delivery and was ill for some time afterwards with anaemia. She only remembers that I came into the 'nursing home' (no mere hospitals in *my* childhood), having been told I had a brother, looked into the cot and said, 'He's no good, he can't play.' Sibling rivalry is, of course, a banal explanation and there's no photographic evidence of antagonism – Geoff the baby lies against me in a studio portrait, we smile with buckets and spades or line up outside the west front of a cathedral. There are some from a farm holiday – the two of us on a cart-horse with a girl between or we're standing on the lawn with the same girl and her grown-up brother, all with broad grins. I look very well and my hands are in the pockets of my knee-length shorts so R.G.N. must have been elsewhere or he'd have told me to take them out and stand up straight. I remember the girl. She was called Ursula and was thought a tomboy. I fell in love with her, so that hiding my wet bedclothes every morning became an urgent matter. This time, though, my shame had a different cause. We wrestled and she won. That was the end of the affair. Geoff already looks more physical than I – sailor-suits, open necks, bare legs and trunks to my full-length bathing-costume. He took to ball-games before I did and in our forties beat me at tennis with a lighted pipe in his mouth.

There is an early memory of audience participation. At a children's party the conjurer said the house was haunted and drummed with his feet and produced a ghost. I screamed and had to be taken home. At five or six, perhaps staying in London while my mother recovered from Geoff's birth, an aunt took me to the Lyceum. It was one of Florrie Forde's last pantomimes but the act that stays is Naughton and Gold as the broker's men, falling from the room above, throwing paint, using a plank for a seesaw and singing 'Ooo, it's a little bit too long, turn it round the other way, turn it round the other way ... Itchy-koo, itchy-koo....' In the late 1930s, before jazz hit me, Uncle Bert took me to Holborn Empire to see a comedian whose name promised well – Fats Waller. He put on a tartan cap to sing 'Loch Lomond' and pulled the piano to the stool when he sat to play. But a hobo act on a unicycle was far funnier. It was a sorry day for music when some humourless sycophant first laughed at Waller's boring larks.

I was stage-struck from an early age and my year had two seasons – the winter for pantomime, the summer for circuses. In Bristol the three theatres for respectable people were the Prince's, the Hippodrome and the Empire, all struggling to hold their own against cinema and radio.

The Hippo, in fact, had almost admitted defeat and during the summer showed films instead. Its unique feature was a dome that slid back slowly during intervals, letting out the hot air but also letting in the rain from any sudden showers. Always upstairs, I hoped for a change in the weather while the dome was open. Then there'd be a view of rows of open umbrellas in the orchestra stalls below.

There was a fourth, the Theatre Royal, but it was known as the Old Gaffe and was for tarts and ruffians. My grandma was very shocked when I told her I was going there to learn acting in the late 1940s.

'You watch your step, young man. 'Tis nothing but brazen huzzies down there.'

The huzzies, of course, had long since gone, giving way to the Arts Council. The Bristol Old Vic had the same lack that Ken Tynan afterwards told me was the main shortcoming of the National Theatre Company – not enough tit.

The Hippodrome and Theatre Royal survive, both doing better now than the cinemas that threatened to kill them off. The Empire and the Hippo both did pantos but those at the Prince's were more lavish, its dames funnier, its flying ballet more alarming. They were presented by someone called Prince Littler. I pictured him as a real prince made littler by a witch, a dwarf whose only remaining pleasure was to stage fairy-tales every Christmas. For me, it was a total experience – after weeks of expectation, the dressing-up, the fears we might be late, Mum's repeated appeal to us to 'go Number Ones' ('I've been Number One already', 'Then go again – I don't want you squirming as soon as we're sat down like you did last year'), the mad place itself, where cupids and gods held torches with electric bulbs inside their glass flames, the band in the pit with its amazing array of drums, the plush tabs and magical scrims and the interval drop-cloths filling the great proscenium with adverts for local shops. I watched everything – the man on the follow-spot spinning his colour-wheel meant as much to me as Cinderella's Shetland ponies. Some way into Act One, the little prince sensibly got the Principal Girl to sing a soppy song about being in love with a lady with long legs. It was like the songs my mother sang – about dark strangers and wishing-wells – and it was the signal for a stampede of wetlegs (always including me) to go Number One again.

Afterwards there was the programme to read from cover to cover and six months spent reconstructing the whole event on my toy stage or in Mum's dressing-table looking-glass. In Dad's wardrobe were some old props from his days as an amateur pierrot or smoking-room comedian – a grey topper and silver-knobbed cane, a vicar's collar and felt hat.

'Did you ever hear my vicar turn, boy?' asks the father in *Forget-me-not Lane*.

'Once or twice,' says the son but his dad goes on:

'And furthermore, dearly beloved brethren, let me scotch the rumour freely circulating in the parish that if the curate wore his trousers the same way round as his collar, there wouldn't be nearly so many christenings to perform. (*Returns to normal voice*) Bit smutty, boy? Used to go down well at the travellers' dinner.'

Amongst the junk piled high in our lofts, there was even a song-sheet, with which I tried to persuade my non-existent audience to join in a chorus of

> Ours is a nice house, ours is,
> We've got no rats or mouses.

My last play, *Poppy*, brought this embarrassing ritual to the stage of the Royal Shakespeare Company, a belated revenge on those dames and barons who'd tried to make me shout a response. My refusal was an early snobbery. I already sensed that I wasn't one of that coarse mob but would in time find my proper place up there with Them, on the stage.

As time went on, my poor brother became the audience or supporting cast. We used more of my parents' everyday clothes – Dad's bowler and straw boater, Mum's high-heeled shoes or evening dresses. By spring, panto had palled and I started hanging about Horfield Common where gangs of roughs put up the red and green marquee that signified Bertram Mills's Circus. The animals arrived at Ashley Hill Station – direct from Olympia! – and paraded past our house. Girls on palominos or elephants waved at the empty street. Watching from the bedroom window, we once saw a camel pause to nibble our privet hedge. Two strong boys had a hard job urging it back into line. Years later, when I first read Eliot's 'Journey of the Magi', it was this unhelpful image that came to mind at his mention of 'the camels galled, sore-footed, refractory'.

My own circus played from then to Christmas. I rigged a tent in my back room, an old sheet for the big top, the hoop from a cask of pepper for the wall of the ring, and real sawdust from the local sawmills. The aroma of sawdust still brings back Gillam's mills, the sad whine of planks clean cut by the spinning blade. In the world before plastics, wood was everywhere. It tore clothes, splintered into hands and feet, lay stacked in piles waiting to be used by builders. We made dens in these woodpiles, staking claims, defending or attacking rival gangs to keep them. Radios, gramophones and radiograms were of wood too. A table model wind-up acoustic gramophone made the music for my circus, placed behind the tin soldier bandsmen. Sousa marches suited best but Dad's old dance records of Abe Lyman or Red Nichols and his Five Pennies were beginning to interest me more. On his new push-button radiogram I listened to Roy Fox, Lew Stone, Ambrose and Jack Hylton on the National Programme. As if to atone for their failure to produce a car, the Co-op had come up with a range of radios called Defiant and shaped like Aztec temples. Dad spent a lot of time on the floor behind his radiogram trying to mend it but nearly always had to call The Proper Man, in this case his friend and fellow-traveller in Electrical Goods, Monty Graves. This dashing figure smiles from the snaps and groups, seeming always in focus when others are blurred, his dark hair brilliantined to a patent-leather shine. He looks like a popular entertainer, which indeed he was – in Co-op circles at any rate. Dad ruefully admitted that in Monty he'd come up against a talent greater than his own. They were both teetotallers but Monty's drunk was better received than his. Dad's Jew sketch – Ikey on the telephone – was still a success, with its 'Voss you dere?' recurring as a catch-phrase. I was almost unaware of anything Jewish until news began appearing of their persecution in Germany. To us they were exotic creatures with beards and funny hats. Nearly all English Jews were in London; from the top deck of the No. 15 bus we saw the shop-fronts at Whitechapel – Isaacs, Jacobs, Weinstein and Abrahams. A Jewish family lived next door to Aunt Lil, jolly people who had some records of Harry Roy's band. Harry Roy was a Jew too. Dad had grown up with the Cockney's awareness of Jewish neighbours. I wouldn't call him anti-semitic, any more than he was anti-Scottish for telling jokes about tight-fisted Jocks. He took aboard the ready-made set of national types established long ago by *Punch*: Irish were stupid, Italians sold ice-cream and ran away from trouble, Germans drank beer and worked too hard, Darkies didn't work hard enough, the French ate frogs and were pansies, Yanks were called Otis and bragged a lot, Jews and Scots were both mean but the Jews were crafty with it. Dad was not even subtle enough to know when a joke was out of place. 'One of my most popular songs was "Sergeant Solomon Isaac Stein". Always went down well. But by Jove, boy, there was one function where it got me in a spot of bother. I was halfway through and they started throwing pennies. I got off quick and asked the reason. I'm dashed if it wasn't a Jewish dinner! Shows you can't be too careful.'

Racist jokes didn't interest my generation, perhaps because so many of the comics we admired, both British and American, *were* Jewish; more likely because we didn't understand the need to make them. Our spirits sank at the mention of 'An Irishman, an Englishman and a Jew'. In fact, we hated jokes altogether. As puberty approached, we began to see the adult world as a gallery of grotesques. Dad was an easy target, he encouraged us to laugh at him but was slow to realize that we weren't *with* him any longer. His favourite recitations were no longer in demand at functions. Monty was now the star and compère of the Travellers' Dinner, so Dad began to perform them more at home. One was the story of the wrestler Bendigo, which began:

What, never heard of Bendigo?
That knocks me out.
Where's your Board School teaching?
Whatchya been about?

The other was about Jeremiah in the Turkish Bath: 'I was pushed and pummelled, pummelled and pushed, till I scarce knew where I was at. Then he says to me, Just lie on this table and I'll finish you awff.'

At this he took up a stance like Macbeth seeing the dagger, hands out to ward it off, eyes rolling, the voice rising to a bellow: 'Finish me awff? FINISH ME AWFF! I'm darned near finished awff already.'

Encouraged by our mocking laughter, he might find this too much for him, tugging a handkerchief from his pocket to mop the tears of mirth that had started to his eyes.

But this is too soon. Before the war he was still a dominating father, usually away from Monday to Friday, his authority gradually undermined by our grandmother's indulgences. There was no love lost between them. Her easygoing ways opposed his Puritanism – the smell of her stout in the larder, the way she had cut holes in her shoes to ease her bunions, her Bristol speech with its lilting rhythms.

'Violet,' he often asked, 'I wish you'd ask Ma not to answer the door of Palatine Lodge wearing an old cross-over pinafore. It looks so dashed infra dig.'

My poor mother would pass this on to hers, as tactfully as possible.

'What's th' odds?' Nan always said. It only encouraged her. Next Friday she would greet his return wearing not only her pinnie but odd shoes ('it do help my corns') and a man's trilby hat.

My mother, now nearly eighty-three, has just spent Christmas with my family. We walked along the canal towpath through Regent's Park with my wife, her parents and our teenage daughter, who wears the collection of old clothes that passes for modish in Camden Town.

'I can't get used to Catherine in a trilby,' my mother said, 'I keep thinking it's a man.'

'But don't you remember, Nan used to wear a trilby?' I said.

She stared open-mouthed. 'She never did. Nan? A man's hat?'

'She used to hang it behind the door of the brush-cupboard.'

'Never! A broad-brimmed felt hat with a high crown, yes. Never a trilby.'

During the walk she drifted towards my wife and I could see her complaining about the slander. Thelma tried to turn her attention to the zoo's polar bears but they were nothing to the trilby.

Perhaps the man's hat too was later on, during the war or after.

Whatever the truth, Dad grew to be a doom-laden misery, turning up like bad news at Friday midday, sometimes early enough to catch me listening to Geraldo on his radiogram. The bad report card I had probably brought home from school to be signed would be hidden if possible till Sunday night after I'd gone to bed, in which case we'd only have gloom at Monday breakfast; otherwise my form position could spoil the weekend.

'What's this? Vi, have you seen this ninny's card?'

'Don't go on, Dick.'

'Twenty-fifth in Maths? Out of a class of twenty-eight? I think we are safe to assume, Peter, that your proficiency in arithmetic does not enable you to subtract twenty-five from twenty-eight but I will do it for you. Three's the answer, boy.'

'Well, I'm not bottom.'

'Not bottom? What's "not bottom"? Three coons with less brains than yours!'

'Raymond Lyle's twenty-seventh.'

'Who's Raymond Lyle? Is he the boy with the runny nose who beat the drum in the Salvation Army?'

'No,' my mother said, 'that's Albert. Albert was poor, you know very well, his father couldn't pay for him to go to the Grammar.'

'Unlike Muggins here,' indicating himself, 'who seems by the results to be throwing his dough down the jolly old drain.'

'Raymond Lyle's Dad's got a farm out Almondsbury,' I said.

'I see. A farm? Well, I dare say long division doesn't matter much to a hewer of wood and drawer of water.'

It only mattered, I thought, if you were a pusher of pens or a seller of bacon.

'He's nearly top in English,' my mother said.

'Nearly top? Nearly top's not good enough, Vi, not if he wants a decent job in the Civil Service.'

'I don't.'

'Hold your tongue, Sonny Jim! You must stop considering those beneath you, the Raymond Lyles, and instead develop the habit of feeling you're behind. Behind people like Tom Graveney, for instance. Where's he in the form?'

Tom Graveney, he knew very well, was always top. He was the golden boy and later achieved national fame as a test cricketer.

24

'I don't want to be like Tom Graveney.'

'Don't worry, you won't be. But you can *aspire*, boy.'

'Do leave off, Dick,' from my mother, 'he doesn't want to be a cricketer. The ball's too hard. It hurts his hands.'

'Shut up, Mum.'

'Don't tell your mother to shut up. You'll feel the back of my hand in a minute. Now say you're sorry.'

'Sorry, Mum.'

'You don't have to say you're sorry to me. . . .'

'Don't contradict me, Vi. I wish you wouldn't spoil him.'

'And I wish you wouldn't come home every Friday and make our lives a misery.'

And Nan, if she had been unable to get away to her flat before Dad's return, would chip in: 'We may have been poor but we were happy. We liked a drink, a laugh and a song.'

'Ma, please do not interfere with matters about which you know nothing. Incidentally you are not so poor nowadays that you need answer the door in a cross-over pinny and –'

'Don't raise your voice to my mother.'

Some weekends, when he was not worn out by his travelling, he would try tuition, plodding through the archaic sums of his Board School teaching.

'We don't do it like that these days,' I'd tell him.

'Hold your tongue, Noodle. You couldn't be much more behind than you are now.'

'I could be bottom.'

But he was as hopeless at teaching as at mending gramophones, painting bathrooms or hewing wood. We had to call The Proper Man. Several, in fact – tutors hired by the hour to help me calculate in acres, cram the Kings of England or learn the piano.

'Wasn't I even any good at music?' I asked my mother recently.

'You wouldn't try. You used to run to the window when the cows went up the road.'

Cows? Where were they *going*? Then I remembered – the slaughterhouse. Those herds of cattle, only ever going one way, regularly disturbed my music. Mum wouldn't try to teach me, though she gave lessons to others for money in the back room on her old upright, her framed credentials hanging on the chimney-breast. From here came painful performances of 'Für Elise' and 'Rustle of Spring', from the middle room (when Dad was home) Furtwängler playing Beethoven, and in the upstairs back (beyond Nan's weekday room) we'd be cranking the table HMV for Jack

Hylton's 'O Ya Ya'. Or was Mum's teaching later? She was still singing, I remember that, obliging at the Travellers' Dinner with 'Only a Rose' or 'An Old Violin'. Her teacher was a woman whose husband owned at least four cinemas in Bristol, one of which – the Metropole de Luxe – had been Cary Grant's local flea-pit before it was dolled up in the 1930s. Whenever the star came home to see his mother, every year or so, he would call at the Metropole, announce himself at the box-office and sit for awhile in the back row. He remembered it with gaslights and so do I. But I preferred my cinemas modern – the Odeon, the Orpheus, the Embassy. They had the best decor but the outdated Palace had the best organ. I swallowed the cinema wholesale, dodging football and cricket afternoons to sneak off to the Scala or Premier for U films or asking strangers to take me in to those with A (for Adult) ratings but I had to do without H (for Horrific) until much later. All the same I saw a series of monster movies with Boris Karloff, Bela Lugosi and Lon Chaney, all of which meant even wetter beds for my mother to deal with.

Having supped full with horrors (a double bill of Dracula and Wolf Man), I'd run home through the dark streets, terrified at every corner, to face – one week in five – the wrath of Dick. Reaching the front door, I'd yank the brass knob and keep the bell tinkling a-rhythmically on its spring till someone (Mum or Geoff, I hoped) let me in, then cry 'Look out' and run past them and up the stairs, two at a time, to the lavatory, not shutting the bathroom door behind me because of what might be in there, waiting in the dark. Afterwards I had somehow to get down those stairs again, a flight of twenty-five, divided by a half-landing where an unlit passage led to Nan's bedroom. From the bathroom landing, another flight led to the attics. The deafening rush of water released by the flush might cover the approach of vampire bats or misshapen creatures scraping forward under cover of noise and darkness, so my survival depended on a well-lit return down the stairs. No longer possessed by the need to pee, I would plan this descent like a bank robbery. Some archaic arrangement of switches meant the lower hall could not be lit from upstairs. If Dad were home, he would probably be in the front room with his Brahms or Delius while Mum was in the dining-room with Anne Ziegler and Webster Booth or more often a radio drama. As I mentioned earlier, his span of attention was short and he never read a novel through or stayed awake for a play. His meanness – later a mania – was as yet only a foible, but turning off lights was a lifelong pleasure. Reared in the gaslit Stratford house, electricity must have seemed sinful, even in the forty-watt candlepower of Palatine. He'd come from the front room on some errand, find the lights on, turn them off saying 'Dear oh dear' and go back to the

Brahms, leaving me stranded in the lavatory. It was no use calling out – he could no more hear over the front-room acoustic gramophone than Vi could over the radiogram. Between bathroom and living-room I was at risk. If the creatures missed me from the attics, they could leap out from the dark void of the passage to Nan's room. What was worse, her wardrobe stood just beyond the end of the passage and she took to leaving a dress on a hanger, dimly lit by the glimmer of the street-lamp through her window. You had to steel yourself not to look and later *to* look, to stare at the filmy shape at the end of the tunnel. I got this journey down to three seconds flat, taking the stairway in two great vaults, hands on banister and dado-rail, feet swinging to land with a crash on the lino of the lower hall. Two more steps took me to the living-room door and safety. A moment later would come Dad's predictable cry 'Is that you, crackpot, jumping down the stairs? How many times do I have to tell you to walk down one by one?'

As I grew older, the limits of safety provided by the firelight were pushed back. Learning to face the dark meant laying the ghosts. I began to analyse the horror films, sorting the contrived shocks into cuts, fades, close-ups, superimpositions and noting shock chords on the music-track. 'Don't spoil it!' my children say, watching these old films on TV, when I tell them a whole scene was made from two intercut takes. Did my imagination survive? Or am I setting too high a meaning to this interest in film analysis? Was it only wanting to be Up There With Them?

As a man I fear drowning but not the dark, though remembering the stairs of Palatine I felt for a moment the old panic. Jonathan Miller called this process 'catching at the mouse-tails of memory' and his metaphor brought to mind my mother's fear of the mice who nested in the broom-cupboard. She is the only woman I've seen behave as they do in comics, running from the scullery, shrieking and climbing on to a chair or table. Later she took to beating and banging on all the doors she could find, calling to them to clear off and leave her in peace. Sometimes we'd see the poor things scrambling for their holes while this immense human panic went on far above. Altogether now –

Ours is a nice house ours is
We've got no rats or mouses . . .

Wishing not to be frightened meant I lost all sense of mystery. Ghost stories had to end with explanations. Conan Doyle and H. G. Wells knew their business, Poe was an amateur. Thousands of boys like me sent off to mail-order Magic shops to discover the banal secrets of conjuring. I could never manage the sleight of hand and went instead to see Dante, the

American illusionist, at the Prince's, a Proper Man if there ever was one. His assistants levitated, changed places, vanished onstage and at once ran down the aisle from the rear stalls, shouting.

I reconstructed these illusions on the only proscenium stage I had – the double door from our kitchen into the greenhouse. My brother, wearing a velour curtain, had a long run through the dining-room and front hall, then back down the passage before he could reappear with a shout behind my inattentive audience – Mum and Nan forever fussing with their cigarettes.

My circuses had a cast of three – Geoff and me and our Scottie dog. Geoff was the trick-tricyclist; he reared up on the two back wheels, stood up on the pedals and circled faster and faster between the apple trees, finally careening on two wheels as I shouted bravo! from the side. A physical coward, I was not much use as circus performer but was good at shouting and posting bills in the street outside to announce our shows.

'That's a picture of lions and tigers,' Geoff protested when he saw my advertisements. 'We haven't got any wild animals.'

'We've got Mac.'

'He's only a Scottie.'

'I shall go on and say we're sorry the lions and tigers couldn't turn up today but here is the amazing Mac.'

'What's he going to do? He can't do anything.'

'He can jump through a hoop.'

'He did once.'

The hoop was the one that had earlier served as my toy circus ring.

'Thassa swizz. They'll want their pennies back.'

Geoff needn't have worried for even at those prices we had no takers.

Perhaps my lack of physical courage came from being short-sighted. I was not yet wearing glasses but could never keep my eye on a ball at speed or deflect a flying fist in the playground. To deal with bullies and gangs I formed alliances with stronger, steadier boys. The most notable of these was Toby Wainwright, my opposite in every way. He lived with his parents, grandpa and sister in the corresponding corner house one block away. This made Palatine seem poor. It looked over the orphanage playing-fields and beyond to the poorer parts down the hill where Nan had her flat. There was a lawn at the back and further still a vast tract of kitchen garden, outhouse and garaging sandwiched between the parallel terraces of York Avenue and Station Road. Toby's people had been farmers and, when the war came, the sheds and pens became a menagerie. A goat, a pink sow, chickens, geese and rabbits lived here in a smelly mess of sweet swill, shit and compost. I would later marvel at

Toby's steady way of breaking a fowl's neck or slitting a pig's throat. They let me collect the eggs. I sipped the warm milk Toby had just drawn from the goat.

His people confused and attracted me. The father and his brother ran a motor-cycle shop near The Horsefair and in the summer Mr Wainwright went motor-bike racing in the TT trials on the Isle of Man with Toby's mother in the side-car. Photos showed them in helmets and goggles or taking a sharp corner, one wheel off the ground, like Geoff in our circus. I'd never known a grandpa or sister and Toby's were the sort you might have invented – Gramps an upright iron-grey countryman sucking a pipe and leaning on a stick and Eleanor a blonde beauty, brave without being butch. The adults all smoked and drank and went to church. Toby was a chorister at St Bartholomew C. of E. overlooking St Andrew's Park. His example persuaded me to join. He and his people did everything by example, never by insisting or prohibiting.

'Good idea, boy,' said R.G.N. when he heard I was a probationary choirboy. 'Get you out of the house on Sunday. Don't forget to thank God for the many blessings He has showered upon you, not least such a wonderful father.'

'Oh, he's sure to,' said Mum, knotting my tie, 'I don't think.'

'Take no notice of Old Mother Hubbard, boy. You tell the vicar all about Yours Truly then ask the age-old question: Why was he born so wonderful?'

'Why was he born at all?' said Vi.

'Hold your tongue, O.M.H.,' he said, delighted, turning his attention back to the Co-op Sunday paper, *Reynold's News*.

My days in the choir were numbered. Fourteen, I think. The dressing-up, of course, appealed to me, larking with surplices in the vestry, but I cannot pretend to have found (as others say they did) anything theatrical about church. The services were slow, the houses thin, there was better singing in school assembly. I longed for distraction and soon found it. The second Sunday, the organist was plagued by wind and belched repeatedly at his console. A giggle passed through the chancel like bush-fire. The vicar, pausing in his lesson, frowned a reprimand into the organist's mirror, quelled our laughter with another glare and resumed. We composed ourselves, avoiding each other's eyes. The organist suppressed his burps, the danger seemed to have passed. Then we grew aware of a regular but resonant snoring. The poor man had fallen asleep. The vicar nodded to the curate to wake the organist, but before he could reach him his body had slumped forward on the keyboard and a great discord sang out. I had done my best not to laugh, but the church was swaying now and the stained-glass keeled over as I swooned, scattering hymn-books. The next I knew, the pews, the mock-Gothic arches, the brass lectern, were all the wrong way up, my arms were hanging loose, as the sturdy vicar carried me from the chancel by my ankles. In the vicarage his wife gave me sweet tea. I had literally fainted with laughter. Toby never insisted I go again, though he kept on with it till his voice broke.

At school he was my playground protector, stout, strong, gentle. I pointed out which boys were enemies and how to smite them. My gang would take prisoners and, if they did not agree to come over to our side, Toby would put the squeeze on, trapping them in a corner of the playground railings and pressing his great bulk against them till they gave in. I armed our gang with Co-op pins R.G.N. had brought home, supplied by the C.W.S. as small hand-outs for branch managers, like trinkets to trade with savages. My men would prowl among rival gangs, each with a pin, jabbing arses, arms and legs, threatening a squeeze from Toby if they didn't give in.

I helped Toby with English composition. Just as I was so near bottom in maths, I was always top in Modern Languages and History. After school, I'd save the bus fare by sitting on the cross-bar of his bike as he free-wheeled down Cotham Brow.

' Put the brakes on, Tobe!' I'd yell at him over my shoulder, seeing the railway arch come closer. It seemed we'd never pull up in time to avoid the main-road traffic, but somehow we managed to level out and come up hard against the kerb by the sweet shop and spend my bus money on a Crunchie bar or liquorice pipe to share as we took turns pushing the bike up the facing hill to Ashley Down.

'There are the Arches,' my wife and I had said to Joe Melia as we'd driven into Bristol. 'It's a railway bridge over the road.'

'Really? The Arches?' Joe said in the back seat, craning to look in a parody of rubber-necking. 'Christ, I'm glad I saw them! The Arches!'

As war came, the liquorice pipe and sweet cigarettes gave way to packets of five Woodbines bought at Hancock's on our way past the station to our hideout in the woodpile. As the men were called up and building ceased, stacks of timber and bricks were left wherever the new roads died away. Various gangs laid claim to these ready-made dens, where sweets, cigarettes, matches, tapers, candles and banned pictures could be stored. Toby, Geoff, Inky Black and I occupied the pile where the uncompleted road reached up to destroy the last fields of Purdown and here we smoked our Woods, Weights and Radex Navy Cut (the Co-op's answer to Players), the latter supplied to Dad as another bribe for retail managers, stolen from his drawer by me and hidden up our bedroom chimney. We had worked hard reconstructing the pile of planks till it was now a closed box with a room inside big enough for several boys to sprawl.

The end of my wholesome friendship with Toby came one summer evening. We were in the pile and its entrance was closed by the square of plywood that served for a door. I suppose it didn't matter to Toby whether he smoked or not – his people did and looked well enough – but Dad's calling it anathema gave it the colour of sin to me. We lay by the light of a candle, puffing and inhaling our Wild Woodbines. When I read later in Shakespeare of a bank being quite overcanopied with it, I guessed it must have been another kind, just as there seemed to be another Olympia, another Dante. The plywood door fell open and a low-class Bristol boy's voice said: 'Yer, oo's this? Two sissies smokin' in our den.'

Toby and I must have spoken with broad accents too, as everyone does in provincial England unless they learn otherwise, but we talked like the BBC beside boys from beyond the railway, from Eastville and Mina Road, where Mum came from and Nan still lived. Their speech was an urbanized Somerset, quicker, more glottal, with no aitches and few consonants, rather as Scouse is to Lancashire. Speakers of Bristolian still use the second person singular, like Shakespearean rustics caught in a time-warp.

'What's thee doing yer?'

'This is our den. We were here first,' I said.

'Christ, they'm bloody sissies all right.'

'Oh, bai jove, I say I say,' said his unseen mate behind him.

I was not yet fluent in their dialect, as I would be in a few months, so I said nothing but looked at Toby for reassurance. He was holding his Woodbine, watching the glow.

'Thee better get out if thee knows what's good for 'ee,' said the first boy.

'This yer's always been ours.'

'Thee gonna get out or what?'

'No. Are we, Toby?'

'Then we'm coming in and you'm bloody for it.'

They struggled in – no easy business for they were a little older than us and heavy. The first boy wore boots, which were almost as frightening as his accent. The second one closed the gap behind him. I looked at Toby, urging action, but he would not meet my eye. He could have taken on both these slum kids and beaten them hollow. Knowing this emboldened me.

'You'd better get out. Eh, Toby?' I said.

'I say, Toby, old boy, old boy, what be you gonna do about it? Beest thee not gonna take us on?' the other boy taunted him.

'I reckon our Toby's bloody pissing hisself,' said the first more boldly, seeing that Toby hadn't stirred.

'Tell 'ee what, sissy, we'm gonna have to take 'ee prisoners.'

'They'm no better than bloody Jerries.'

'Thee's'll have to tell us what thee'm doing in our den.'

'What's thee called?' the second boy demanded, grabbing my lapel.

'Shan't tell you. Shall we, Toby?' but my friend's fat face gave no answer, only blushed in the candlelight.

'Get the string out and tie his wrists,' said the first boy and his mate did as he was told. The first one took off my shoes and socks and with string from his pocket bound my ankles. Then they tried to provoke Toby again.

'What's the matter with thee, Fatty? Ain't thee gonna help thee bloody mate?'

He pinched Toby's cheek but Toby only turned the other.

'Right, thee'm a prisoner too.'

Far from resisting, Toby untied his own laces and offered his wrists to be bound.

'We'm gonna have to torture thee, Sissy, if thee won't give thee's name.'

He waved the candle about my bare feet, still hoping for action, then under Toby's, slightly singeing his toes. Toby winced a bit then smiled at me. I turned away and said to the trespassers: 'I'll get my gang on to you.'

'If they'm all sissies like thee and Fatty, I shan't trouble.'

'Let 'em go, they'm a couple of nancies.'

They took our cigarettes, untied us, and made us crawl out.

'Thee mind out we don't catch thee yer again! In our den.'

We put on our shoes and socks without speaking then walked down the hill and across Muller Road towards the railway embankment.

'Tobe –' I said.

'Yes?'

'Why d'you always bounce like that when you walk?'

'Do I?'

'Yeah.'

'I expect because we're a farming family. It helps us lift our heels out of the soil.'

'Yeah. I see.'

It was something to say. Neither of us spoke again during our walk home through the pedestrian tunnel and up Station Road. I left him at his house, parts of which are among my dream landscapes. ('I live on the Pacific Coast but every night I dream of Tudor Manor,' says Queenie in *Born in the Gardens*). Toby's house appears as an upstairs landing with sunlight through a stained-glass window, and many white doors opening into bright bedrooms. It is afternoon but party guests are moving gracefully in and out. There's a heavenly serenity.

'Why didn't the father get called up for army service?' asked my wife when she read what I'd written of the Wainwrights. The question had never occurred to me but an answer came at once: they were conscientious objectors. Toby's father organized the air-raid precautions, became chief warden and instructed volunteers how to use a stirrup-pump but that, of course, was only dealing with attack, it wasn't even defence. If the boys in the woodpile had gone further, would Toby at last have shown his strength?

The male figures of my childhood all, for various reasons, failed to act like men. They spurned strong drink, tobacco, rough ways and a good fight, so it may be I turned for such qualities to my grandma. Perhaps she stood in for Dad, away five days a week and losing ground with every absence. A strong survivor of two husbands, she had brought up three children by working long hours for slave wages in a factory; her answer to life was yes when his was no. My mother has usually chosen strong women as her friends. Perhaps Nan was The Proper Man we were always expecting and so is now remembered in a trilby.

And then again perhaps she only spoilt us and so grew more lovable, where poor Dad struggled to be a parent. As I now know from my own experience of both roles, mothers and fathers can no more win than their children. Only survive, forever scarred.

The middle-aged father in *Forget-me-not Lane* winces as his teenage son goes out, slamming the door.

'Great coon!' he calls, then speaks to himself: 'Oh, listen to me. Like some Andy-Pandy twitched about by Old Butterfingers up there. But if he let go, perhaps I'd fall to the floor. We're all in the genetic trap.'

He goes on to remember his salesman father:

'Poor man. Thirty years too late I can see what he must have been suffering, separated from his beloved wife five days a week, packed off gladly Monday mornings to share commercial hotels with heavy-drinking, dirty-joke-telling travellers. And on Friday welcomed back as warmly as a Messerschmitt.'

3 Shake Off Dull Sloth

> The conflict (with his mother) went far back into his childhood, apparently to his fourth year. Before that time he had been a weak and always sickly child, but his memory had turned that difficult time into a paradise because he then possessed the unrestricted affection of his mother, not divided with anyone else. When he was not yet four, his brother was born. In reacting to this intrusion, he transformed himself into a headstrong and unmanageable lad who constantly provoked his mother's strictness. He never again got on the right track.
>
> *From Freud's essay on Goethe*

One way of coping with pain is to go into a trance. To dream so as not to be hurt. And, if my brother's arrival was painful to me at five, perhaps I fell asleep so as to shut out more distress. For some years I took nothing in. If true, this would explain how little I remember from that time until puberty brought problems too intense to be ignored, excitements that finally woke me.

Such was a therapist's tentative suggestion and to me it struck the note of truth, a possible answer to the question of why I made so much water. To attenuate the pain, my infant mind went into an oblivious sleep, so deep no signals could reach me, from which I woke too late in the wet bed with tepid pyjamas and acrid sheets. Or did I never wake at all? Sometimes it seems I am one of a great silent shoal of dreamy fish. Once or twice I've turned tail and hunted with the sharks, but more often I browse vaguely among the swaying fronds. Writing is only dreaming made useful and the urges I have felt to upset people may be symptoms of my effort to stir myself.

Of course it's only half true. The therapist meant simply to indicate a line of enquiry, to ask a promising question. It may be no more than a smart version of Lil's tea-leaves. What's clear is that, at about the age of twelve, my memory begins. Britain, too, stirs in its sleep and slowly pulls itself

34

together. A moment everyone of my age remembers is the Chamberlain broadcast. We were at war with Germany. It was sunny. I was at home with Mum. Dad was away. She embarrassed me by weeping.

'What's the matter?' I said.

'You don't know what it's like. You don't remember the First.'

But she was wrong – I knew it like the back of my hand. We were never allowed to forget it. The strange and wonderful ritual of Armistice Day came in with winter. All vehicles stopped wherever they were, people in the street paused on the pavement, took off their hats and waited, at eleven on the eleventh day of the eleventh month. As junior boys we joined the Upper School in the Great Hall, put in our place by a thousand towering seniors, the high vaulted roof and the thunder of organ and massed voices mourning the glorious dead.

> Time, like an ever-rolling stream,
> Bears all its sons away;
> They fly forgotten as a dream
> Dies at the opening day.

To avoid Mum's tears, I went out the back and leaned against the dusty dark-green trellis, staring at the worn patch of earth between the apple trees. I sucked the slat that was level with my mouth, giving it a shine that faded as the saliva dried. I can taste it now. What would happen? Not the trenches. Would it last long? Perhaps as long as the other, by which time I'd be sixteen. But surely you couldn't be a soldier if you wet the bed. I had seen the film of Wells's *Things to Come* and thought it more likely there would be one massive air-raid on London and the country would surrender. One way or another, this was the end of the world we'd known. I stood there trying on emotions that were too big for me.

In the event, for some time, life changed only in detail – the lights went out for five years, we were given gas-masks in cardboard boxes, which we carried about like charms, and local sign-posts were taken down to confuse the invaders expected hourly to drop from planes and try to find their way to Shepton Mallet or Keynsham. Buses only showed numbers, not destinations. Some vague dreamer in Bristol Tramways had a vision of German parachutists queueing for the double-decker to Westbury or a tram to Bedminster Down. This was a typical measure, only a little less mad than the length of string someone sent in as a civil defence measure to tie across the road between two trees and knock invading Nazis off their bikes. Easy now to see that no one knew what to do. The BBC had given all its variety performers orders that when radio announcements changed from 'This is the BBC' to 'This is London', they should go at once, by whatever means they could, to Bristol. It was thought to be safe from raids. Within nine months bombs started falling on Bristol too and millions of people heard the explosions during a live broadcast of ITMA. After that they moved to Wales. The BBC Symphony used the grocery showrooms of the Co-op depot as an emergency studio. Dad hung about, eavesdropping on the musicians.

'Don't talk to me about Sir Adrian Boult, Peter.'

'I wasn't going to.'

'I heard him presenting his good lady to Mister Gosley, our grocery manager. You know what Sir Adrian looks like, of course, very imposing, very much the bandmaster, bald head, waxed moustache. And d'you know in what terms he introduced her, boy?'

'Should do, you told us often enough –'

'Not "Allow me to present Lady Boult" but "Have you met the missus?" The missus!'

Mum knew her cue. 'I'd rather be called the missus than Violet Annie Ladysmith.'

'Hold your tongue, Goldflake Gertie.'

'Did Mister Gosley introduce *you* to him?' I asked, rubbing salt in.

'Did he aitch-ee-double-ell! No, Friend Gosley, as I may have told you, is one of that benighted breed, the Masonic Brotherhood. He never extends a courtesy or favour to any but his fellow crawlers. Those who rise by kissing b.t.ms.'

'Dick!'

'When it comes to the Masons, Vi, I don't mince words. In fact, there is none that can properly express my contempt for those of my colleagues prepared to creep for advancement. Notice that, boy, "there *is* none" – not "there *are* none". "None" is singular.'

'I thought you told us you were trying to join.'

'How else am I to recommend myself to the powers-that-be? Now the war's started, your mother will be alone here with you two great coons. In the event of air-raids or invasion, my place is with you, but how can I hope to be taken off the road unless I somehow ingratiate myself with Friend Gosley? Look at Friend Graves – when did he move from traveller to buyer? Six months after joining the Masonic Lodge! So don't make yourself look small by talking big about that about which you know nothing.'

Somehow even Sir Adrian Boult was tarnished by this encounter with the creepie-crawlies. Dad went over to the other camp. 'Sir Thomas Beecham, he's the boy. Not so imposing as Boult, of course. Very much the great I-Am, Sir Adrian, very much the Big Cheese. Very Land-of-hope-and-glory. Sir Thomas is altogether different, more like Bert Orritt.'

Despite his efforts to learn the oaths and rituals of Freemasonry, he was never admitted to the lodge and so, he maintained, never got promotion to buyer and the home posting he deserved. For the rest of his life he fretted over this injustice and on the night of his death read to me a lecture on the theme 'You scratch my back, I'll scratch yours'.

In one way he was lucky to be a grocery traveller. He had a petrol allowance and ran both cars on it. He still set off most Mondays with his case of samples and order-book, with its carbon sheets and sharp indelible pencils, but as the war went on, it can't have escaped the neighbours' notice that he brought home more samples on Friday than he took out on Monday. A few eggs here, some bacon there, a wedge of Cheddar, butter, tins of spam or salmon. An elaborate show of secrecy went on as we smuggled this loot into Palatine Lodge.

'Black market,' says the boy in *Forget-me-not Lane*.

'Not at all,' says the father, 'I'm in the distributive trade and fragments are bound to fall off now and then in the process of conveying the goods from hither to yon. Who said that? Hither to yon? Was that the Old Man? I'll give him a kick in the pants. Boom.'

He'd kick himself, imitating a comic called George Doonan, trying to make us laugh and expiate the guilt that was more thrilling to him than real sin was to others.

This was all by the way to me.

Puberty struck me harder than the war. They're inseparable in memory. At the moment I became aware of the need to be sexually attractive, it occurred to me that I had bad sight. The few street-lamps allowed in the black-out were beamed through narrow masks. My left eye saw a clear image, my right a blur. One of the ways I mocked superstition was by challenging God to blind me. Was this myopic astigmatism a sign of His incompetence or His mercy? Snapshots show that for some time I had tended to glance sidelong at the camera, narrowing my eyelids in sunlight. Then suddenly there I am in horn-rimmed glasses, to me a handicap as severe as hare-lip or hunchback. In those days, film actresses wore them only in the early reels before they realized they could manage without, and turned from ugly ducklings to swans.

In my day and night dreams now I seduced everything under twenty that wore a skirt – my cousin, Princess Margaret Rose, Judy Garland, a girl I saw each morning on the bus. Seduction meant rescuing them from some danger – flood, fire, rape, Nazi jackboots, grinning Japs – then a long embrace during which the girl smiled at me, admiring my blend of quiet strength and unassuming good looks. I switched roles too – Errol Flynn one moment, Olivia de Havilland the next, and in the final moments both together – an androgyne like the variety act in which a male dancer wore a costume, part black suit, part white ball gown, with a false female head and one false arm of each sex. Masturbation had started, though the technique of tossing-off took some time to master. At first I made no connection between the dreams of girls and these pleasant experiments. It wasn't at all clear how anyone else could be included in such a solitary act.

I was now a member of the Upper School and, under the hammer-beamed roof of its Great Hall, we would gather, 700 of us, for morning prayers. My gang had its share of braggers, recounting marathon wanks as we sat on benches waiting for school to assemble.

'How much spunk d'you get when you toss off?' asked Issy Whittington.

Cliff Brown thought about it. When he spoke it was clear that his confusion, like mine, was technical.

'How d'you measure it?'

'I mean roughly. You know – enough to fill a thimble?'

'About that, yeah.'

'How about you, Nick?'

'About the same,' I said. 'About a thimble, yeah. You too?'

'Yeah, but how many times a night can you rub up cream?'

These exchanges ended with the entry of the Sixth Form to sit in the transept of the hall facing the podium and, soon after, the headmaster himself, in mortar-board and gown. We scraped to our feet as Shiner Cheyney struck up the first hymn in the organ loft.

> 'Awake, my soul, and with the sun
> Thy daily stage of duty run;
> Shake off dull sloth and joyful rise
> To meet the morning sacrifice.
> Let all thy converse be sincere,' droned Issy Whittington,
> Thy conscience as the noon-day clear,' intoned Cliff Brown,
> 'Think how all-seeing God thy ways
> And all thy secret thoughts surveys.'

The other members of staff stood in Victorian stalls, eight on each side, bawling out the tunes in deep voices. We first-years still sang treble, despite our male potency. Going from the top of the prep into this vast cavern of hoarse giants was a move from Lilliput to Brobdingnag.

There were no women and all the staff had long since perfected styles in which languor, sarcasm, rage and incredulity were nicely mixed. At the main door stood a uniformed porter called Sergeant, always at boiling-point, a cane clenched in one fist, bellowing across the playground 'That boy! Over here, at the double!' I learned in time that he too was only posing, his bullshit a sustained joke, to hide his partiality for boys like me who'd never learn the drill. Behind the gym there were two courts for a violent game called Fives, which frightened me more than the air-raids.

Subjects began fragmenting: science into chemistry, biology and physics, sums into algebra, trigonometry and geometry, while to French and English were added Latin, Greek and German. A scratch wartime staff struggled with this ambitious curriculum. As the younger teachers joined up, more and more ageing derelicts replaced them. Biology became Archer, a burly man with an iron-grey stubble, Cockney accent and pockets full of specimens.

'All right, settle down – what's this?' producing an emu's egg, a rabbit's skull or most often a live amphibian.

'Axolotl, sir!' we groaned in unison, for the creature was as familiar within the school as Alfred, the zoo's gorilla, was in the city outside.

'And what is the natural habitat of the axolotl?'

'Lakes, sir!'

'Or – ?'

'Ponds.'

'Precisely.'

'Shall we take him down the pond, sir?'

'I think he'd be happier, don't you?'

Archer had started digging a pond for the study of plant and animal life, using us as pressed labour. It was sited beyond the playing-field and proved in the end to be a popular project, both with the few boys who liked digging and with the rest of us who dodged away, when Archer's back was turned, down the bomb-shelters in the field for a crafty smoke and the latest bulletin on our erections. The pond was abandoned uncompleted when Archer was found in the Bursar's office reading some confidential report on his own misconduct.

My mind has drifted away like an unmoored dinghy. Archer came much later, of course, as schools scraped the barrel for temporary staff. In the beginning they were all frightening, even the legendary 'Fred' Perry, Head of English, Chief Librarian, known to generations of old boys by the same Edwardian blue serge suit, worn every day till his retirement in 1960.

'Mister Nichols – ' clapping his hands for attention, speaking quickly in the flat Lancashire accent, 'since you seem unable to grasp the meaning of these immortal lines, shall I put them in terms even you may understand?'

'Please, sir.'

'Am I right in assuming you have ambitions to be some kind of humorous writer?'

'Sir.'

'For example, the editor of *Punch*?'

'Don't know, sir.'

'Would it be safe to say that aspiring to be editor of *Punch* you may fail
and only succeed instead in becoming the editor of *Comic Cuts*?'

'Sir.'

'But that even this – to someone of your turn of mind – might be a
gratifying achievement? Then didn't Tennyson put the case well when he
wrote those lines – will you read them out, please, Mister Nichols?'

> "Tis better to have loved and lost
> Than never to have loved at all – sir.'

The only instance of official encouragement I recall. But, to be honest,
what was there *to* encourage in this myopic namby-pamby boy, who looked
studious but wasn't, never caught a cricket-ball, his only score at football
one own-goal and who was always giggling furtively with a gang of other
brats? He could read aloud with unusual fluency, of course, and seemed to
have a perfect ear for the right sense – whether it was his own compositions
or *Macbeth*. Probably didn't *understand* but sounded as though he did. You
had to be fair to the others and not give him all the leading parts to read.
Then he'd look resentful and you could feel you'd done the right thing to
take him down a peg. Do him good.

We waited for war to start and watched while Poland, Denmark, Norway,
the Netherlands and France all went down like skittles. Anyone who was
alive then will remember the strange mood of fear and optimism as the
truth sank in that we were alone in Europe. This book is the story of a
private life, but for the first two years of war no Englishman could separate himself from the nation. He could try, of course. That thousands did try
– to run away, to bribe, to profit – can be seen in Angus Calder's *The
People's War*: 'About two million left for Wales, Devon, Scotland and other
quiet spots. It was reported from Southampton that five thousand people
left for America in forty-eight hours.' Official evacuation had been going on
for a year and the greatest shock for most middle-class British was the
discovery that there was a whole population in the great cities that had
never seen a lavatory. Evelyn Waugh had a lot of fun equating their
poverty with criminality. He affectionately laughed at the posh cowards in
their funk-holes, but his malice was kept for the retarded children from the
slums.

All good Christian stuff.

It was decided that my brother and I should be sent to Canada to stay
with one of my mother's many relatives there. A government scheme had
been started and 200,000 applications were received, again mostly from
the better-off. My dreams changed, their objects were all American now –
Judy Garland was in the lead over Deanna Durbin, Bonita Granville and

Ann Rutherford, all of whom took it in turns to fall in love with the shy boy from Bristol, England, so diffident it was hard to remember he'd already lived through a hundred air-raids.

'It wasn't bad at all really,' he'd say, if pressed, 'most of the time the sirens sounded and the guns went off but not that many bombs were dropped.'

Not one of these snow maidens could resist his quizzical smile, his understated jokes, his way with a cigarette. They wore bright-coloured woollens like the girls in the Coca-Cola adverts in *Saturday Evening Post* and *Collier's*. We sat together for hours in the drug-store feeding the juke-box, Sonja Henie took me ice-skating (I was a natural), and afterwards tobogganing and when our sledge capsized on a bend, we rolled over and over together down the snow-covered slopes outside Quebec. Even the local boys couldn't begrudge my conquest of their prettiest girls.

'Peter, listen a minute –' said my mother.

'What?'

'I'm making a list of things to pack for you to take when you go.'

'Okay.'

'How many rubber sheets will you need? You don't want to spoil Auntie May's linen.'

'Oh, shut up, Mum.'

'Well, it's got to be thought about.'

'Long as I've got my shrapnel collection.'

'Your shrapnel collection won't stop you wetting the bed.'

Every morning I left the house promptly to search the streets round about for fragments of steel shell-casing that had fallen that night from the ack-ack fire of the great guns on Purdown. The bigger the piece the better. By September 1940, I had a biscuit-tin of these metal chunks, each worth hard cash in Canada. Or so we heard. I was more interested in their aphrodisiac properties. Only a medal or a uniform could be more sexually arousing than shrapnel.

This dream came to nothing, of course. In September the *City of Benares* was sunk in the Atlantic and seventy children drowned. My parents decided I'd be safer in Bristol, especially as I couldn't swim. A few weeks later the bombs began to fall in earnest. Whenever Dad was on the road now, Nan came to stay. My brother and I started every night in the twin beds upstairs, but when the alarm sounded Mum and Nan half-woke us and helped us to blunder down the stairs to the hall cupboard where we drifted off again. If Dad were home, he'd carry us down, my mother bringing dry pyjamas in case I'd already wet myself.

I wrote earlier that no one of my age can forget the moment war began with Germany. It seems I was wrong. It's stayed with me as a week-day, with my Dad away, my brother and grandma nowhere about, only my mother and I alone at home. This would have done for a deliberate mistake in 'Puzzle Corner' on 'Monday Night at Eight'. Did you spot it? 3 September was a Sunday.

Perhaps my vivid memory of the sucked trellis is of the day France fell, 22 June. With an enviable sense of theatre, Hitler signed the armis-tice in the old railway carriage near Compiègne. It's still there, of course, in the woods, the only exhibit in a well-kept museum. French school-children in parties, war veterans, tourists of the battlefield from Agin-court to Dunkirk, all make pilgrimages to this spot where the Germans surrendered in 1918. What they will not find here is any reference to the replay in 1940. A lot of Foch but no Hitler. In fact, France never fell.

During the summer holiday which followed, the Battle of Britain was fought. It was more a battle of *South-East* Britain really. We listened to the daily scores on the Defiant and cheered when our side got more than theirs, but we saw very little until the Bristol raids started in September. My future father-in-law, unemployed for most of the 1930s, had come from South Wales to find work in Bristol. He got it at Bristol Aeroplanes, where they were making Blenheim and Beaufort bombers and Beaufighters. The Luftwaffe came one morning and in less than a minute killed 250 people. Next day they came again but were seen off by Hurricanes. This is from books and hearsay. As it was during term-time, I almost certainly saw these raids out in one of the trenches under our sports field. Every classroom had posted instructions. When the warning went, we evacuated in an orderly fashion, following coloured arrows either to the dug shelters or the basement stores or, if we were lucky, across the road to the underground laboratories of Bristol University, where we sniggered at human foetuses pickled in glass jars. At home we'd taken to sleeping in the downstairs passage, reading the action by sounds, trying to identify the rhythmic rumble of Theirs and the reassuring steady note of Ours. We worked out a code to tap mes-sages to the next-door children through the dividing wall: 'one of ours, one of theirs, ack-ack' and so on. The gunfire was noisier than the falling bombs for the main batteries were on the hill near our woodpile. During the first true blitz in November, we went out to watch the blazing city, an orange sunrise, spectacular beyond the orphanage, with a barrage balloon on fire in the dark smoke above. Next morning the bus was alive with rumours that the school had been destroyed by incendiaries. We were inconsolable when we rounded the corner to find the Prep smoul-dering and the main building unharmed.

During lunch hour we explored the neighbourhood – the university's hall had gone, the City Museum and the Prince's Theatre. Hoses, pools of water, charred timbers and furnishings filled Queen's Road and exhausted firemen and police ordered us away. I was sorry to see these buildings go but such sudden havoc was exciting, it promised an end and a new beginning. I shared the joy of the pyromaniac and I wasn't the only one. Tots and teenagers felt it too. Future councillors saw the razing of the old city and saw that it was good. In the great demolitions of the 1960s and 1970s they would knock down most of what was left. Armed with more sophisticated weapons, they'd replace the old, unplanned muddle of streets so clearly unsuited to the age of the car with a new, unplanned muddle of streets even more clearly unsuited to the age of the car. A good many Bristolians trying to live with this terrazzo tat in the 1960s would long for another Luftwaffe, another blaze, a fresh start.

The Co-op clothing factory was another disappointment. Bombed early on, it was soon repaired and back at work, which meant no relief for me from the regular visits with R. G. N. to get me measured for cut-price suits. The manager would meet my father and me at the door and lead us through the vast workshop where hundreds of girls stitched and hemmed at benches to the sounds of 'It's a lovely day tomorrow' from the speakers. They seemed to have prior knowledge of our arrival for, as soon as I appeared – skinny and spectacled – a great chorus of cheering and whistling drowned out machines and music and died only as we went out of sight into the manager's office. This was the world's longest journey – a fifty-mile walk lasting ten years – and had to be faced again after a tailor had measured my narrow chest and inside leg and clipped off one or two coupons from my ration book – just for show – and Dad had slipped them the usual packets of Radex. Even today I can induce clenched bowels and red ears by remembering the fresh cat-calls and hooting of that return trip across the factory floor.

The raids became regular during the cold winter of 1940. In December the boys of both schools were paraded on the terrace to watch the visit of King George VI, who must have been kept busy cheering people up after the raids. He and his family set us all an example of frugality when they had a line painted round the inside of the bath at Buckingham Palace to signify that if the royals could manage, so could we. Dad, always glad of an excuse to go short, at once followed suit.

'Tell you what, Buzfuz, let's you and I share, thus pooling our allowances and enjoying a ten-inch bath.'

'D'you think the Royal Family do that?'

'What?'

43

'Share twenty inches?'

'They well may.'

'Wouldn't half be soupy by the time it got to Princess Margaret Rose.'

'If you're complaining about being second, have it first, I don't care tuppence.'

'I don't either.'

'Then I'll go first. I want to listen to Sibelius's Second on the Home Service while I'm making out my reports. And – crackpot –'

'Hello?'

'Mind you wash out your lug-holes. D'you want some help?'

'No.'

I agreed to be second and use his bath because I'd lately taken to wanking under water. It wouldn't do to have R.G.N. discover the stretchy threads of semen floating round his knees. I could imagine the scene.

'Noodle, where are you? What have you been a-doing-of?'

Better go last, taking over the exhausted bathroom, its green walls sweating with condensation, the soap melting in the dish, the Valor oil-stove turned up high. A wartime sauna. Please, Princess, share my ten inches.

Margaret Rose's father met our headmaster, Mossy Moore, at the gate to the playing-fields. The OTC played the anthem, we all cheered and watched as he inspected the guard, saying as little as possible. It was somehow comforting that he stammered. After his speeches no one commented on what he said, it was always 'I thought he got through very well, only had to stop three times.'

The novelty of his appearance on the field did not last long. It was nearly time for Radio Rhythm Club Sextet on the Forces Programme. Or perhaps it was Lew Stone or the Squadronnaires or some other band that played something resembling jazz. In any case, we were spoilt for celebrities at the Grammar – Sir James Jeans came to explain the canals on Mars, a huge man called Tyrone Guthrie, an actor called Gielgud who only did Shakespeare and – when, I'm not sure – W.H. Auden made the Sixth laugh at jokes that were beyond the rest of us.

One thing was sure about headmasters and toffs generally – they thought jazz was a shocking row and that was reason enough for loving it. *Real* jazz came slowly, of course. We took what we could get – dance music to begin with, then swing and Dixieland and finally the hard stuff. This road I travelled with the boy who was to be my closest friend until we were sent to opposite coasts of India after the war. Cliff Brown was the nephew of my mother's best friend, Mrs Monty Graves. His father had a sinecure in some insurance firm but had chosen never to grow up.

The first time I visited Cliff's home, a modern semi in the sort of street my mother coveted, with ornamental cherries all along the verges, the father and son were flicking pellets at each other with elastic bands. Cliff's mother, plump, pretty and delicate, protested in vain. What he and I felt for each other seems now a kind of calf-love. Ours was the only uncritical friendship I've known. The first drop of doubt was fatal, but while it lived we developed our skills of mimicry and caricature and our love of jazz, films and comedy, all subserving the great necessary theme of our adolescence – making fun of our elders. Cliff was in another First Form at the Grammar but we sought each other in morning break, at lunch and after school. His gifts as a cartoonist put him far above our untalented art teachers. He could draw figures as effortlessly as other boys kicked balls or solved equations. His way with a picture matched mine with words and our shared skill at mimicry matured in no time into a secret weapon against which the adult world had no defence. A range of influences contributed to it – the *Dandy*, *Beano*, ITMA, the Crazy Gang, the Marx Brothers, Hell-zapoppin', James Thurber, Ogden Nash, Abbott and Costello, Hope and Crosby, Red Skelton, the comedies of Preston Sturgis, women like Martha Raye, Cass Daley, Betty Hutton and Nellie Wallace. Under his influence, I neglected the grammar of French and Latin to learn the grammar of film and jazz. His graphic skill was widely known and in constant demand for forging parents' notes for the entire school, but we kept it to ourselves and used it to get off sports and spend the time instead in the Embassy, Premier, Orpheus or Scala watching the films through three times in a day until we had learnt, say, the Contract Scene from *A Night at the Opera* or Abbott and Costello's classic *Blow that Horn*. Common experience, of course, for boys of our kind throughout the world. Though we didn't know it then, Philip Larkin, Kingsley Amis and John Wain were doing the same in other parts of England, Barry Humphries, Michael Blakemore and later Clive James in Sydney, Gunter Grass in Danzig, Josef Skvorecky in Prague and all those other Europeans about to be starved of jazz and Hollywood for the duration. *Boys* of our kind. Not girls. Girls enjoyed our jokes, yes – humour was all we had over the he-men – but somehow never managed to distinguish between the Marx Brothers and the Three Stooges, they were still listening to Joe Loss when we'd moved on to Charlie Barnet and still on Charlie Barnet when we were already groaning with delight at Pee-Wee Russell. Blitzed by their eyes and lips and breasts, we sent out the Spitfires of our mockery. We scandalized them with our family portraits. Cliff's drawings and my text depicted R.G.N. as a bald eagle, with ill-fitting teeth, advancing to clean out someone's ears with a cry of 'It's beyond my comprehension, Crackpot', or my mother as a gin-swilling, chain-smoking harpie stuck with this old killjoy but ogling soldiers behind his back. Mrs Monty Graves, Cliff's aunt, was tinted scarlet to represent what we saw to be her titanic struggles with indigestion. His father hid from his mother the nudes of *Men Only* behind the *Bristol Evening Post*. She would have moved across the room to reveal this but was too obese to rise from her chair. In real life she was suffering from some mild form of thyroid deficiency but our attacks gave no quarter. Nor expected any. I was shown as a gangling weed with lank hair, a pillar-box mouth and Harold Lloyd glasses. Cliff was pink-cheeked and infantile, a series of shudder-lines showing his excessive and spasmodic way of moving. We enjoyed a kind of invulnerability by saying worse of ourselves than any of our enemies could. To deal with louts or yobs, we developed a parody of Bristol speech with few consonants and a plethora of arr's. More than once I got a bloody nose for using this to bullies in our local park.

Our comic strips and sketches put the adolescent point of view. It was as though Swift had written ITMA. Old women's teeth hung lopsided in their ape-like faces, middle-aged mothers and aunts struggled with hideous undergarments – those corsets, suspenders and brassieres known to us as 'organizations' – teachers were gargoyles, each with his own distinct flavour of halitosis. Words foundered. For example, 'haemoglobin' may have been red corpuscules to our science teacher Freddie Flood; to us it was the catch-phrase of a leprechaun who bounced up like a jack-in-the-box and shouted 'H'Oi'm a goblin'. Anyone appearing suddenly anywhere reduced us to tears of laughter. What people *said* didn't matter, only their manner of speaking, their efforts to be posh, to hide their stammers, control their dentures, sound their aitches or disguise their German accents. Nazi saboteurs were everywhere. A young geography master, recently appointed, who must have been unfit or a conshie, had been parachuted in, we thought, during the daylight raid on Filton. His classes were a clamour of 'Heil Hitler' and 'Gott in Himmel!' and 'Zis is Funf speaking.' Cliff and I refined the general uproar with fine distinctions between Anton Walbrook, Conrad Veidt, Albert Basserman and Sig Ruman, the last turning up in *A Day in the Death of Joe Egg* when I was nearly forty. The accidental sensory impact of films was all-important. Guns in films weren't like the ones we were hearing every night in the raids – the sound-tracks couldn't cope. 'Boom' was nowhere near it. A sort-of preparatory hawking in the throat was closer. Noticing that broadcast applause in a crowded hall was like the sound of slowly exhaled breath, we could then do a thousand soldiers joining Vera Lynn in 'We'll Meet Again' by singing in a sustained whisper. It was an abstract, nothing like the real sound, as we knew very well for we had ourselves become entertainers and heard a hall of soldiers singing.

I am surprised to find how early this happened. In fact, my memories of the war seem to be mostly of its first two years. I was already appearing in shows early in 1941, during the worst air-raids, a fact authenticated by the death of the singer Al Bowlly, killed by a bomb in his London flat in March of that year, which cannot have been long after he had topped the variety bill at the Bristol Empire. I was part of a supporting act of local discoveries. Now that Bowlly has become a cult, regarded as a major figure by Dennis Potter, I should like to be able to offer a vivid memory of his act. In fact, I was only interested in a half-naked girl who danced with a python, dimly lit by coloured spots while the band played bits of Ketelby. The climax of this nearly unbearable display came as she struck a pose (required by the Watch Committee's regulations) and ripped off her bolero, allowing a brief flash of breasts before the lights went out and the front-drop fell. I remember envying Bowlly, who seemed to be always in her dressing-room or fondling her in the wings. The snake-charmer's were the only tits I saw in the first twenty years of my life. She was brought back to life in the 1970s by Stephanie Lawrence as Miss 1940 in *Forget-me-not Lane*.

Another figure in that play was a conjuring queen called Mister Magic and it was he who in real life presented the local discoveries, including me. His stage name at this time was Will A. Mays, but he had other aliases in the court records and was no stranger to the *News of the World*. He rented a bed-sitting room a short walk from Palatine and, when he learnt I couldn't swim, promised to teach me free of charge. I assumed we would be going straight to the Public Baths round the corner and had put on trunks to save time. He told me no, it was best to start with some exercises on dry land and he'd help me off with my trousers. I said I could manage and, when I'd done so, he asked me to sit on his lap and he would show me how to move my legs. It seemed a pretty silly way to learn but it couldn't be left to Dad, whose idea of teaching me was to duck me under and shout 'Come on, piecan, push with your arms!' I remained unresponsive to Will A. Mays's efforts – he was old and fat and it had never occurred to me for an instant that people of the same sex could enjoy one another.

This blank in my education must be counted as another failure of the day-school system. At Clifton College I'd probably have learnt much sooner. Whatever I gathered during nine years at the Grammar was out of school hours. In the case of the conjuror, I grasped the basic principle quickly, made my excuses, pulled on my trousers and ran home. A few months later Dad found an item in the Sunday paper. The poor old bugger had been reported by another boy and was doing six months in Horfield Gaol.

'You had a lucky escape there, Peter. Only confirms what Brother Robb said – the theatre's full of nancy-boys.'

'Is that what he was?' my mother asked, reading the column.

'Of course! They're everywhere. Our chief buyer in Fancy Goods, suede shoes, pronounced squint, they say you were only safe near him if you wore tin trousers.'

Soon after that Cliff taught me the breast-stroke in Bristol North Baths, though I still can't dive or swim under water.

The incident confirmed Dad's view of show business as a gang of bankrupts, lechers and drunks, not one of whom could expect a pension. My mother tried to understand.

'Well, they say even Ivor Novello sleeps with all his leading ladies.'

Before her marriage, she'd auditioned for Carl Rosa.

'I had to give up singing when you came along,' she said.

But in 1940, when the call came, she was ready. It was through her that Cliff and I joined the Bristol Wartime Entertainers, a pool of amateurs who added to the miseries of local army and air force personnel by driving out to their camps most evenings to sing, dance and laugh away their cares for them. We gathered at the offices of the *Evening World* and formed loose groups or parties with one concerted opener and a finale with a string of individual turns between. Our opening chorus went:

> Goodnight,
> Got your torch-light?   YES!
> Got your gas-mask?   YES!
> All right? All right!
> Goodnight, goodnight, goodnight.

I was the baby and came next with a couple of comic monologues about Albert and the Lion or Runcorn Ferry or the Jubilee Sovereign. I wore a flat cap and woollen scarf and recited in stage Lancashire. Next came a peroxide blonde tap-dancing to current favourites. She can't have been more than five years older than I but was already as unattainable as Princess Margaret Rose. The sight of her bare legs, browned by Miner's liquid make-up, caused an uproar which ceased only when she'd gone and the compère promised she'd come back later with more of the same. My mother appeared in one of two evening gowns – satin or velvet – and sang from her repertoire of ballads: 'One Fine Day' from *Butterfly*, 'Because', 'Bless This House', and

> Up in the attic away from the deen
> Someone is playing an old violeen. . . .

From *The Chocolate Soldier* came 'My Hero', for which she always said she had had many requests.

'Come, come, I love you only,' she sang to the assembled troops. Those with a taste for the classics showed it by applauding Violet loudest. Cliff's act went well with everyone. He already contributed regular cartoons to the local paper and from the print-room pinched supplies of newsprint to cut into squares and fix to an easel. With a wodge of cotton-wool dipped in black ink, he sketched figures of the day, played tricks with lines and always somehow managed his caricature of Churchill's face from a doodle by someone from the audience. This led to our finale – Violet sang 'There'll Always Be An England' and the rest of us appeared to take our bows and join in the final chorus. Recreated in *Forget-me-not Lane*, this had them roaring but I watched with mixed feelings. There was more to it than that. They jested at scars that had never felt a wound.

The deepest injury I sustained one night in an army hospital ward. The rum-tee-tum lines with their obvious rhymes must have given me a false sense of security. Suddenly there were no more in my head, no hope of improvising such stuff and no one to prompt me. For some time I stood looking helplessly from bed to bed. The patients waited. After a pause of several years, I said 'I'm sorry, I can't remember,' and blundered off. Warm and sympathetic applause followed The Miserable Mirth-Maker to the passage outside where I cried with shame – not so much at *my* dry as at *their* pity. I determined that never again would I give any audience the chance to patronize me. In my years on the stage, I dried many times but no one ever saw me lost for words.

It would be dishonest just to belittle those times for they were often exciting. We always played on when alerts had sounded and sometimes had to shout over anti-aircraft fire from another part of the camp. Once I was reciting to a full hangar of airmen when the tannoy began calling fighter crews into the sky. 'Carry on!' shouted the others as I stood waiting for the duty personnel to scamper up the aisle. Some moments later came another call, then another; I'd wait, watch them go, pick it up again and somehow reached the end. Even now, tarnished as this scene is by film and television cliché, I remember it with pride.

Some of the smaller units were the most isolated and the most in need of amusement. For these a motor-coach was converted into a mobile theatre. At the driver's end a tiny stage, eight foot by five, was equipped with a mini-piano and some lights. We artistes waited outside and jumped aboard when our turns came round. Somehow the peroxide blonde coped with this limited space, tapping bravely on the spot. Even I, who worshipped the ground she danced on, have to admit that her roller-skating number lost a lot in these conditions. Sometimes, afterwards, she'd sit beside me on the way home.

'And as we approached the city,' says Frank in *Forget-me-not Lane* , 'the sky was orange, searchlight beams were tracking the bombers, a balloon burned over the houses, ack-ack pounded away ... and my hand was crushed beneath a dancer's thighs!'

My brother Geoff had started twitching with loss of sleep when the raids got regular. The doctor said he needed rest and quiet, somewhere in the country. My parents knew of a hotel in the Mendips that had been taken over by a London private school for the duration and Geoff was sent there as a boarder. This meant that my mother had no children under twelve at home and was conscripted to work for Bristol Aeroplanes at Patchway. Geoff hated the Mendips so much that he ran away several times, on one occasion walking back to Bristol. I went to stay with him once or twice, fell in love with the head girl, wet the bed and renounced her. When the Germans raided the factory, my mother had to go to the shelters 'with all the rest of them. It was terrible. Some of the women had gone to the toilets to wash their hands and got caught.' It was her turn to start twitching so Geoff came back and she left the factory.

The man next door was a traveller too, a freelance, Dad said with pity, for it meant he could expect no pension. When he was on the road, his wife and children came to share our company and the protection of a father. Dad was unnerving, though, a cat on hot bricks, bobbing in and out from his firewatching duties, looking daft in the helmet he'd been issued, an upturned bowl in grey fibre. When their father was home, we went in there and sang and played I-Spy. One night the blast blew in their black-out screen. It was a lark at first but, once the novelty had worn off, we went back to sleeping in our beds. One Sunday morning in April 1941, after a perfect night, Mum woke me to say that Nan had been bombed out. The night before, she'd left Palatine for a drink with a friend but had never returned. The sirens sounded and a raid began. As she was closer to her own place than ours, she'd gone there rather than to 192. She was about to open her front door when her niece Maud, who lived in the next house, asked her to go and share their Anderson shelter. Nan's sister Hannah was already there and Nan wasn't with them long before a high-explosive bomb fell in the street and burst a gas-mains, lighting the streets around. The bomber made a second run and it was then that Nan's was hit. For some reason, Hannah's family now decided to run for it. Nan and her sister, both in their late sixties, had to be helped over the back wall. In the great blaze of the burning gas-leak, they reached the local school, but the shelters there had no room for them and they made their way off through the streets.

Mum and Dad meanwhile, alarmed when she did not return, searched her ruined house and at first took her for dead, but finally traced her to a cousin's place where they'd found refuge. This was the excuse Mum had always wanted, an unanswerable reason for moving Nan into Palatine for good. They rescued what they could from her first-floor flat. The looters had called and there wasn't much – a wooden chair and a tin trunk. Next morning, a picture of the debris was in a national newspaper. In the foreground crouched a girl with a doll's house she seemed to have saved from the wreckage. An inspiring image.

'Brazen little hussy!' Nan said indignantly, 'I ain't never seen 'er. She'm a stranger.'

Nan stayed with us until her death, vague and easily upset, suddenly waking from a doze to ask if that was Them she could hear coming back. Her room at the end of the passage smelt of old age. There was only space enough for a cheap stained wardrobe, a high bed with a feather mattress and a dressing-table with drawers that stuck. On a glass tray before the mirror she kept her hairpins and a switch of her own hair, shorn in the days when it was still brown. Every morning she fastened this to the grey wisps that remained, unaware of the strange effect, as though a grey and a red squirrel had curled up together on her head.

When the air-raids ended, our share of the war was over. From now on we simply waited for it to end. To people like ourselves who were comfortably off, the shortages seemed hard but most were better fed, clothed and paid than ever before. We settled down in our cosy fortress to sit out the siege. Churchill huffed and puffed, carefully avoiding any mention of ordinary people, about whom he knew nothing.

'He's never been on a bus,' his wife told their doctor, 'and only once on the underground.'

He came to Bristol after the raids and did the V-sign and promised we'd pay them back. From then on things got steadily worse until, lucky for him, Pearl Harbor brought in America. Hitler couldn't win now but then neither could we. The pink-map geography I was still learning would soon be history. But the Yanks were coming, that was all we knew. We'd parodied Churchill's 'Give us the tools and we will finish the job' because a tool to us was a penis. When the first wave of black Americans came, the girls of Bristol cheered up.

Our leader's call had been answered.

4 Over Here

'You ought to see the 21 bus-stop,' said my grandma, 'all they nigs sitting on the wall with they brazen hussies! Decent people waiting for the bus and there they was a-loving of 'em!'

The orphans had gone early in the war, leaving the great houses to become an ARP centre and then an American barracks – first for blacks and later whites. The blancoed gear and tight-arsed trousers and nifty jeeps pointed up how drab we were. How humiliating it must have been for British adults to cope with this! A British captain got less pay than a Yankee private. But to us teenagers, who weren't even in the race, their invasion was a godsend. We put up no resistance. Loving jazz, we saw the blacks as somehow sharing the glory of Ellington, Bechet and Armstrong. They brought gum, they drilled like the Rockettes, they were friendly and every one seemed to be a millionaire. From all over Bristol, brazen hussies flocked to the orphanage on wooden wedge-heeled shoes, in brushed angora sweaters and snoods or turbans, at first only the real pros, but hot on their heels the good-time girls, amateurs of every kind – bored teenagers, fast tarts and middle-aged women whose men were in the desert. We reeled at the age and appearance of these crones. How could those handsome blacks bear to touch them? Mum explained that most darkies would find *any* white woman fascinating.

Rows of tarts sat on Toby Wainwright's wall by the main entrance to the camp. Respectable families were scandalized but before long they surrendered too – girls who'd learnt elocution, been to secretarial college or who were writing letters to North Africa Sealed With A Loving Kiss. Catching a bus meant running a gauntlet of sexual derision from the waiting women. Miserably conscious of my glasses, sallow skin and school cap and tie, I would brave the calls of 'Hullo, lover' and 'Ain't he handsome?' Cliff and I took some revenge by following them of a summer's evening up to Purdown where they lay with their exotic lovers, sometimes ten couples to a field, doing whatever it was they did. We sneaked up on them, trying to fill the gaps in our education, hoping for a flash that would tell us what this had to do with wanking. Used condoms were as common on our pavements as Lucky Strike packs. Later, when the whites arrived, it became our pastime to climb down the Somerset bank of Avon Gorge and throw pebbles at the shoals of Frenchies being carried out to sea on the ebb tide. Not all were effective. A year or so after the blacks left Muller's, several local girls gave birth to coffee-coloured babies, having claimed they'd got pregnant before their husbands went to war. It was said that the wrath of their white GI boyfriends was greater even than their husbands'. The blacks got posted elsewhere and sometimes appeared in the city centre and racial skirmishes would break out. One was so grave that double-decker buses were used as barricades to separate the feuding factions. The films were coming true. The sculptor 'Nibs' Dalwood got on a bus one night at Temple Meads Station. There was one other passenger and a conductor. As the bus moved off, a GI ran from a side-street and jumped on to the platform, where he was gunned down by another who'd been chasing him through the blackout. He fell into the road, dead or dying, but the conductor didn't stop the bus, only turned away and fiddled with his tickets. When Nibs asked the other passenger to bear witness, the man refused to answer, just stared ahead. The day they all left by train to join the Normandy invasion, my grandma said 'They brazen hussies turned up at the station 'awlding up their brown babies and chanting "We want our 'usbands, give us back our 'usbands!"'

The week before they left, the whites were confined to barracks and an army of Bristol women of all ages stormed the camp singing 'Don't fence me in'.

Incidents like this took the gilt off. By the end of the war, a poll showed that Yanks were only slightly more popular than Poles and less than Czechs, Danes, French and even Italians, who were one of the official enemies. But in the beginning, they were welcomed with open arms and legs, if only for nylons, cigarettes, K rations, Scotch, V-discs, the American Forces Network radio station and Yank-style picture magazines. These papers were given to girls and later sold in bundles to secondhand bookshops near the Horsefair. Each had a full-page pin-up girl and so began a collage that covered the four walls of our back-room den. We haunted Lee's Ice-Cream Parlour on Gloucester Road. Memory suggests that we spent our sixpences on sundaes and sodas, but no ice-cream was made in England after 1942. Perhaps we drank Dried Milk Shakes while listening to Bob Crosby's 'Vultee Special' or Gene Krupa's 'Tuxedo Junction' on the juke-box.

One afternoon I sneaked off sports to see an American troop show called *This is the Army*, doing a few dates for the public at the University's Victoria Rooms, which has a Graeco-Roman façade, ornate bronze fountains and a statue of Edward VII: In this unpromising place, I took a knock-out blow – my first American stage musical. A big band played in the pit, the all-male chorus line was like a machine-gun and near the end, almost unexpectedly, the tabs rose and there, in Doughboy's uniform, beside a canvas tent, sat Irving Berlin. In person, not a cartoon. In a quavering voice he sang

> 'My British buddy,
> We're as different as can be –
> I like my coffee and cream
> And he likes his tea.
> But we're in there pitching and on one thing we agree –
> When the job is done
> And the war is won
> We'll be stretching hands across the sea.'

A forlorn hope. In fact, as soon as they'd dropped the atomic bomb, the Americans betrayed every promise they'd made. Churchill and Roosevelt had said one thing but Truman did another. Like a landlord from Dickens, they made us pay every penny of our debts and, having robbed us, knocked us down and left us bleeding.

One day, hurrying to the bus after school, I blundered into Mrs Roosevelt. She was leaving the Gas Company showrooms, converted for the war into a welfare centre of some kind. This memory turned up in the late 1970s when we visited Hyde Park, the Roosevelt family house in New York State, and found that Eleanor's bedroom and F.D.R.'s were separated by his mother's.

Our own variety theatres had never closed. London's had, in the early days, and that had meant better tours for the provinces. Before the Prince's was burned, I saw Beatrice Lillie and Vic Oliver in Coward's *Tonight at 8.30* and Robert Donat in *The Devil's Disciple*. Jack Buchanan was its last attraction. About this time too my parents had seen *Murder in the Cathedral*. They'd expected a nice mystery but it was 'nothing but moaning nuns'.

In my twenties, struggling to get an acting job, I went to the agency where Uncle Rob claimed to have spent his days. I used his name but they seemed not to know it. Had this too been a lie? Was he only another Bob Cratchit? He certainly sent my father tickets for the Hippodrome to report on acts they'd booked. So it was that we saw the last of Billy Bennett, Revnell and West (The Long and Short of It), Morris and Cowley, Nosmo King (with Dad forever explaining how he made up his stage name), Bennett and Williams with their phono-fiddles, Arthur Prince and his dummy, Robb Wilton and Will Hay, Jimmy James and Monsewer Eddie Gray, not to mention the jugglers, acrobats, mono-cyclists, exotic dancers, animal acts and mouth-organ and accordion bands. It must have been tame compared to its heyday in Dad's youth but enough survived to bring the colour to his cheeks. He struggled valiantly against this glamour, dreading the filth of Music-hall that was always threatening the decorum of Variety. He longed, as I did, to be up there. My brother and I remember in different ways the packed second house when Dad finally became the star. I say it was Ronald Frankau, known for smutty innuendo in a posh voice, a not-very-likeable top-liner, more revue than music-hall. Geoff says it was a supporting act. In either case, the jokes were getting bluer, though I wasn't sure what they meant, when Dad suddenly shouted 'That's enough. Get off! Women and children present!'

After the usual shock, some of the audience jeered. The comedian took heart from this.

'Thanks very much, sir, and very welcome they are too! Both the ladies and their little ones! Now – to continue –'

'Oh, no you don't! We don't want your filth. We don't want performers who have to resort to mentioning the private parts of women to get a laugh.'

My mother leaned across Geoff and me and whispered 'Dick! Dick!', but she might as well have reasoned with a drunk. This was his moment and he felt it. We all did. 'I sat there,' says Frank in *Forget-me-not Lane*, 'hot under the collar of my utility shirt.'

Again the comedian carried on but Dad began a slow handclap, each beat for us a gunshot.

'Don't knock your pipe out at me,' said the comic.

By now the gallery were booing and hissing and suddenly Dad was on his feet and moving down the aisle to a point near the stage where everyone could see him. To the mounting roar of derision, he bowed with absurd dignity. Somehow he'd won. All the comedian could do after that was cue the band and go into his exit song.

It was nothing to do with disapproval. In another theatre during a dance by girls in tights, he went comically down the aisle with a pair of those rented opera-glasses to his eyes, shouting back at me 'Not bad, eh, boy? What d'you think of the redhead?'

The slow bow he later perfected for other audiences. Geoff was on a bus when some football supporters got on, rowdily telling each other about the funny old bloke who'd berated the crowd for their behaviour and, when they started jeering, had bowed slowly, three times, provoked a roar of joy, then raised his hat in a grand gesture of thanks.

All this was impossible with which to live. Cliff and I had a hard time exaggerating his oddities. The noise he made when he ate sounded to us like the rhythmic crunch of an old sound-box in the groove at the centre of a record. Or like men marching in mud. On the beach he wore a full-length costume with shoulder-straps and a rubber bathing-helmet fastened under the chin. He removed his ankle-bandages and the scraps of cotton-wool from between his toes, transferring two of these to his ears. He left his teeth in a towel on the sand. Orifices intrigued him – he seldom caught sight of Geoff or me without asking if our ears wanted cleaning. If we weren't quick on our feet, he'd grasp a lobe and set to work with a twist of handkerchief. He showed endless resource with handkerchiefs : before our very eyes they became spikes, towels, face flannels, tablecloths, handbags and, by means of a knot at each corner, hats. Laying out a hankie in his lap, he'd peel an orange without breaking the rind, split it into segments and eat each piece with grotesque relish, making that noise like men in mud.

I try to recreate him for my children who don't remember.

'Old Mother Hubbard here, my good lady, has been asking why I tore up her clematis in the back garden,' I say, doing his voice but at the sa e time pulling a handkerchief from my pocket, 'well, I have to explain that for me it belongs to that variety of plant I refer to as Members of the Lodge,' holding out the handkerchief by two corners as though to warm it at an open fire, ' – clematis, wistaria, honeysuckle, ivy, you've got it, boy, yes, creepers!', and I bring the warmed handkerchief from the fire and place it between my legs, holding it there to warm my genitals as he did, 'creepers, crawlers, Masonic types, don't talk to me about clematis!'

When he reappeared on Friday, we no longer thought 'You home again?', we said it to his face. Poor man, we both hated him. He loved touching us but we wouldn't let him.

It was my wife who first showed me how tactile he was. By an amazing coincidence of the kind he loved, she met him when she was a girl in Swansea. She'd been sent back there during the Bristol raids, just in time for the Welsh blitzes. Doing the South Wales societies, he'd made friends with a manager who lived in the street where Thelma was staying with her aunt. She remembers a children's party at the manager's house and Dad as a huge, jolly man who played the piano, joined in the games, lavished presents on them all and carried the toddlers piggy-back. They were always fond of each other, though he could never call her name to mind. Stella, Bella, Tessa, Velma ... he'd usually give up. But then, as time went on, he wasn't sure of anyone's.

'Bert, Tom, Rob, Fred, Harriet, Buzfuz, what's your name? Peter, yes, all right, I know.'

Thelma remembers two visitors to her Swansea suburb – Dick and Haile Selassie, whose son taught at the Bible College next to the house where she met Dad. After Mussolini's conquest of Abyssinia, the Emperor lived in Bath. One day he came to visit and Thelma and the other children were lined up to cheer and wave. This is what she remembers when Rastafarians carry on about the Lion of Judah.

After the raids, she and her mother rejoined her father in Bristol and there they settled within half a mile of Palatine Lodge and she began at Colston's Girls. She already knew my brother, but living beyond the railway cut her off from the civilized world. She came literally from the other side of the tracks, where Captain Dowsett kept dog-kennels, where there were open hills and gasometers and the real city fizzled out into madhouses and alien parks. During the war the whole quarter reeked of simmering pig-food. The blacks paraded on a waste-ground near her house and were made welcome in many homes. Later, when the same people tried to welcome the whites, they found they wouldn't go where the blacks had been. Thelma was eleven or twelve when she hung about the houses of older women while they painted their faces and curled their hair with sugar and water before going out to see what they could find. The one she most admired worked her way from buck private to major between 1942 and the Normandy invasion.

At this time, Thelma and I hadn't met. Nor had either of us met the other Bristolians of about our age who'd later mean something in our lives: the actors Robert Lang and Robert Stephens; the future artistic director of Glyndebourne, John Cox; the sculptor Hubert Dalwood, the painter Francis Hewlett. At Colston's with Thelma were the future actresses Margaret Whiting and Valerie Newman and the outlandish Patsy Chidgey who later became conformable enough to marry a Nobel Prize winner. Most of these lived within a mile or so of Palatine Lodge – Lang and Hewlett were at Cary Grant's old school, Fairfield, on the other side of the tracks, transformed in the film star's *Who's Who* entry into Fairfield Academy, Somerset. Lang would be in the National Theatre Company in 1969 at the right moment to play the Bristolian Ash in *The National Health*. Another actor, Peter Jeffrey, began his career in my end-of-term skits at the Grammar and in the 1970s appeared in my play *The Common* on television. As a boy, he lived a few hundred yards along Ashley Down Road in a grandiose Victorian folly called Tudor Lodge. His father, a prosperous wine merchant, had a family of nine daughters and two sons, of which Peter was the younger. By local standards the Jeffreys were indecently well-off. The 'grounds' were large enough to contain a tennis-court and inside there was a billiard-room with Gothic windows. The place teemed with boisterous sisters and his mother seemed, not surprisingly, tired. Peter and I played Mills Brothers records on his portable gram and tried to imitate their imitations of muted trumpets. Was there a real suit of armour in the hall? I certainly remembered one when I used the house as the setting for *Born in the Gardens*.

His father decided the Grammar wasn't good enough and Peter was sent to Harrow. Years later, after his father's death, the house was sold to a spec builder, pulled down and replaced by a gimcrack terrace. While it stood, Tudor Manor was a focal-point – not an aspiration, it was too old for that, more a place by which to measure others. For example, Cliff and I made it our destination on the walks we took when I was dressed in my mother's clothes. Tuesday afternoon was Sports and also the day Vi went with Cliff's aunt to the pictures. There was no need to traipse up to Golden Hill to catch their horrible cricket balls. Cliff would forge a note tomorrow. Instead we'd raid Mum's wardrobe for a dress, high-heeled shoes and a turban. Then Cliff would make up my face with any lipstick, eyebrow-pencil and rouge we found on her dressing-table and together we'd set out for Tudor Lodge.

What a smasher I must have been, even without my glasses, hobbling short-sightedly with Cliff as my guide-dog! The tricky bit was staring out any neighbours we passed. Toby Wainwright's mother might be trimming their front hedge. Once past their house, the way was safe till the American sentry at the main gate of the orphanage. I don't remember getting a response, though I couldn't have been any more grotesque than some of the tarts they took to Purdown. But this was the point of the dare – to get past the sentry. At Tudor Manor, we turned back and I hobbled home. I have forgotten how often we did this; like many of our hobbies, it didn't last. Cliff liked animals, especially reptiles, and for a while we kept a lizard and a grass-snake we'd caught in the back garden. Cliff used to take it for walks in his inside pocket, frightening girls by suddenly allowing the beautiful head to appear between his fingers. One day it escaped. Our next-door neighbour came upon it and cut it in two with a chopper. She told my mother afterwards but Mum never let on where the snake had come from.

As the war went away and the siege wore on, the old life returned. Older people moved pins about on maps tracing the to-and-fro of armies. England seemed to us to go to sleep again. Everyone dreamt of After, a wedding-time when bells would chime, a gay tomorrow with no more sorrow, just you wait and see. But the present was boring. My brother started keeping a diary.

'Bought some Ovaltine tablets,' says one of the few entries, 'and we shared them out.'

He was old enough now to share a lot with us – not only Ovaltine tablets but games and jokes and music. He was called Tich and got treated as Tich. One photo shows him in Dad's vicar set holding a bottle and acting drunk beside a sign advertising the Band of Hope. Geoff was back at the Grammar now and on prize day joined Cliff and me and 900 others to sing with choir, orchestra and Shiner Cheyney on the organ, the school song in Latin, the only words of that language I remember.

> So nobler and so worthier
> Be she, whate'er befall us,
> Be this our noblest boast for her –
> Bristolians men do call us.

It's better in Latin. *Sumus Bristolienses* was a great noise, I know, though it might have offended our new headmaster John Garrett, a fastidious snob, friend of the famous and intellectual groupie. With Auden, he had co-edited the famous anthology *The Poet's Tongue*. He spoke only to the Upper Sixth and the Upper Sixth spoke only to him.

'The public behaviour of the lower forms', he said at one assembly, 'is execrable.' Pause. 'Which means very bad.' Knowing smile. Laughter from the Sixth. He spoke to me only once. I was now in a sort-of academic ghetto called Transitus but my behaviour was even more execrable than that of the Lower Sixth's. 'An old queer' Evelyn Waugh called him in his diary. I saw him once years later in the London tube at rush-hour – a short, nervous man bewildered by so many of the common sort. The gown, the dais, the carved chair had all made him seem tall. I went back lately for the first time to address the Sixths myself and was entertained to school dinner on that holy podium by the present head, his wife and the head boy and girl. Yes, girl! The gloomy corridors, otherwise unchanged, thronged with females who made no secret of their sex. I loitered, a dirty old man, the only male who was at all amazed at this Great Step Forward. If there'd been girls in my day, would it have made any difference to my life? My son has been to mixed schools mostly and still looks confused. In any case, we weren't boarders. In the evenings we could hang about the surface shelters in St Andrew's Park, sneering at the girls in our new gang, hoping one of them would take to us. But with boys like Inky Black about, this wasn't likely. Inky became our Proper Man. His father ran a music-shop in one of the old arcades and lent us instruments when we formed our rhythm section. Inky was our Count Basie, tinkling away in the upper octaves while Stan Coates picked out guitar chords like Freddie Green, Cliff made the hi-hat whisper for all the world like Jo Jones and I did Walter Page on double-bass. Or would have done, but Mr Black couldn't manage a bass so I did what I could with an old cello. First we listened to the Parlophone Super Rhythm Style Series (with the smart blue and gold labels), then took our places to copy every note of 'Basie Boogie' or 'One o'Clock Jump', ecstatic at the lovely sound we made, whispering 'genius' as one of us caught a fine nuance. Inky was the undisputed leader – strong and good-looking, the John Wayne of the static water-tank. He protected us from bullies, laughed at our jokes and helped himself to the prettiest girls. He was afraid of nothing. He even made a successful play for one of the WAAFs who looked after the barrage balloon that was tethered in the park. It was always breaking free and floating away over the houses, while the WAAFs ran after it to mark where it came to earth.

How long this happy time lasted I have no idea. There is only a generalized memory of girls I loved but never told, of smoking in the bandstand, showing off tricks with bicycles by the sundial and the smell of mown grass on summer evenings.

The old life hung on like the sound of a plucked string. Through the forty years since then, it has been accessible during illness. Lying in bed with cold or fever, with the will gone and only memory working, the sounds and sights of the last of my childhood have come back. Horses' hooves on asphalt, bringing milk or coal or vegetables from the market garden, the Salvation Army Band on Sundays, right outside on purpose to provoke the Old Man. At least four of them were from a very holy family who lived a few doors off.

'You listening, Buzfuz? I was just telling Old Mother Hubbard here that, if there is one group you can safely set beside the Masons as A1 creepers, crawlers *par excellence*, it's the dashed Salvation Army.'

Dad was a happy man the day we heard that one of this family was going to jail for theft.

'Didn't I tell you? Eh, Goldflake Gertie, didn't I say they're hypocrites?'

'Oh, well, of course you're always right.'

'Not always, no.'

'And always telling the world about it.'

'Verily, verily, I say unto thee, blessed is he that bloweth his own trumpet lest it be not blown at all.'

'I feel sorry for his mother,' said Violet.

'Just let his old man come round beating the drum outside my window on a Sunday morning, that's all. Just let him try.'

Others came on bicycles – the sweep thrusting his brushes up the chimney, bringing soot down into the room Mum had covered with sheets; the lamplighter turning on the masked streetlights; the post-office men who put on pointed spurs to climb the telegraph pole beside our back wall.

I hear Dad clipping the privet with his shears and the rapid approach of a friendly local gossip.

'You're doing a good job there, Mister Nichols.'

'Good afternoon, Mrs Rushworth. How are you these days? Keeping busy?'

'Not specially, no.'

'Well, I am. Good day to you.'

I failed to qualify for the School Leaving Certificate, stayed another year, took it again and scraped by. I left after nine years without ever winning a prize or distinction of any kind. Cliff and I spent a year in offices – he in insurance, I in the Board of Trade. Obviously the war was won – it was only a matter of when they blew the whistle. We'd still be taken for the army. Bed-wetting could have kept me out but suddenly that had stopped. Cliff decided to volunteer for the air force and I did the same so that we could stay together. We longed to leave, for now we saw this was the way to break the string. We suffered agonies of boredom, haunted the local railway stations at night to get a vicarious thrill of travel and stood on the footbridge over the line at Montpelier as the engine coughed out bursts of steam and smoke, smelling of coal, enveloping us entirely as we mimed elaborate deaths. In our new trilbies, we climbed the bank at Ashley Hill, read the signals and felt the shuddering rail. One or both of us put halfpennies on the steel, then lay together on the scorched grass staring at the sky. A frantic whistle not far off brought the Cardiff-Temple Meads express pelting past, its passengers strangely calm in such a turmoil. The guard's van's light receded and we picked our halfpennies from the rail, flattened, misshapen and a little warmer.

Sunday evenings on Blackboy Hill, we tormented the evangelists from the pentecostal church of the Mount of Olives. Our favourite butt was Henry Colman, whose name could be read inside his stiff collar, but we drank cider with the fascist Webster, later a star at Marble Arch.

One night in that same Hippodrome, I was shaken by Olivier's production of *The Skin of our Teeth* by Thornton Wilder. Bristol went to see Vivien Leigh, hoping for more Scarlett O'Hara, found itself at an expressionist comic strip and walked out. Cliff and I stayed to cheer. I wish I had started from there, not followed so many false trails, before returning to that path in my first stage plays.

In moments of extreme boredom, I formed a habit that persisted through my twenties of paying a penny toll to go halfway across the

Clifton Suspension Bridge, lean on the balustrade, gaze down into the Avon Gorge and contemplate suicide. Hundreds of feet below were Hotwells, the road to Avonmouth, a well-known pick-up place for whores, the muddy river-bed with usually only a trickle that became a river at high tide, and the branch railway to Portishead. We all knew of people who had thrown themselves over. The temptation was nearly irresistible at times. Something surely would hold you, as it always did in dreams. In the last century a woman had been saved by her crinoline and floated down. I didn't mind hitting the road or railway – good and sudden. It was all that mud that worried me. I'd seen a film where Robert Newton went under in a bog, while his rescuers looked on helplessly.

'No,' said Nan, 'they do never land in the h'Avon. They do almost h'always 'it the tennis courts.' Game, set and match.

But it was the mud that turned me back to the Bristol side, along the Promenade past the zoo and across the Downs to catch the 83 bus home. This was Clifton, the tourists' Bristol, an imperial village where the rich slavers and chocolate or tobacco merchants had built a public school for their sons and a zoo for their trophies. I knew a way into the zoo through an exit turnstile and spent a lot of my time staring into the ill-tempered face of Alfred, the oldest gorilla in captivity. In fact, he'd not been Born in the Gardens but captured as an infant. During the war he was frightened by a low-flying aircraft and, like my grandma, never properly recovered. He can be seen now, stuffed, in the City Museum, but it's not the same.

A week before we were due to be called up, Cliff and I went cycling in Wiltshire with my brother. Geoff was ahead and suddenly applied his brakes, Cliff went into him and I flew over both and landed on the road. I was slightly concussed and had some scratches. They took me to a cottage hospital and kept me there a week, my face all gentian violet, long enough to delay my reporting for duty. Cliff and I might have been separated anyway but this was better, clean and easy.

The war in Europe was over. We expected to be posted east to fight the Japanese. Then the bomb was dropped and all of a sudden there was no war, those that were left gathered at the Tramways Centre and danced and sang but most people took no notice. Still slightly scarred, I reported for duty the day after the Japs surrendered.

'This', said Einstein of the Bomb, 'will change everything except the way Men think.'

Part Two Man

Well – what's the contribution I can send?
Turn back and read what I've already penned
So jauntily. There's little left to say...
I'm not the man I was. Nine years have passed;
And though the legs that marched survive today
My Fusiliering self has died away;
His active service came and went too fast.

He kept a diary. Reading what he wrote
Like some discreet executor I find
The scribbled entries moribund – remote
From the once-living context of his mind.
He wrote as one who craved to leave behind
A vivid picture of his personality
Foredoomed to swift extinction. He'd no craft
To snare the authentic moments of reality;
His mind was posing to be photographed;
'If I should die...' His notebook seldom laughed.

'A Footnote on the War',
Siegfried Sassoon, 1926

5 Bengal Days

An uncultivated lout at the Grammar School, I became a pacifist aesthete in the air force. With little Latin and less Greek, it was easy to feel unlettered in Transitus; in a billet near Kettering the ability to read a two-syllable word without hyphens put me well ahead. There were four of us who had gone through some form of education, and qualified to be called 'Cambridge', 'Einstein' or 'Foocking Brains'. We stood for civilization in the barbarous life of square-bashing.

For three months we'd be cheek-by-jowl with wood-hewers and water-drawers, young men whose only reading so far had been *Beano* and *Dandy*, who would later become the cooks and drivers and stores-bashers. No wonder we felt ourselves the Oscar Wildes of our intake.

So much for the aesthete. The pacifist needs more explaining. Our teens had been spent at a time when no one cared for youth. To be glamorous was not to be young but to wear a uniform. The war had starved us of the toys adolescents usually enjoy – clothes, new music, dancing, ice-cream, cigarettes, travel, lighted cities. War's first excitements had given way to a grey utility and we resented it. Following the Second Front on maps was something our parents did. Those hectoring newsreel voices were among our most intolerant imitations. We only wanted it to end. After the Allied invasion, the newsreels brightened, the rhetoric got more jovial, it was only a matter of time. Then one day the smile was wiped off the voice of Movietone. The eyes and ears of the world were faced with an item that could not be rendered into by-jingo and 'Well done, Tommy'. The armies had arrived at Belsen. The mystery tour was over. We'd come through the tunnel and our eyes were dazed by the scenes that haunt my generation. This was why the war had been fought; for these grey spectres picking over their blankets, these pits full of corpses, these heaps of teeth and spectacles.

At about the same time came a film that glorified war. Olivier's *Henry V* had colour, movement, heralds and fanfares, music and above all language that stood my hair on end. Like all British films of the 1940s, this now seems to speak for a posh minority, but not then. We thrilled at the *shared* victory, the king's nocturnal conversations with his soldiers, the Robin Hoodness of it all. When Private Michael Williams spoke of the arms and legs chopped off in battle, we felt for the king as he vainly tried to make a case for war. Ten years later, when I played that soldier for the Bristol Old Vic, the memory was green and I pitied John Neville who, as a man, didn't believe a word the king was required to say. Later still, of course, we learnt that Agincourt was won not by gallantry but by the long-bow – the Maxim Gun and atom-bomb of its time. But in 1945 it was possible to believe in a band of brothers. The four of us aesthetes went, on one of the few nights we were allowed out, to see the film for the third or fourth time in the nearby steel-town of Corby. Running through the wet streets for the last bus back to camp, we swore to be brothers forever, our boy-faces lit by flashes from blazing foundries.

Of course we didn't include the other erks in our billet. One of our four was from the Welsh valleys and said the plebs would have to be educated before they could become brothers. Some of them, it seemed to me, had a long way to go. The boy who'd worked in fairgrounds, for instance, on the Moon Rocket, and who woke us every night with his cries of 'Come along there, please, for a bigger ride and a better ride and a faster ride!' till someone shouted 'Poot a foockin' sock in it, mitey!' and if that failed, threw a boot in his direction. 'Sorry,' the boy would say, waking, 'was I foocking doing it a-foocking-gain?'

Boots are what I remember of these miserable months. Boots had to shine at all times, they had to crunch on gravel and scrape on tarmac and come crashing down on floorboards. They had to be laced up and laid out for kit inspection. But it was because of boots that I got a blessed day or two in bed at sick-bay, having one of my big toe-nails removed. I slept for thirty-six hours and woke with the hope that I'd be invalided out, as Dad had been with his varicose veins. But no such luck, I was soon back with the rest, trying to slope, order and present their cumbersome rifles, blanco their webbing, and break the code of their unintelligible commands. 'They' were the NCOs, caught to perfection in Wesker's *Chips with Everything*, members of a motley called the RAF Regiment. They wore a joke costume, part-khaki, part-air-force blue. I/c our billet was a solemn Corporal Nym of a man from the Black Country, whose fate was to be stuck with not one aesthete but foocking *four*! Basic Training was cast as a contest between billets with Passing Out Parade as the Olympic Finals. A long-time drop-out of the School House system, I scorned this incentive. The other three musketeers were with me. We set our minds to resisting. On glorious autumn days in requisitioned fields, I unscrambled our corporal's orders.

'Squaah – uuhh – d – by the left – qui-ick ... wait for it, wait for it – march! Ite, ep, ep, ite, ep! On the command ep incline, squad will advance ep incline. Ite, ep, ep, ite, ep. Squaaah – uhhd – ep in – IPE!'

I headed the right-hand column of three, staring ahead into a heavy morning mist. On the command, while the rest of the squad inclined to the half-left, I marched off confidently to the half-right, proud – in spite of my scorn for such antics – that the three ranks were behind me. My pace was sure, my eyes front, my rifle sloped at the right angle, free arm swinging, thumb uppermost. It was some time before I realized I was alone.

That night the corporal called me to his billet and spoke sympathetically.

'Don't you know your right from your left, airman?'

'Yes, corporal.'

'Then why can't you obey the foocking commands?'

'Dunno, corporal. Can't seem to follow the footwork.'

'Never learnt ballroom dancing?'

'No, corporal.'

'Why not, lad?'

'Didn't like the music, corp.'

'The music?'

'Corp.'

'Victor Sylvester?'

'Yes, corp.'

'What's foocking wrong wi' it?'

'Well, it's very commercial, corp.'

'Foocking right. He makes a few bob, I'll bet.'

'I couldn't listen to it.'

'All the classics, is it? The Warsaw Foocking Concerto?'

'Not at all, corp. That's commercial too –'

'Anyroad, dancing wouldn't help you on the range so how is it that on target practice the airman next to you got ten out of five and you got nil?'

'That's because of my helmet, corp.'

'What's your foocking helmet got to do wi' it?'

'Well, when you told us to throw ourselves down and begin firing at the target in our own time, I found the respirator pack slid up my back and pushed my steel helmet forward on my head, which not only hid the target but pushed my glasses askew and I couldn't see a thing.'

'Look 'ere, lad, you'd better pull your finger out, else you'll let the whole foocking squad down. Even your three mates are beginning to shape oop.'

This was true. And during the remaining weeks, they all gave in to *esprit de corps*. I ended up a brotherhood of one.

Few details of this miserable time remain with me. The glorious autumn turned cold as October passed. Exercise and outdoor life gave us an appetite for the cookhouse food and I put on two stone. The educational side of our basic training was left to a demented flying officer of the regiment who lectured us on protocol.

'When you address a non-commissioned officer, you will come to attention and reply, using his rank, whatever that may be. Corporal, Sarnt or Flight-Sarnt. A warrant officer you will address as "sir". As, of course, you will all commissioned officers. These begin with the rank *below* my rank. What is that? Yes, pilot-officer. Then comes *my* rank. What is that, anyone? Flying-officer, yes. And *above* my rank?'

Now a bitterness soured his face. It was like Dad mentioning the Masons.

'Flight-Lieutenant, yes. And what is the rank two ranks above my rank?'

'Squadron Leader, sir!'

I have forgotten almost everything else so it must be admitted he knew how to teach. There were some films, too, about venereal disease. They seemed to have been borrowed from the Americans and left me with the impression that you got gonorrhoea off cues in pool-halls. As we didn't know of any pool-halls in East Anglia, we reckoned we were safe on that score.

I remember too the oath of allegiance to king and country.

'Right, get a move on, lads, it's freezing in here. Pass these Bibles round, airman.'

'Not enough to go around, Flight.'

'Two airmen to each Bible. Come on, we haven't got all day.'

'Still not enough, Flight.'

'How many airmen not got their hand on a Bible?'

'Three, Flight.'

'You all C. of E.?'

'I'm an agnostic, Flight.'

'That's C. of E., lad, don't waste my time. We've put in a requisition but fook-all's come through. Right, it'll have to be three hands on the nearest Bibles you can reach. Now repeat after me –'

It was in this manner that I vowed to lay down my life to serve and protect the stuttering man who'd turned up at the Grammar School and prevented me getting home in time to hear Radio Rhythm Club.

There'd been some threats that any airman who didn't pass out would be put through the whole business again but, knowing our corporal's feelings about me, this didn't seem likely.

Come the day of the parade, I was left behind as billet orderly, rather than spoil the squad's chance of qualifying. Leaving out the rotten egg was apparently a time-honoured RAF tradition. Not *very* time-honoured admittedly. The air force itself was only ten years older than I.

Our squad returned triumphant to the billet, having come high in the lists. My three friends were flushed with pride. That night there was a booze-up in the NAAFI and the four of us debated how long one should remain in the awkward squad. At fifty-five, I'm still there and can safely assume I've left it too late ever to pass out. An everlasting billet orderly, polishing the coke-stove while Proper Men are forming up elsewhere.

Uniforms still had some allure so soon after the war. On my first leave a fast piece came home with me and lay on the sofa of our back room, the one with the collage of girls. For some time she suffered my fumbling and, on my fifth trip to wind up the acoustic gramophone, said 'You aren't very good at this, are you?'

This was the moment for me to say 'No, can you tell me how?' but, though the memory fades to black to that point, I know that pride and fear prevented me. When she left, I was still a virgin.

Cliff was sending letters now – not so much written as drawn – from his transit camp where he'd fallen in with a boozy crowd. It had taken no time for us to fly off our opposite ways. His humour was the same, but NCOs and officers had replaced our parents as the monsters of his cartoons. The envelopes were decorated with girls and goblins. Somehow, though, it was clear he was more at home in the NAAFI than he'd been in his mother's semi.

There were times in the 1940s when the entire army, navy and air force seemed to be travelling by train. Civilians were asked 'Is your journey really necessary?' while servicemen were shifted about like counters on a board game. Military admin. couldn't decide what to do with 2231747 A.C.2 Nichols unless they had him in the flesh, waiting in some transit camp – Padgate, Lancashire; Kettering, Northamptonshire; to Bristol on leave; and Morecambe, which like most seaside towns had become an unarmed camp for the duration. We paraded in a fairground among the shuttered helter-skelter tower, dodgem enclosure and moon-rocket, in the lee of boarded-up side-shows to shelter from the wintry breeze off the Irish Sea and waited, like the rest of Europe, for a movement order.

'Hurry along there, please, for a better ride and a cheaper ride and a faster ride,' said the boy from square-bashing, in his element. We, the new recruits, found ourselves outnumbered by non-commissioned air crew.

'Right,' the duty corporal would shout, 'fall in here in ranks of three the aircraftmen.'

Perhaps twenty of us would muster smartly, eager to please, all bullshit, forage caps one inch above the right eye.

'And over here the corporals.'

Very few of them, long-serving tradesmen promoted for doing nothing.

'Right. The sergeants fall in with them.'

A very few more.

'And just here will the flight-sergeants form up?'

And 150 fully trained air-gunners, navigators, bomb-aimers and wireless operators would slightly alter their positions, cheering ironically, bleating like sheep, continuing their cigarettes and conversations. This was not what they had signed on for.

'We don't hold with bull in the RAF,' says Kevin Cartwright in *Privates on Parade*. 'I joined under age to get a crack at Jerry. Soon as I passed out Flight-Sergeant, ready to go on ops, old Adolf packs it in. Right, I thought to myself, see if we can't chalk up a few Nips. No sooner reached Ceylon than old Tojo says *he* don't want to play no more.'

Every day we were sorted into *ad hoc* platoons and marched along the deserted promenade to perform some time-consuming folly.

'Right, you lot, get this pit filled in.'

'But, corporal, I think this is the one we dug up yesterday.'

'Air force doesn't pay you to think, lad, only get stoock in.'

These Sisyphean labours weren't meant for air crew NCOs. During our marches along the prom, they'd slope off in pairs to pubs and cinemas, the corporals and LACs turning a blind eye.

Our next posting was North Weald, Hertfordshire, where we spent most of our time clearing chitties, a treasure-hunt which had us crossing windswept runways for the initials of storesmen, medical orderlies, chaplain's clerks and aesthetes in the education corps. I wished Cliff had been there to fake all their signatures so that we could dodge off to nearby London. I did this once, without leave, running the gauntlet of military police at the barriers of Euston Station. Having risked this much, all I could think of doing in the capital was visit Bert Orritt and Auntie Lil. I found them folding printed handbills on their table with the plush cloth pushed back.

'You don't mind if we carry on, do you, Peter?' Lil said, head askew, eyes squinting in the smoke from her Players Navy Cut. 'It helps out a bit.'

'The folding-machine in my office was blitzed,' said Bert between coughs, 'and we make a bob or two for every hundred.'

I never saw Lil again. She died of bronchitis two years later, while I was still in Singapore. Bert got no pension from his firm and ended in a twilight home, finally dying of lung cancer.

Our chitties cleared, we went through a series of FFIs – Free From Infection tests – to ensure we hadn't picked up the clap or syphilis. Often we had one in the morning and one before tea. No one knew how we were expected to have caught a dose in the meantime as we were confined to barracks with no access to billiard cues.

In December I reported to an air base in East Anglia. There was, as usual, a fuel shortage and the camp buildings were being stripped of any furnishings that would warm the huts. My intake took a door off the bog and burned that. We felt ourselves to be veterans now. You only had to be stationed somewhere for a few days to have the edge on new arrivals. With every new posting, of course, you returned to Go. Would a time ever come when we'd feel in front?

I left Britain for the first time one frosty morning in late 1945. Obsolete Liberators had been converted to troop-carriers and eighteen of us sat in two facing rows in the bomb-bays, our knees interlocked, in near darkness. We wore all the clothing we could, as there was no heating and we'd be flying at 12,000 feet – great-coats over uniforms, balaclavas, two pairs of socks, gloves, scarves, Mae West jackets and blankets. It's from this moment that my earliest writing survives. I'd decided to send home two parallel accounts of my life abroad: on one hand personal letters with news, gossip and appeals for cash, on the other a properly written diary, sent piece by piece, a vivid account of my great adventure. Sadly, it is the last that survives. Though jotted down in pen or pencil on whatever paper came to hand, it is clearly meant to be a literary composition, eighty-seven chapters, each with its snappy title – the first 'Tense Present', the last 'Prologue'. The tone changes over the two years and four months but only superficially. Reading it now, one longs for more facts, fewer purple passages. 'A high-pitched burring sound startles us,' I wrote of the first moments of our flight, 'then the deeper tones of aircraft engines harmonize to produce a symphony of man's power.'

It took eight hours to cross Europe and when we came down it was in Tripolitania to re-fuel. It's all there in Chapter Two, called for some reason 'Perfect Past'. The scent of desert sands, the palms, the full moon directly overhead. 'I thought of this new world and its wonder – this morning East Anglia, tonight North Africa!'

We were given food under canvas at tables with cloths, served by

Italian prisoners of war. Except for the odd visit to Lyons' Corner House on trips to London, this was the first time I'd been waited on. Our next leg took us to Cairo, landing shortly before dawn, which brought another rush of blood to the head.

'Behind the mountains in the distance, a red glow was silhouetting every contour of the hills. Between these mountains and our lorry lay a bank of white mist and as the sun suddenly appeared it seemed like a beacon shining through to us. Yes, "a thing of beauty is a joy forever" and cannot be destroyed by the factual analysis of some geographer. The sunrise was a great experience which I have not the power to describe or even intimate to you. Please bear with me.'

Shades of R.G.N. and the Silvertown Explosion! Of Fitzpatrick's travelogues and 'Nature Notes' from the *Grocer* magazine! Of prepositions being bad words to end sentences with! This was a style out of which I should take some years to grow. 'Standing like parts of a child's game on a distant hill far off, stood the three pyramids of what is Man's Eternity.'

We stayed at Mena for a fortnight, six to a tent, eating in the open, still wearing air-force blue. Aside from daily genuflections to Sphinx and Pyramids, I went twice into Cairo by liberty-truck. My reactions to the city were to be expected of an adolescent who'd never left North Bristol. 'Strewn along the road were natives of all descriptions – selling, begging, in a long inhuman chain till we reached the city boundaries. Many ancient Egyptian trams were crammed with natives of all classes and I thought of those at home who grumbled because their bus was a minute late.' We found in Cairo what we were later to find in India – dirt, poverty, crowded trams, thieves and beggars, service canteens and cinemas. First we saw the YMCA, then the Lady Tedder Club and presumably drank lemonade or tea and ate cakes. We were robbed by shoeshine boys and ran for the liberty-truck and camp. Nobody had told us anything. Forty years ago the other ranks weren't required to know. Where were we going? Why? For how long? What were the natives like? Air force doesn't pay you to think, lad, only get stoock in. Stoock in to what? NAAFI, Union Jack Club, YMCA, Lady Tedder canteen. Who's Lady Tedder, Corp? Never you foocking mind, lad, *you* won't get nowhere near her.

So tuck into your Christmas dinner, lad. It may be Egypt, those may be the foocking Pyramids but here come the officers to serve your turkey and stuffiing and plum pud. Service tradition, son.

'I have seen the way certain Egyptians enjoyed Christmas,' I wrote on 29 December. 'Hundreds of them yesterday were working like slaves at the Pyramids, pushing trucks, kneeling down, beaten by what seem to be Foreign Legion men. While people sleep off their dinners at home, slaves sweat in the desert.'

None of your business what the wogs do to each other, lad. Get your kit laid out for inspection. Tomorrow you're off to the Persian Gulf.

My final posting was to a small maintenance unit at Bally some five miles north of Calcutta but there were four more transit camps before I reached it. Now we were wearing khaki drill, half-hose and black shoes. We slept under mosquito-nets and learnt to avoid the sun. In some camps there were no beds and we made do on cookhouse tables. The last lap was by train from Calcutta to a small halt beside the camp. I was to spend the best part of thirty chapters here, from 'Bally At Last' through 'Rigor Mortis Sets In' to 'Halcyon Days'. Reading these breathless pages now fails to bring back the last complete year of the Raj. Our base was not unpleasant – a motor transport unit set on both sides of a disused runway. The admin. block, where I clerked in the orderly-room, was of stone. Our quarters were in part-timbered bashas with open verandahs and thatched roofs, set around pools that had to be constantly disinfected of mosquitoes. The only cool in Bengal came from ceiling fans that never stopped, night or day. The houses of a village surrounded the camp and by night the chimneys of a match factory threw out a spray of glowing cinders.

Those Bengalis who worked on the camp were lucky. Even to be the bearer of a British untouchable was better than life in the match factory. I paid Ram, the bearer for our billet, one rupee a week (then a shilling and sixpence) and for that he polished my shoes and badges, made my bed, fetched the laundry when the dhobi-wallah had it ready, guarded us from the thefts of loose-wallahs and supervised the other menials – sweepers, water-bearers, char-wallahs, fruit-wallahs and took our khaki drill to the durzi-wallahs to have it mended or altered. Alterations had to be done at once to change our gear from that of 'moon men' or 'zombies' to the look of the long-serving men we met on our arrival. Many had been there for years. It is generally said that it was their sort who had voted Churchill out six months before but, in fact, less than half the men serving overseas voted at all. Bevin had drawn up the plans to release them but there were five million and it would take time.

It was already taking too long for the brown, case-hardened men I met on my arrival. One was alone in the billet as Ram brought in my kit and made up one of the charpoys – rope beds on a wooden frame with only a jute palliasse for mattress. This grizzled corporal lay on his, eating peanuts, watching me without expression. He had been in the East for four years and had a three-year-old daughter at home he'd never seen. I hoped she wouldn't be coffee-coloured. His reports of the place were non-committal. He only wanted home.

'You billet orderly, Corp?' I asked.

'Don't Corp me. I'm Stan, all right? And there's no orderly. Ram takes care of the basha.'

'You off duty then?'

'I've finished, son. We've all finished, we've been here long enough. We've told them we're not working again till our number's up.'

They were conscripts or wartime volunteers who thought of their job as done and were now on strike. The few mentions of this episode in the British press always called it a mutiny. It was far from a local affair. From Cairo through India to Burma and Ceylon, for all I know to Malaya and Singapore, the wireless operators co-ordinated this early show of the only weapon labour has – concerted action.

I soon had my shorts taken up to the length of French knickers, bought some chapplies and wore only ankle-length socks. My skin went through painful pink, flaming red and deep crimson before maturing into the mahogany that marked out men from boys. I mastered the lingo, that mixture of service slang and basic Hindi that had been spoken by BORs since Kipling's 'Barrack-room Ballads'.

Morning and late afternoon, with a midday siesta, I crossed the broiling runway to sit beneath the office fan making out movement orders and railway-warrants for those lucky men whose time was up. The magic group numbers came in Proms (or promulgations) from RAF Records not far up the Gloucester Road from Palatine Lodge. It was all done according to trades. Just your foocking rotten loock if you happened to be a balloon operator and somebody in Gloucester decided there weren't enough of them left in. Then they'd put the brake on their release and let out some fitters or cooks instead. The average level was running at about group twenty-seven and, as I was sixty-nine, it was best not to count.

The time-expired men remained in the bashas, appearing only at the mess to be fed or at the free film-show or the canteen to drink beer. They watched as I left the cookhouse counter with my metal plate of food and made for one of the shaded tables in the open compound. A kite-hawk swept from a tree and seized my dinner and I tried to dodge the great wings and dropped my plate and irons. The old hands laughed and shouted: 'You won't foocking make that mistake again!'

News reached Whitehall that one of the armed services had stopped work and envoys appeared to reassure the rebels that it wouldn't be long now. Our commanding officer called us to the assembly hall, apologized for making us parade and begged silence for a pink-faced, white-kneed man in fresh k.d. The veterans jeered and barracked him, calling to the fruit-wallah for more peanuts and bananas. The CO wound up the meeting with an invitation to drop in at his office for a chat any time we felt like it – 'My door's always open.' The pink man headed for his next unenviable meeting, the veterans to their charps and the rest of us to our duties. 'We are the masters now,' Attlee was supposed to have said when Labour won and the rank and file believed him. How did Britain strike these men when they got home? When the demob leave was over, the gratuities spent and the uniforms thrown out, how did they take to five more years of rationing? Or does the history of our decline suggest that they *never* recovered?

The hall where we'd assembled served also as cinema, theatre, church and school. Every evening there was a free film – usually, I remember, a farce with the grown-up Shirley Temple called *Kiss and Tell*. A mixed audience of British and Indian other ranks gathered while a Geordie corporal laced up the projector. Fruit- and char-wallahs went on trading till the show started, allowing credit to mount till pay-day when they would wait outside, remembering the unit's debts without writing a figure down. With only one projector, there had to be a break between every reel. If Corporal Steadforth took too long, someone would yell: 'Come on, Geordie, get your finger out!'

'If you can foocking do better, come and foocking do it!'

'I facking will and all!'

'Like to see any Cockney foocker take my job so now then!'

When the film resumed, it was seldom the one we'd been watching. *Brief Encounter* would become a Crown Film Unit documentary about colliers. More audience participation. More temperament from Geordie Steadforth.

'Not my foocking fault they've sent the wrong foocking reel, is it?'

'You were meant to show the facking short before the main feature!'

'*Tikh hai, tikh hai*. Shall I take this off and look for the foocker now?'

Usually they'd vote to leave it on and the first film would continue after another break. Or a quite different one might start, perhaps the last sequence of a thriller. The following week another job lot of reels would turn up and we'd watch the last of *Brief Encounter*, the second of Shirley Temple and the first of the mystery in any order Geordie got them from the cans.

I took the cinema too seriously to enjoy moments when moth or mosquito were trapped in the frame and flickered grossly over Celia Johnson till a cry went up: 'Hey, Geordie, dekko the bleedin' picture. You gone to kip or what?' and finally the dark image of Geordie's forefinger would wipe away the insect while Trevor Howard kept a stiff upper lip.

I dreaded the sight of an American uniform in any film. Errol Flynn had made an infamous thing in which he'd taken Burma single-handed, but this only partly explained the howls of rage that came with every mention of the US army. In one a GI was shot on a high place and fell to a grisly death below. A cheer went up and when it died one of our veterans called out 'Sweeper!'

Geordie Steadforth was a regular, not a conscript. His air-force trade was blacksmith. Perhaps he'd joined when the RAF had horses. Only long service could give a man that vocabulary. From Hindi he had got *dekko*, *tikh hai* and *tunda pani*, from Arabic *bint* and *shufti*, and from the air force 'increment, inventory, requisition' and 'promulgation'.

He was one of nature's corporals, not the first or the last I'd meet during my spell inside. In time they coalesced round Geordie like filings round a magnet and emerged thirty years later as Corporal Len Bonny in *Privates on Parade*, to be fleshed out so truthfully on stage and screen by Joe Melia. A Geordie Steadforth with more than two stripes was unthinkable. Promotion had gone instead to my immediate superior, the sergeant of our orderly-room, who ran the entire unit. A sweet-tempered giant with Battle of Britain moustache, he was so capable that he left the adjutant and CO with nothing to do. A model of tact and industry by day, he would be seen by night roaring drunk, stark naked on a bicycle, or wading fully dressed into some malarial pond.

You didn't have to be doollally to work there but it helped. Doollally was the Doctor Fox's of India, Deolali transit camp near Bombay. All occupying forces suffer some sort of madness – and no wonder. No one had spared five minutes to tell us why we were in Bengal. No more, I suppose, than they'd said anything to those dazed squaddies in Palestine, Cyprus, Malaya, Korea, Vietnam, Algeria, the Falklands. What do our gallant lads think they are doing in Belfast?

India made no sense. The sights and smells appalled me. The main streets were a freak show of amputations, piebald maniacs and sacks of flesh swollen by elephantiasis. The village beside our camp was an excremental slum where only the cows had tolerable lives. I never blamed this misery on British rule. Not until my fifties did I discover that the Ganges delta had once been a garden of plenty where corn, rice and fruit fed the people, cotton clothed them and jute gave them ropes and sacking. Then the merchant venturers of the East India Company had turned it over to poppy. From Benares to the Bay, the prime cash crop became opium. Auctioned in Calcutta, shipped by fast clippers to Canton and forced on

the Chinese at gun-point, the drug was also the ruin of Bengal. A long
drawn-out vengeance for the Black Hole turned Calcutta into the arse-
hole of the empire.

But at the time I made no such connections. It didn't occur to me that
grammar school history, Warren Hastings, Suraj-al-dowlah, Clive and
Plassey had anything to do with the signs on every wall – Jai Hind, Quit
India, British Out. We agreed, of course. The sooner we were out the
better – for us. For them it would be the last hope gone. We obviously had
not brought them much in our 200 years' occupation but that was their
fault. A people who would suffer this without revolution must be innately
inferior. For when the Bengalis took to violence, what was it for? To kill
each other. Hindu and Moslem spent 1946 rehearsing for the massive
slaughter that followed Partition. For about half that year Calcutta was
officially out of bounds to us but, with what now seems to me reckless
pluck, we went in anyway, to spend an hour or two in some canteen or one
of the air-conditioned cinemas. No violence was done to the British or to a
dwindling rearguard of Americans. Savages to one another, the Indians
were decent enough to us.

The only way in was to hitch a lift by jeep, car, lorry or bullock-cart.
Journeys were often made by all four. My first time in I had the eerie
thrill of being the only European in a busload of natives. The same day a
friend and I rode a tonga, an open coach drawn by a scrawny nag. We
successfully beat the driver down from his first demand of three rupees to
one, a technique we later used with taxi-drivers and rickshaw boys. Not
till I was in Singapore did I read in Mulk Raj Anand's novel *Rickshaw Boy*
that their average life-span was twenty-eight. Not till I read *Pacific
Overtures* did I learn that the rickshaw had been invented by a man from
Chicago. It remains the perfect colonial vehicle – a way of using cheap
labour at the same time as it helps reduce the population.

I soon mastered other necessary imperial skills. I learnt to eat at the
window-table of a restaurant while children in the street begged for
bakshish and, when they got none, turned to shoo scavenging kites from
the heaps of waste and pick the rubbish over for scraps.

Which is not to say many Indians could have stomached the food we
ate.

'What you got, John?' the boys from Bermondsey would ask the smiling
waiter.

'All the usual eggs and chips, sahib,' politely pointing to this section of
the vast menu. 'Eggs and chips with bacon or with tomato. Or sausage,
eggs and chips possibly. Baked beans and eggs and chips. Sausage,
beans, eggs and chips.'

'Always the same old thing. Ain't you got nothing different?'

'On these other pages, sahib, you will see our many curries. Beef, lamb and vegetable curries. Biriani, tandoori chicken, with many chutneys, chilis and –'

'No fear, John. Ain't you got no other way of doing eggs?'

'Certainly, sahib. Nice omelette?'

'*Tikh hai*, son. Sounds all right for a change.'

'Cheese omelette, yes, burra sahib.'

'Portion of beans and plenty of chips, mind.'

'Naturally, yes. And for sweet?'

'Apple pie and ice-cream and iced beer. *Juldi-juldi.*'

'Thank you, rajah sahib.'

I left India after a year without having tasted Indian food. I didn't see the ancient banyan in Calcutta's botanical garden. I explored no temples, heard no songs, saw no dances, knew no Indians. For a few rupees I could have lost my virginity any night. Along Chowringhee, the ponces called 'Hullo, Johnny, you want nice girl? Almost white, working way through college? Nice clean girl, burra sahib. Hey, Rajah, you like jig-jig? My little sister, just thirteen, my mother? Hey, John, you like jig-jig my brother?' Sometimes the pimps were at the reins of tongas patrolling the pavements. In the open carriage behind, their whores scowled from padded-leather seats. The army is said to make men of boys and this was certainly a chance. The air force can't be blamed. Others took it. Some had whores and the luckier ones found Eurasian girls. We never used that term, by the way. To us, anyone of mixed blood was Anglo-Indian – Anglo for short. Pure Indian women were no temptation – they were either poverty-stricken or in purdah or otherwise hidden by gauze veils and shrouds like tents and yards of shawls. When they chewed betel-nut their gums looked bloody. Their rarely seen faces were disfigured by caste-marks and embedded jewellery. We untouchables never met middle-class Indians of either sex, though we might glimpse them crossing the pave-ments from their limousines to dine at Firpo's. I had no idea that, away from Chowringhee, Central Avenue, Chatteranjan Avenue and Dalhousie Square, this was the intellectual and artistic centre of India, or that a few years earlier it had been the long-established capital of the Raj. New Delhi was only the Basildon or Milton Keynes of capitals. Nor would it have reassured me to know that Calcutta was the centre of political unrest for the whole sub-continent and the scene of a congress to decide post-war Communist Party policy for the whole of South-East Asia. Communists were bogey-men. In this belief, at least, I was ahead of

American public opinion, Senator McCarthy and Richard Nixon. A year after leaving Calcutta, I came to believe communism was India's only hope and in this I was well after Nehru, who'd said so in 1937.

The hammer and sickle flew above crowds along with stars and moons and spinning-wheels. One Sunday I hitched into the city to meet a friend. Chowringhee and the Maidan, the great park around Fort William, were deserted. An out-of-bounds order meant that even the Phoenix armed forces club had no customers. Early afternoon, we decided to make for camp but by this time a huge assembly blocked the centre and all approaches to it. Politics, religion, fireworks, atrocity, snake-charmers and bands attracted a swarming multitude of brown faces and white clothes. My friend had gone another way and I was the only white man in the only white quarter of the city. My Chapter Thirteen ('Meeting on the Maidan') tries to convey my alarm. This can be measured by the fact that I was *glad* to catch sight of two military policemen in a jeep.

'D'you think there's any chance of reaching Central Avenue?' I asked them.

'What you doing here anyway?' said the Lance-Jack driver. 'You'd best get off the streets, airman. They don't like us at all.'

I struggled back along the crowded pavements to the Phoenix and watched from an upstairs window till the tumult had shifted from Chowringhee across the Maidan towards Victoria Memorial. I left again and in Central Avenue was picked up by the only white man I'd seen – an old Scot, an engineer who'd been in India since 1919.

I asked him: 'What's this demonstration all about?'

'Oh, don't you know? Jinnah's there. He's telling the Moslems to kill more Hindus.'

'He's the Moslem leader, is he?'

'God Almighty! They don't tell you erks much, do they? Yes, he's the wallah that's going to make a unified India impossible. More important in many ways than Nehru or Gandhi. He'll never be the head of India but if there were a separate Mohammedan state, he'd be the boss, the Burra Sahib.'

'Is it going to come to that?'

'Have to. And God knows what else. Once we're all gone, once you chaps are on the boat to the UK. It's going to get a lot worse before it gets any better.'

He dropped me on the Barrackpore Road as he was going north to Dum-Dum (where the bullets come from) and I walked the mile or so to camp through the scenes that had so suddenly replaced the orphanage and Ashley Down – paddy-fields ploughed by ox-teams, white cows wandering among the mud-hut villages and palms, dhobi-wallahs beating the clothes against stone ghats by the river, kites and dogs squabbling over refuse. . . .

During the next few days' hullaballoo (from *holo-bolo*, to make a noise), some of the boys from my basha had been to town in an armoured car to collect the mail. They had found the occasion to open fire on some looters but weren't sure how many they'd hit.

'I lapped it up, mate,' one of them said. 'I'm going in again and this time there won't be no foocking errors.'

'Pure sadistic ignorance,' I wrote home. The chapter 'Calcutta Has a Party' ends: 'I am convinced that till we root out this bloodthirsty element from among the people themselves, wars will never cease.'

Here is the embryo of that belief in perfectibility that was later to grow into a sub-Shavian socialism which put all its faith in the power of education.

'Education is everything,' says the young soldier in *Privates on Parade*. 'Once they understand, men will stop worshipping gods that don't exist and learn to love one another and that will mean the end of war. It is going to be an enormous task. . . .'

How could I have believed in this after my own experience at school? Simple-minded political idealism takes no account of facts. It's sealed off from reality, a state of mind very close to religious faith, very close in fact to 'worshipping gods that don't exist'.

At about this time I made my first attempt to escape from the air force into an entertainments unit. In India it was known as Welfare Productions and an audition was arranged for me at the HQ in New Delhi. I hitched to Howrah Station, where the population of a sizeable town seemed always to be camping with all their household goods, and found room in a second-class compartment with four other BORs. We slept on shelves that hung from the roof and by day stared from the open windows at 'an India about which I had only heard'.

(D'you hear that, Woodbine Winnie, young Buzfuz seems to be learning to write good English at last!)

'Monkeys climbed around the stationmaster's office, camel-trains awaited their loads, women in gorgeous sarees tended their well-attired children, white flamingoes flew over a stagnant pool. Thus passed the longest railway journey I had ever taken – though short for India, beginning on Tuesday evening and ending at the same time Thursday. . . . At Delhi posters proclaimed from every board that I had chosen Victory Week for my visit.'

'Had my first decent meal for days at the Wavell Canteen just outside the station. This was the most amazing place I had seen since my arrival in India – eggs, tomatoes, chips, bread and butter, fruit salad, ice-cream and a pot of tea for Rs. 1/4!'

One of my four friends from square-bashing met me at Racecourse Camp. A shortage of hard facts in my journal at this point suggests an embarrassment too painful for words. 'The auditions were, of course, absurd. We were ordered back to Calcutta.'

Meantime we managed to enjoy our stay among the tidy avenues of Lutyens's garden city, with its fountains and bicycles. I decided that 'there is much beauty in India if you know what to look for'. (For what to look, you great pudden! If you know for what to look!)

'A Utopia for service life! Buildings of indescribable magnificence, streets of beautiful design, a racecourse adjacent to the camp, WAAFs in plentiful supply, cool breezes at night, far away from the India others know and loathe – far away from the Muslem Madmen!' That was in Chapter Fifteen, but in the next we read: 'Riots began while we were there and fires were caused. While watching the races from our charpoys on the balcony, we saw a string of Indians join hands across the track in the face of the galloping horses. Luckily they lost their nerve and broke away in time but we heard later that one of the horses had died of a heart-attack.'

The air display I mentioned was part of Wavell's Victory Week celebrations – another chance for my cruel tongue to do its worst: 'Though this was to celebrate the end of the war, they had to give us a demonstration of rockets, bombing, paratrooping, smoke-screens and everything else we long to forget.'

We spent some time exploring the Safdar Jang Tomb, but only because we were determined to take a picture of my friend sitting on the tomb smoking his pipe.

My chapter from Bally on 1 April makes no mention of Dad's birthday. Perhaps a letter went with it. All that's left is a complaint about the heat and humidity and a longing to visit Tibet! Wherever I was, I wanted to be somewhere else. Watching the trains go out in Bristol, marching through Morecambe, eating Christmas pudding beside the Sphinx, counting the hours in Bengal. I never liked it *now*.

My friend with the pipe heard of a local drama skive and this time we were taken on as actors to tour up-state in a West End play about airmen who'd been shot down in occupied France. It gave us three weeks' rehearsal in the comfort of the Sixty Club on Chowringhee Road but 'we were thoroughly bored with the stupid manner in which it was being conducted'.

('Well, he may not have remembered my birthday, Vi, but how's that for style?')

'Our first show was at Bally – a disaster! The next was Barrackpore – even worse! Apart from the torrential rain, failing electricity, terrific humidity and all the insects Bengal can provide, the show itself was quite a dead loss. For a month now we've had average temperatures of eighty-five with humidity of ninety-five per cent. This means the sweat runs down one's forehead into one's eyes and makes every stitch of clothing soggy. Eat a meal and you sweat like Niagara. Take a shower to cool off but by the time you've made the exertion of rubbing dry, you're damp with sweat again. As I write, sitting here in the race-track at Barrackpore, flies are crawling over my arms and legs, on the notepaper and around the frames of my glasses. The race-track's empty – a ghost of former days. It's now the property of the RAF – and so am I!'

'Kankinara is even filthier than Calcutta. The further you get from the city, the more squalid the villages become. There's a constant odour of dung about them.'

I made no note of the curious little state of Chandernagore – literally 'City of Sandalwood' – which we could see from across the river. It had been a French colony since 1815 and continued to be until three years after the British left. We scanned the place for signs of France but only saw one European in khaki drill with a gendarme's cap. Why was he there? What anomaly of empire brought him to this sweltering outpost?

Our last date was Kanchrapara – an isolated collection of huts. 'No one expected a show so we didn't give one. In the morning we parted company with the other members of our troupe, whom we loathed. Soon after that I returned to Bally. The long, endless existence goes on.'

This meant that every morning I made out railway warrants and movement orders, at midday ate tiffin in the mess, enjoyed watching the new arrivals lose their meal to the swooping kite-hawks, returned my irons to the basha and, while the others lay under the electric fans dreaming of home and trying to keep their dripping sweat from smudging the letters they'd written their girls, I went back to the office. Again I started the fan and took from my desk drawer the work I had come to continue in the only time I had, the baking afternoon when the mad dogs and I had the place to ourselves. It was on that air-force Remington that I typed my first real plays. *Francis is my Brother* – what was that? The title is all that's left and that's only in my head. Was it hagiography? Christian apology? A plea for kindness to animals? No. Only a light comedy on West End lines, set in a drawing-room in Surrey with French windows letting on to a terrace. I'd never been in Surrey nor seen a

terrace. And French windows? But these were the only models I had –
Noël Coward, Maugham and Rattigan and something called 'George and
Margaret'. This stockbroker culture had reduced the British to a race of
quacking suburbanites. The only balls were on tennis-courts. Its leading
lights were mostly homosexual but never said so. It was so insulting a
national stereotype it might well have been written by an enemy.

I wrote travesties of other styles too – Oscar Wilde, Eugene O'Neill,
Thornton Wilder, Kauffman and Hart, Priestley and Shaw. I dabbled in
expressionism, a few samples of which I'd heard on radio. It might have
been at about this time that *The Statue* rolled off the Remington: an epic
on the lines of *Julius Caesar* which took place in an unidentified country
(sure sign of upcoming rubbish) and had a cast of several hundred
townspeople who swept on from time to time to raise and later raze a
monument to the tyrant of the day. No connection with Calcutta. Nothing real was allowed in. I'd lived through a world war and was now
present at the end of an empire but all that came from the orderly-room
were dramas of Godalming and No Man's Land.

Later these were all destroyed. My parents' letters have also gone. I
can only imagine their replies to such outpourings as Chapter Twenty-
One, 'Nostalgia', in which I contrasted my wonderful life in Ashley Down
with the present in Bengal. 'Imagine yourself not in a grand hotel or even
a simple home. Picture instead a white-walled billet with rows of
creaking wooden beds, topped by khaki mosquito-nets; the shuttered
windows with no glass trying to keep out the ever-insistent sun but
admitting from time to time the nocturnal loose-wallah (or thief), his
naked body greased to escape the grasp of his captors. And picture the
mosquitoes, the transparent and green lizards, the long black scorpions
and the elaborate beetles, visualize if you can the monsoon flies that come
in hundreds, live for a hectic hour dashing against the walls till they kill
themselves, leaving a pile of white wings on the stone floor. Listen to the
screeching of a million crickets and the croaking of a billion frogs. And all
the time that incessant voice of the bus-driver shouting his destination
"Shambazar, Shambazar!"'

'Picture it if you can!'

It can't have been easy for Dick and Vi to do as they were told. Dad's
reply would usually be on his 'Humorous Entertainer and Dramatic
Monologues' notepaper in faultless copperplate.

Dear P, yours of the 10th instant to hand.

Note your remarks re high temperature, humidity, insect population
and presence of native bandits. Worrying this and should advise you

keep all valuables under lock and key. Loss cannot easily be afterwards rectified. Yours truly cannot forever be reimbursing a Pudden like yourself, albeit indirectly feeding the hungry mouths of the starving multitudes of our far-flung empire. Ye olde man's motto has ever been 'Prevention is better than cure' and, though generally averse to blowing his own trumpet, The Big Cheese reckons it 'ain't arf a bad idear'. Suggest you adopt same re personal bric-à-brac. Things here seem much the same. A return to pre-war conditions appears not to be an imminent prospect and Messrs Attlee et al have much to do to get dear olde Englande on her tootsies again. Your consumption of bananas, ice-cream, free cigarettes, etc. etc., sounds some consolation for presence of raucous frogs, as here Old Mother Hubbard wonders how we shall manage when bread-rationing comes in next month. Friend Gosley, very much the big I-Am and Member of the Masonic Creepers, remarked that America was despatching supplies of same to us but do not imagine he has learnt same in a private p.c. from the PM this a.m. so shall discount it till I hear it from authorities. Imagine you are in state of anticipation for your proposed itinerary (not 'itinery' as in yours of 20th ultimo) to cooler parts. We hear from his parents that your old friend Cliff is now in India too. You, of course, know more re his progress. Am enclosing message from Violet Annie Ladysmith in same cover to save postage.

All the best, Dad.

Hers would be shorter:

Dear Peter,

Just a line to let you know how we all are at 192. Weather lately a bit warmer. As Dad has told you all the news, don't think there's much left for me to say. Must rush now to catch the post.

In haste, love, Mum.

PS Am baking you a cake for your birthday.

Bread rationed? Let them eat cake. Or at any rate send it to Calcutta. On my nineteenth birthday in July, my mates ate a slice each and drank my health with hot sweet char from tin mugs.

Cliff's letters were another matter. They came in richly decorated envelopes. Goblins were shown writing the address, pin-up girls embraced dragons, jazz bands rode on elephants. Impatient men in the sorting-office added comments: 'Why don't you grow up?' (a question easier to put than answer), or 'Little things please little minds'. The letters themselves embarrassed me when I opened them in the billet – one was stuck together from many pages to form a centipede six feet long, neatly folded, with a spine of text supporting a body of pictures. I replied in kind with sketches, stories, playlets and parodies. We afterwards admitted that we'd each begun to feel bored by this but had no idea how to stop.

My letters home never refer to it, though in Chapter Twenty-Two we read: 'From Karachi I was hearing bad news. Cliff had taken to drink too suddenly, I thought, and seemed proud of the fact. I tried to stop him by letter but it seemed hopeless. I left that job till September.' We planned to meet halfway across the sub-continent for a leave in one of the hill-stations north of Delhi.

The comparative cool of eighty degrees in the monsoon season was followed by enervating heat. The medical room was full of men treating their prickly heat, tinia, dhobi itch and sunburn. I went swimming and caught a cold. We spent hours in cinemas in Calcutta more for the air-conditioning than the films.

Meanwhile the Cripps conference ended in deadlock and Nehru declared that Congress was not bound by any of its proposals. Jinnah responded: 'This day we bid good-bye to constitutional methods.'

To put it mildly. On 16 August he declared a Day of Direct Action and Calcutta gave India its first real foretaste of civil war. 'For three days', I wrote, 'murder and wrecking have put the city off the map to British troops. Regular broadcasts under the name Caterpillar have given us news of the situation. The latest figures are 240 dead, 1,500 injured. The fire department has been called 900 times since the riots started. Every announcement is greeted by cheers from the bods in my basha. Elaborate defence regulations are in force and all of us are doing extra guard. I myself completed a twenty-four-hour stretch this morning. Armoured cars cruise constantly and men are seen everywhere with small arms. On Friday the orderly-room staff was ordered to throw bricks at the stores staff, seizing the chance to shout their opinions of this section and calling upon the Gandhi-wallahs to come out and fight. No mail has been collected and we're on emergency rations.'

Odd that I left out a guard-duty in the city.

We were sent in, sitting in the back of a fifteen-hundred-weight van, armed with stens, to patrol the streets. The worst was over and we had orders to fire on any civilians breaking the curfew. Of course this had to be done – should have been sooner – but I agonized as I stared down the empty alleys and avenues. Could I train a gun on a citizen of a city where I'd no business to be? In fact, the problem was notional. My marksmanship on the range, when all my fire went into the next man's target, showed that, as long as I aimed carefully, no harm would be done. In any case, the only living creature we saw was a vulture picking over a dead bullock.

'The riots eventually stopped,' I wrote, 'leaving 4,000 dead and countless injured.'

Richard Attenborough's biopic suggests that Gandhi was entirely responsible for ending the carnage but the presence of British troops may have had a bit to do with it. This was an Indian quarrel, not part of the anti-British feeling that had for a time united the various factions in a common cause. No British were harmed.

'My own affairs of late', I wrote, 'do not improve a grim situation. I was relieved of my wallet in a Calcutta cinema – 120 rupees, £9 10s., the savings of many long months waiting for leave. I am now scraping together what I can for my leave in two weeks' time. The rain has come again and the camp's been flooded. It's brought with it every type of reptile and just now the char-wallah showed us a five-foot python he'd killed near the basha.'

A Moslem holiday followed close on the massacre and unluckily for me came on the day my leave started. 'Trouble was expected and no transport left the camp. Miraculously I reached Howrah Station, the train for Delhi, Kathgodam and Naini-Tal! Fourteen days in the hills! Calcutta and Bengal are behind me now. I'm going a thousand miles closer to England. The train shakes and rattles. I struggle with a blunt pencil.'

Eight pages of flamingoes, camel-trains, beggars and flooded plains took me to Delhi. Another train to Muttra, a village I called 'a thing likely to become extinct'. 'A great many soldiers, eggs and chips, darts, rest and reading happened all day and someone even set the village on its feet by starting the rumour that Gandhi was coming through in the next train. The whole population turned out, including the mayor and chief constable. They filled the station and we joined them on the platform but when the train came, Gandhi didn't.'

Cliff didn't come either. Of course I missed him but it was such a relief to be cool that nothing else mattered much. The next few chapters try to convey the sharp sensations of cool breezes, forest waterfalls, white clouds below us as we climbed the hills, the cosy room, its fireplace, the thrill of a shower ('like standing under thawing ice') and of sleeping under blankets. In an age of easy travel it takes some effort to recall the excitement, but I was only among the last of a long line of British soldiers and civvies to describe the ecstatic relief of the hills. 'The skin around my mouth wasn't damp with sweat, my shirt wasn't clinging, my prickly heat had gone. And to see men in pullovers and suits again – almost like home! And at night there were lights on either side the lake, some reflected in the water, some shining so high on the hillside that I confused them with stars in the clear black sky.'

I befriended some other men and we took out boats and rode horses to Cheena Peak, and I stretched my poor prose on the rack in an effort to describe my first sight of the Himalayas – across the rolling brown foothills the blue distance, and beyond that, glistening eighty miles away, the range of Nanda Devi rising to 25,000 feet. I remember (but don't mention in the diary) the dandies, mountain litters carried on shafts by four local boys. Rickshaws were bad enough but I drew the line at these. The sight of a fat memsahib being lugged up the mountains to her friend's cottage almost put me off coffee and eclairs in The Shady Grove, which is where I spent most of my time. Otherwise I took a good many artistic photos with my beloved Voigtlander.

I arrived back at Howrah, Calcutta's station, at seven in the morning and took five hours reaching camp five miles away, travelling in four different vehicles.

Vehicles were all-important. Ours was a motor maintenance unit but that was a misnomer. Our function was rather to sell obsolete jeeps, trucks, staff cars and heavy lorries to civilians before they were flogged illegally. Fleets of vehicles were driven across the plains to vast auctions. Elsewhere, we heard, whole armouries were sold by officers and NCOs in private deals. Rumour had it that fighters and bombers were peddled part by part and lay in private stores awaiting reassembly as soon as we'd gone. The unit was being run down. Most of my office work had to do with posting or repatriation and our billet emptied as men went home or further east. The string charpoys stood like skeletons. Ram, the bearer, was making do with less each week, for we still paid him only a rupee each. The char- and fruit-wallahs were pressing us to settle our debts. It was common for men to go home without paying.

We had to share out the extra duties and I was put in charge of the fire section. We had a pump on wheels, a lot of hose and the means to make foam. Luckily the Indian Other Ranks knew how to handle this. I was only the token white.

There wasn't much chance of a fire anyway. The 'rains' had come again. One 'rain' is not enough to describe this deluge. 'We are in a downstairs billet now but the roof and the floor above us don't stop the downpour. It soaks the floor, the beds, the nets. The paper on which I write is damp and matches hardly make a flame. All the lights are on all day because it's as dark as dusk outside. A minute ago one of the bulbs spluttered, cast a shower of sparks around me and finally blew into fragments. There's only one consolation – it's cool.'

Cliff had sent a letter shaped like the Indian rope-trick, in which he explained (in a message that rambled up the length of rope) why he hadn't made it to Naini-Tal but that he'd got leave in Calcutta and would be arriving on 1 November.

'But', I wrote in prompt despair, 'Calcutta is again out of bounds! Once more the goondahs have killed and plundered and put a stick through the spokes of the community wheel! It is too much! He's bringing all his personal possessions with him: gramophone, records, letters, books, photos, drawings – and here I am, hopelessly cut off!'

And later: 'Why is the city still out of bounds? Things are reasonably quiet now – only six men were killed today and thirteen people injured. The Viceroy is on a tour of inspection. Surely our military presence would curb the bloodshed – and also mean that I could see Cliff!'

Again I broke bounds, going in with two new friends, Dave and Johnny. Dave was my first real toff and he evidently took my breath away. 'Mad, cultured, intelligent, immoral. His passions are women and the poetry of Rupert Brooke.'

Not that I remember seeing Dave with a woman. Johnny, a tough little nut, was never without one – always the same one: Florence, an Anglo-Indian, who smiles from the snaps I took with my Voigtlander, elegant on the diving-board of the Victoria pool or with her head in Johnny's lap. Thirty years later she reappeared as Sylvia Morgan in *Privates on Parade*. Before I left India, Johnny was suddenly posted to Ceylon. Florence met us later in a club. She asked us if we'd heard from him, then started crying and told us she was expecting his baby. I asked him why she hadn't told him. 'I did,' she said, 'that was my mistake. He put in for a posting right away.'

'If I'd known, I'd have told the CO.'

'Oh, he knew as well. Johnny told him. Why else d'you think he was posted so quickly?'

In the play, Major Flack writes to his wife: 'There's a young soldier here I'd like to invite down to the mill-house when I get home. He's in a spot of bother at the moment but I mean to help him out of that, as I would my own.'

I met Cliff in the Sixties Club, spotting him in the darkened dormitory by a glowing dragon painted on his tin trunk in phosphorescent green.

He was the same – rosy, shabby, cherubic with the same way of drawing hungrily on strong cigarettes – but I was different and we both knew it.

'You're getting all la-de-dah,' he said.

In *Forget-me-not Lane* this happens later – after Frank gets home. His friend had spent his service in Germany, not the East.

'It's so small,' says Frank, looking at the old back room, 'but otherwise unchanged.'

'You've changed,' says his friend, 'you've got a posh voice.'

They are embarrassed. Frank studies the collage of pin-ups.

'Like a record?' says his friend. 'One of the old ones?'

'The acoustic gramophone!' says Frank, exploring the room.

'Acoustic?' – his friend is disgusted – 'bloody hell! Used to be wind-up.'

Frank shrugs. 'Acoustic *is* the proper word.'

But in Calcutta we found 'music, from Egmont Overture to Canal Street Blues, was the one matter on which we were in perfect harmony'.

Otherwise, it is clear from my diary, he preferred Dave to me. They stayed in the city, out of bounds, for a fortnight, while I ran to and fro to sign on as i/c Fire-fighting. They swam, drank, ate and smoked their way through the rest of Dave's money and poured most of Cliff's into fruit-machines. They went to the races and lost 150 rupees. Spending a night at Bally, I left my Voigtlander with Cliff in town and in the morning he found it had been stolen from his trunk. The case turned up under the mattress of the next bed, which had just been vacated by a Corporal Smith. 'Obviously fictitious,' said Dave.

What is obvious now, after nearly forty years, is that Cliff and Dave had sold my camera to back horses. How could I not have seen this at the time? Retarded, even for eighteen.

I got posted to Dum-Dum and it looks to me now that I'd been no use to the orderly-room and even less as fire chief. My replacement no sooner arrived than he went down with malaria, so on I stayed.

A pair of new buckled shoes I'd had made were replaced in the swim-ming-pool changing-room for worn-out ruins. Since then I've always bought ready-mades.

'Spent the evening', says Diary, 'staring at men's feet.'

Cliff went back to Jodhpur. We'd enjoyed ourselves but our friendship was over. It should have ended long before. Now I was free to make new friends.

Winter deepened as Christmas drew near. The temperature went as low as sixty-four degrees at night, cool enough for me to wear a white pull-over I had bought in Naini-Tal. I stayed on as i/c Fires while the new man convalesced. A cake and Christmas pudding arrived from home. I had the Indian Other Ranks in the Fire section spray a coniferous tree with foam. It only slightly resembled a snowy scene but Corporal Steadforth was moved by it and had himself photographed in shorts and chapplies to send home to his wife, who worked in a NAAFI at Aldershot.

The newspapers, tired of reporting death in the city, ran smaller items about tigers marauding among the villages upstate. Temperatures never dropped far enough to silence the cicadas and frogs, or repel the mosquitoes. The latrines were still a zoo, to be avoided after dark. Caught short, my only safe way of sitting on the wooden seat over the pits of shit was to wave a burning copy of the overseas *Daily Mirror* about the cubicle, then over the hole itself, watching the various spiders and centipedes scuttle off. With one hand I unbuttoned and dropped my shorts, holding the naked torch to keep the insects at bay till I was done. Sometimes a noise or movement nearby was followed by a muttered 'Sahib', reminding me that it was some untouchable's job to mind the place.

When there were only three of us left in the basha, our bearer Ram came to say he could not continue. He had a family to support. He'd get taken on at the match factory. I hope I gave him a few chips as a farewell tip but somehow doubt it.

The food gave out as the unit disbanded. I lived for three days on bread, cheese and water. When we complained, the CO suggested we pay a mess-bill of sixpence a day extra. It seemed the only way to guarantee a meal at Christmas so we agreed. A few days into December, though, my new posting came – not Dum-Dum after all but Singapore.

A draft of us assembled at the transit camp in Calcutta. Five gharries took us through the ruined streets to the docks and one of them killed a goat.

During my year in India, no one had told or asked me anything. Keep your nose clean, airman, keep your foocking head down. The wall-eyed Wavell, a plain soldier who put together a book of other men's verse, was posted home soon after and replaced by Mountbatten, the hurry-hurry man. In eight months they'd all be gone. The Indians would have it to themselves. At least I'd learnt that empires were a bad idea.

6 My University

The Wednesday before Christmas, we boarded the SS *Dunera* (London).

A few weeks ago the ship appeared on television in a documentary history of how enemy aliens were treated during the war. Three elderly Italians told how they had been deported to America on the *Dunera*, how she had been hit by a torpedo and how badly they'd been treated by British sailors in the rush for a place in the lifeboats.

Somehow it survived after all. 'Quite an ordinary-looking ship,' I wrote. How was I to know? This was my first time afloat.

'My arm was still aching from the effects of various jabs as we dragged our bedrolls and packs below to the mess-deck. George and I volunteered for a fatigue, cleaning out the recreation room. Might be easier than guard-duty. When all the men were aboard, we had our first meal. Mess Deck E is a shallow compartment with wooden tables and hooks for hammocks jutting from the ceiling. At each table sit sixteen men, the two at the end of each are orderlies responsible for giving out the food and cleaning the plates. They bring it in large metal cans and the tea is in buckets. It's divided among the hungry crew by passing from one end to the other. Those at the far end are lucky to get anything at all. If there's any left over, it's almost fought for, the young sahibs behaving like savages. Our first meal was a kind of steak-and-kidney stew with bread, cheese and tea. I managed to stomach most of it.'

There's not a lot to like about the glum youth who writes these pages. Nothing pleased him. He was so frightened of life that he could only sneer. The chance to travel so far at a time before tourism had spoilt the world went unappreciated. As peevish as an old man, he wallowed in sentimental nostalgia for a home he'd longed to leave. A priggish virgin with little to offer but self-esteem. Reading this stuff now, I blush for him. He wasn't me, of course. He was a fictional character, created for home consumption. These pieces were a plea for pity, aimed at Dick and Vi. I was arresting my own growth by posing as a pompous adult. A great deal more happened than was set down but these chapters are useful now as a mnemonic. A corrective, too, in case I should be tempted to think fondly of my teenage self. If only he'd done *something* but grumble!

Worse was on the way.

'George and I took a stroll on deck and it was then that I became really horrified by the class distinction aboard ship. We peered into the first- and second-class dining-rooms. There the officers and their families chatter over coffee cups on white tablecloths while down below the other ranks fight for a few lumps of tinned meat. Eventually we went below to sleep. A smell of bodies rose to meet us. Hundreds of them lay on the floor or hung in hammocks. I'd slung mine in a clear space but since then the men had piled in and I had to jump, tip-toe, duck and dodge to reach it. Once undressed, I heaved myself up. The rope looked none too trustworthy but, if it gave, there were people below to break my fall.'

We awoke early and went on deck, after a night of body smells, bumping hammocks and 'the rough male kiss of blankets'. While we smoked our cigarettes in the cool darkness before dawn, Calcutta's skyline seemed almost beautiful. That was the last of India. During the following day and night, we cruised sixty miles to the mouth of the Hoogly and, leaving the coast, made a smooth and uneventful crossing to Rangoon, 700 miles off.

Diary makes no mention of meeting David Allford, but I remember a blond aesthete leaning on a deck-rail with the blue Indian Ocean behind him, reading stories by William Saroyan. It's odd how often I failed to notice when important people entered my life. His first appearance is a year later and he can wait till then, though it was on *Dunera* we spent the first of many hours of talk, gazing over the side at schools of fish that skimmed the surface with spread fins. His India had been Kerala in the far south-west. He'd loved it there, made Indian friends and eaten their food. Even now I was hardly aware of the way Indians talked but David fixed Bombay Welsh for me long before Peter Sellers made it an international joke. Now that it was too late, he lent me *A Passage to India*. We agreed that Forster had caught Mr Harris, the Eurasian chauffeur, especially well.

One evening, an Indian concert party performed for an audience of Hindus, Moslems, Sikhs, Gurkhas and BORs. Of the five dancing-girls in the troupe, 'Two', I wrote, 'were lovely. One danced on the rim of a brass plate with bare feet. Strange but beautiful ... disconcerting ... vacant, sultry faces, mobile hands, naked midriffs ... not enough body movement. ...' This is the first sexual reference in the whole journal. How had I coped with the tropic heat at eighteen? I explained in *Privates on Parade* to the tune of 'Greensleeves':

> There came a soldier-boy fully grown
> Who till that moment had held his own

And though he'd served on several fronts
He'd never seen action on ladies once.

Even so! Most of us were still intact when we finally got out. Some were Keeping Themselves for girls at home. An army and air force of conscripts wanked their way round the Orient. We were frightened, that was all. Compared to the Yanks in the orphanage, perhaps we *were* undersexed. After all, the cure for syphilis was said to be savage. The parasol up the penis. Those films put me off billiards for years. But did the army dose us with bromide? Cooks always say they didn't, that it was only a line to bolster self-esteem. My wife tells me I spend too much time wondering how I did without.

At Rangoon we watched from B Deck the disembarkation of military and civilians posted to Burma. Smarting from the inequalities of life on board, we relished the sight of the sahibs and their mems herded into a dirty wooden landing-barge.

The next leg took us from Burma to Malaya, 1,000 miles closer the equator and that much hotter.

'Christmas Day – reveille six a.m., breakfast seven, scrub out recreation room for inspection – need I go on?'

But I do.

'The crowded room, crammed with the reluctant exiles playing ping-pong, drinking char from tin mugs, large heads with vacant faces ... half-nude, sweating soldiers, chewing their Gold Flakes, floating on a distant ocean, not wanting to go anywhere except home. Bawling NCOs, the tannoy calling for attention, guard-duties, the whole stinking cesspool of wasted time and forced oblivion.'

We were served our dinner by the officers, the cruellest insult service life could offer. These public-school boys not much older than ourselves looked as embarrassed as we felt, and carried out this repellent ritual with a show of bravado while we sat at wooden mess-tables muttering 'thank you, sir'. In Egypt I'd enjoyed it but now my knees were brown. Aboard ship you were all too close, we'd seen the first- and second-class mess-rooms with their tablecloths and silver. I think of it now as a crucial moment. A speck of steel entered my soul – and high time too.

One morning we awoke to find the ship in what seemed to be an inland lake. It proved to be the natural harbour of Port Swettenham, our point of disembarkation on the Malayan peninsula. Our kit was unloaded into landing-barges by Japanese prisoners, the first we'd seen. They were as strong as trees and threw the baggage around as if it had been made of balsa-wood.

We spent our first days on Singapore island under canvas while equatorial rain beat down in torrents. On New Year's Eve, I explored the city, paying a dollar to enter The Happy World, one of several vast amusement parks swept away in Lee Kuan Yew's puritanical reforms. On this and other visits, I watched the gracious Malayan dancing where the partners never touched, dos-i-dohing sedately as in some Western square dance. I was always light on my feet and rhythmic but fear of failure kept me off the floor. I'd never learnt the simple patterns of ballroom dancing, in those days almost the only way to pick up girls. Instead I sneered from the wallflower line.

In Singapore there were also 'Great World' and 'New World' and in K.L. 'Gay World' and 'Lucky World', and here I sat among audiences of Chinese to watch the popular versions of Peking Opera. Accompanied by the crash of cymbals, the dramas were keened more than sung by gorgeously dressed principals while prompters in black pyjamas moved through the action supplying and removing scenery and props. If a heroine decided to end it all, she'd sing about it at great length, the man in black would step from the wings and slip a dagger into her outstretched hand. He'd wait while she performed some ritual gesture of suicide. She'd return him the dagger and go off. While the band screeched and crashed, he'd calmly set up the next scene. There is no note of this in my narrative but the memory lodged and surfaced for *Privates on Parade* when I asked that the silent Chinese should 'sometimes move furniture and props, to the accompaniment of percussion, suggesting popular Chinese opera'. The idea was to set this against the equally artificial British variety theatre of my childhood, a symbolic confrontation like the Malayan War itself. Our failure to achieve this in production sold the play short.

It was New Year's Eve, 1946 and, for such a British place, I found few signs of revelry. Some sailors let off firecrackers in the foyer of the Cathay cinema, my first skyscraper, glamorous and modern. In the towering new republic of the 1980s, it looks a squat structure, regarded as an ancient monument, almost in need of a preservation order.

This was a simmering time. Pots were about to boil over. In eight months India would go it alone; in eighteen China would go Red; in a year or so trouble would start in Malaya.

'An Emergency they're calling it,' says Major Flack in *Privates*, 'but that's softly-softly officialese. Everyone knows it's the start of the Third World War.' There was a very good reason not to call it war. Insurance policies were so framed that they wouldn't have covered the damage. To those being shot at or having their hands cut off, it might have felt like war but they were wrong. It was only an emergency.

From 1948 to 1960, over 100,000 British, Indians, Malays and Chinese were kept busy trying to defeat a guerrilla band of 5,000. Major Flack's history lesson goes on: 'The Communists used to call themselves the Malayan People's Anti-Japanese Army; now it's the Anti-British Army. What's that if it's not a declaration of war?'

But why did they take so long to fire the first shot? During the Jap occupation they'd stashed away enough arms and ammo to do the job in no time if they'd acted quickly. 'No sooner had the Yanks exploded that contraption than bands of agitators turned from killing Japs to killing us.'

In fact, there was a three-year hiatus. I discovered the probable reason while researching the play in the Imperial War Museum. The Communist commander had run off with the funds. It is not known whether he was ever caught. I see him growing old in some Oriental funk-hole – Taiwan, Hong Kong, Bangkok – with his jade collection and Japanese car. He gave Malaya time to recover from the occupation and ensured a final British victory.

In a post-war confusion of boiling pots, the press took very little notice. For the film of *Privates* I went to Movietone's studios and reviewed the entire newsreel coverage of the twelve years' conflict. Five minutes at the most. None too good a job – though, to be fair, the media made up for it later in that Barnum-and-Bailey war in Vietnam. Malaya was a direct precursor but was fundamentally different. The Communist cause there was never a popular movement. The Malay states were multi-racial, a post-imperial chop suey (or nasi goreng) with no unifying interest. Except for the aboriginals, the Malays had been there longest – Moslems, farmers, fishermen, in general easy-going people who'd nonetheless given the world the phrase 'to run amok'. The Chinese had been brought as indentured labourers by the British in the last century to work the tin-mines. From India the Tamils had come to harvest rubber. A class of mostly professional Portuguese Eurasians had been centred on Malacca. The planters were, of course, Maugham's British. Having already covered Bengal and Bihar with opium and Ceylon with tea, they went on to smuggle the precious latex tree out of Brazil and brought it via Kew Gardens to the coastal strip of west Malaya. And there they remain. So, I was surprised to find on a recent visit, do the Communists. I spoke of a final British victory but semi-final would be closer. Not far outside the cities, illiterates are warned of possible ambush by logos of a man being shot. An Englishman who seemed to be In The Know told me, as we lounged beside the Kuala Lumpur Hilton's pool, that it was only a matter of time before South-East Asia went over to the reds entirely. And what price Singapore then? More men on bicycles over the causeway?

The first few weeks in Singapore were the usual confusion of transit-camps, made worse this time by the loss of my entire kit. I had only the clothes I wore and something to wash and shave with. My final posting was Changi, the immense HQ of the South-East-Asian air force.

'An RAF city', I wrote home, 'of three-storeyed white buildings set in garden surroundings – offices, billets, clubs, hospitals, theatres, laundries, and so on. There's an airfield and two swimming-pools. The best RAF camp I've ever seen. I call it Changi Garden City.'

On the dark side, 'the people are far too keen, work progresses steadily from eight till noon when a whistle blows, then again from two till four-thirty when the whistle blows again. Too many regulars here, especially a senior warrant officer who's accosted me four times for being improperly dressed.'

Letters from home reminded me that things could have been worse. Friends who'd gone described an England of cold, boredom and shortages, a London crippled by transport strikes. Yet we would all, without exception, have given the sun-soaked beach, the tropic village, the garden city, for all the miseries of Attlee's England.

Three weeks later I was posted again, leaving David Allford and my other friends in the long open dormitories thronged with naked men, the Chinese tailoring women in black pyjamas moving through as invisibly as prompters in the opera, chanting their infinite variations on the two syllables 'sew-sew'. It seemed as though there could hardly be a cushier billet. We had bearers to keep our bedspace clean, collect our dhobi and clean our shoes, sew-sew women to darn our shirts, cinemas, clubs, beaches, and a lively city twelve miles off. Then why couldn't we enjoy it? I've just spent two weeks in New York City, supposedly an exciting place, to attend rehearsals of a Broadway production of one of my plays. I stayed in the splendid town house of one of the city's best-known citizens, was generously entertained and fed on flattery. There was nothing to complain of and yet, the moment the soothing stopped, a painful misery came back, very like that we had known in Asia.

Posted to Number Two Base Signals and Radar Unit at Paya Lebar, I was housed for the night in a house raised on stone piles to avoid the rain, which even as I arrived was falling in torrents. A Jap prisoner escorted me, carrying my kit. He showed me the only furniture – a wooden bed. When he left I would be alone in what seemed to be a rising lake. I offered him a cigarette and for some minutes we smoked in silence, nodding and smiling. Once he'd gone, I sat on the verandah rail, staring at the remnants of the old plantation, and added my tears to the deluge. The same ache as in New York, a nostalgia beyond reason. In both cases I asked why I was there, and in both the answer came back: money. A New York play might pay for my life in England. And Singapore? Why was an enormous standing army kept on till the early 1960s? Because it was the World's Finest Youth Club? Made a Man of You? Those were the reasons generals gave. But most of us were only clerks or drivers or storekeepers, usually working alongside native civilians. We'd have been no use in a fight, even as police. So why weren't we sent home? Because the country couldn't run to it. We were cheap. A private's weekly pay was twenty-eight shillings, rising by only ten shillings in the next thirteen years.

Free foreign travel, yes, but that would have been no consolation to the sobbing erk in the flooded plantation with only the rats for company.

This was the nadir. Spirits could only rise. The moment lives as one when fortunes turned, one of perhaps a dozen in my life. My official diary, though, treats the incident facetiously. No mention of Jap, rain or tears. I was moved into a hut next day and made friends. More amiable than Changi, less splendid, closer to Singapore, the place suited me well.

I bought a satin kimono, egg-yellow with blue dragons embroidered back and front. It cost me two weeks' pay and I promised 'I shall love it till it's old and grey'. It must have been thrown out when I put away childish things, some time in the early 1950s.

'Killer Wimpory looks pugilistic in it for his broad frame fills it well. The effect on me is a shade grotesque, as the shoulders come where my elbows are.'

'Killer' was an amateur boxer with a jutting jaw. He never just came in. He threw open the doors, struck a pose and sang 'Good Evening, Friends!' He and the others in A12 billet were kitting themselves out for civilian life. Their black tin trunks, with the owner's name, number and home address and the instruction 'Not Wanted on Voyage' painted in white, were treasure-chests for the trinkets they hoped would secure them safe passage into civilian life – the watches, lighters, pens, hand-made shoes and shirts, lengths of silk and lace for their brides to run up on suburban Singers. For most of them, sex would start with the honeymoon. Surprisingly few practised on the tarts at Racecourse Road. After spending so much on all that stuff, they probably couldn't afford to.

'Killer' tried to perfect a gesture I later borrowed for poor Eric Young-Love in *Privates on Parade*.

'I'm working out a movement for when I'm back in Blighty to display

97

my Swiss watch, silver cigarette-case and Ronson lighter all in one. I haven't yet included my Parker Pen but all in good time.'

While I was at Paya Lebar, a short story of mine won a prize in a service magazine, the first money I earned from writing – and the last, till my television plays were sold when I was over thirty.

Why so many different postings? Was I useless even as a clerk? From Changi to Paya Lebar, Paya Lebar to Seletar, Seletar to Tengah, I was bounced about the island like a bagatelle ball till I rolled into the hole I'd wanted. Nee Soon is a spacious, sylvan military camp, now shared by units of the Singapore, Malaysian and Australian armies, then a British transit camp. Beyond a ravine, terraced on the slope of the far hill, the off-white block of Combined Services Entertainments stands empty. On the sloping lawn before our billet, where once was heard the patter of ping-pong and the squeaks and farts of amateur bands rehearsing show tunes, all's quiet now but the wind up the ravine stirring leaves on the great overhanging tree that was in our day a sapling. On guest nights the mess-boys strung Chinese lanterns along its topmost branches. Our dining-room was a marquee, with two of its canvas walls drawn up. The forecourt was furnished with tennis-table, upright piano, reclining chairs and striped rattan awnings. These blinds also shaded our verandahs. Hardly comparable with rooms at King's College or Trinity, but this was where my education began. Chapter Forty-Six, 'The Beginning of a New Life', at least shows some awareness but is a worse pack of lies than ever: '"You say you're a straight actor?" they asked when I got to CSE. "They'll have you playing bagpipes in a fortnight."' That sounds like a joke for Dick to repeat on his round of the Great Societies of the south-west.

'I may have mentioned my great pudden of a son? Now in Timbuctoo defending our far-flung empire? You'll be amused to hear the greeting he received on arriving at the latest stage of his itinerary. I had to correct his spelling of that last word. "Itinery? What's itinery, noodle?" I said. But be that as it may. . . .'

And perhaps he sent a letter to me in reply.

Yours of the 10th ult. to hand. Considerable glee was occasioned by your quoted colloquy on newly arriving at Nee Soon. Friend Fish of Yeovil was among the many branch managers who found it amusing. But that may have been the way it was read aloud by Yours Truly, the great R.G.N., the First and Foremost, who said that? I'll give you a kick in the pants – boom! Trust your efforts re. bagpipes are bearing fruit. Could hardly be a worse row, nay a more strident cacophony, than that kicked up by younger brother Geoffrey, who has by fair means or foul acquired a battered cornet and is learning to blow same.

Perhaps you recall our neighbours in the Salvation Army? Yeah, verily, one of their number *was* imprisoned for theft! Well, the father of their household, chief cook and bottlewasher, not to mention Prime Creeper, had the dashed impudence to complain of the sound of your brother's jazz on the Sabbath. This – from one whose own band has rent the air most Sunday mornings with their brazen hymns! I said to him, 'Friend, let he who is without stain cast the first stone', raised my hat, bowed politely, walked off and left him gasping.

If not actually fictitious, the bagpipe joke almost certainly came from one of the 'Hearties' – drivers or electricians, wood-hewers and water-drawers. On the other side, far more alluring, lounged the Arties. All were sergeants, though most wore mufti. I too should be a sergeant as soon as the sew-sew woman could attach my stripes. Our billet was a sergeants' mess but there was no mess-bill and no increase in pay. My first artist was stocky, already balding, mischievously smiling Sergeant John Schlesinger. He and others in his family would recur in my future in odd ways.

'Well, hullo. And what brings you here?'

'To act, to enjoy myself, to escape the boredom of service life.'

'I wish you luck. What d'you make of it all so far?'

'I'd rather not say.'

'Why not?'

'First impressions are generally erroneous, don't you think?'

'Had you heard anything about us before you came?'

'Oh, yes. There's supposed to be a lot of homosexuals here.'

'Really? You amaze me!'

John turned to encourage those who were listening, somehow controlling their laughter. This alarming man was not to be joining the company of *Not So Much the Heat*, a farce about service life in India. He was already in a revue called *Thru' the Hoop*, with his own conjuring act, just back from touring Ceylon. John was one of those who took matters into their own hands, leading several lives at once and apt to slip from one to another whenever he sensed danger. Another was Company Sergeant-Major Marriott, the unit's senior NCO, who spoke to me as soon as John had gone.

'Buy you a drink, son? What'll you have?'

'Thanks, Sarnt-Major. Orange squash.'

'All first names here, lad. Better call me Hank. Here, boy – gin and orange for the new man. Peter, isn't it?'

He seemed middle-aged but was thirty-three, good-looking, carried a cane and wore on his bare forearm a brass crown on a leather band.

'I hope you'll settle down here.'

'Don't see why not.'

'Don't you? Let me offer you some advice. There's two courses open to you. You can join the men or you can join the queers.'

'The what, Sarge? Hank?'

'The queers, the queens, the fairies. There's your gin.'

'Thanks. Cheers.'

'Cheers.'

Not only gin to drink but yet another language to learn!

Pidgin Hindi and service slang would cut no ice with these people. Queers, eh?

'You see, Peter, there's always the threat of RTU. That's there all the time, for all of you.'

'What's it mean, Hank?'

'Return to unit. Loss of rank, privilege, back to all you thought you'd left behind – fatigues, guards, the cookhouse. Whereas, if you play your cards right, this is a cushy number. Mess-servants, private room with balcony, no bull, tours of the Far East, nothing to do but camp about on stage.'

'Camp about, Hank?'

'You haven't met the old man?'

'No.'

'Major Cotton. Likes the ladies. Know what I mean? Nothing camp about him. Get me?'

'Got you.'

'All up to you, isn't it? No one's twisting your arm but I like to offer a helping hand, little push in the right direction. You with me?'

'With you, Hank.'

But not for the first time, I opted for Art though Life might have taught me more. Thirty years later I learnt that, when we met, Hank was out on bail with charges pending for theft, criminal breach of trust and extortion. He had already served six months for illegal possession of firearms. None of us knew much about him at the time. When *Privates* was staged, letters from an address in Finchley Road questioned my portrayal of Hank in the play as a racist, colonial brute. The sender, now a theatrical agent, had been intrigued by the quiet, circumspect sergeant-major in the orderly-room and had followed him one night after the office had closed. A few hundred yards away, Hank was let into a private car by a Malayan chauffeur and driven out of camp towards town. My correspondent and Hank later became friends. He wrote to me: 'Having lived in Singapore before the war, he showed me the true wonders of the Orient.'

Hank lived with his American wife in a house near the Cathay cinema

100

and in a little hut at the end of their garden kept a Chinese taxi-dancer and her dependent family. No real reason has ever been given for his being in the army. While they prepared the case against him, the Special Investigation Branch kept him marooned in the backwater of CSE, where they could keep an eye on him. Major Cotton, our commanding officer, must have known all about Hank through his intelligence dossier. It came out later than Hank too was finding out all he could about Cotton.

The other artists and I knew nothing of this. I had more than enough to do mastering the new lingo. The vocabulary was of mostly familiar words with new meanings – camp, drag, queen, queer, chopper, cottage, gay and auntie. Some were from Romany or Parlyaree – vada, bona, roba.

But unless I got hold of the syntax too, these words would only add artificial colouring. Catch-phrases helped – 'Can't wait!', 'It's the end', 'Let's face it', 'Are you sending me up?' 'Through the roof!' – but when Kenneth Williams told a story, I recognized a master of the idiom. Not until the 1960s would he introduce a wide public to this novel way of talking, through *Beyond Our Ken*, *Round the Horne* and, later, the television talk-shows, but in 1947 it was already there – the impeccable diction, nasal resonance, flared nostril, upturned chin, and the whinnying laugh like a horse played slow. At nineteen, his virtuosity was complete, owing nothing to anyone, waiting only for public taste and tolerance to change. His name is seldom mentioned in my journal so there's no way of knowing if he was already fluent in the Lewis Carroll sex-inversion that was later to thrill a nation.

'Did you hear Montgomery's coming out? It's *true*! She's on her way. Louise Mountbatten called her into the Admiralty. She said, "Now look here – "' – the cut-glass voice, deep and resonant, with the staring eyes – '" I want you to go on a tour of Asia and Australia. Clementina Attlee wants it, Winifred Churchill wants it, that old queen Ernestine Bevin wants it. The natives there are seething with disaffection, shrieking filth against Our Sovereign Lady Georgina the Sixth. The sight of you camping yourself silly might possibly pull them round." Well, Monty was livid! She plonked her beret down on his desk. "I won't," she cried, "if God had meant us to go that far, He'd have given us wings or webbed feet."'

The cast of *Not So Much the Heat* also included Stanley Baxter, who like Kenneth had been seconded from an army corps – signals or service. Their respect for each other's talent made their friendship a wary one, as evident now in their mid-fifties as it was in their adolescence. Kenneth frightened me and some years passed before I understood him. But I wrote then: 'It's with Baxter I find the most in common. Dark-haired, of medium build, with a plastic face and body always awry in some particular. A straight actor, producer and writer of cryptic stories and obscure poems. On his wall is a picture of Picasso. Spent a miserable period of his life as a Bevin boy in the coal-mines near his native Glasgow. Vehemently berates mining, miners and all concerned with the excavation of coal. Loathes trivialities, excess heartiness and shallow etiquette. Lives for art and for the stating of his beliefs through art. Doctrine Shavian, though he dislikes Shaw's plays. Prefers drama and serious art but is always willing to take part in revues and other frivolous entertainments. I have not yet decided whether I like him or not, but apart from myself he is probably the most brilliant of those at present residing in this abode of knowledge and female impersonation.'

He was also among the first to help me write better. Beside the snapshots in my album, he read such captions as 'The Sands of Time' or 'The Mystic East'.

'You must stop writing that sort of thing,' he said.

'Why?' I blushed, knowing already.

'Don't you see, it's banal. Secondhand. Pretentious too. Claiming more notice than it deserves.'

There's a picture of him in my kimono, 'studying a script', smoking what seems to be a little pipe but which holds a cigarette upright in its bowl.

The arties weren't all performers or peacocks. Kenneth Williams shared a room with Purdy, a clerk from Bristol who – in the absence of any real authority from CSM Marriott – ran the orderly-room. He was infatuated with one of the servicewomen who lived in another billet nearby but, like most of us, had no idea how to further the affair.

'Touch her up!' advised Kenneth.

'Yes, but how?' said Purdy.

'Titillate the clitoris.'

'But where is it?'

'I don't KNOW!'

The problem was driving him to drink. Unlike the rest, he was a *paid* sergeant but his mess-bills for gin were more than he could afford.

One night he was awoken in the early hours by a hideous screaming nearby.

'Did you hear that?' he whispered in the dark.

'Yes,' said Kenneth.

'Thank God!' said Purdy and went back to sleep.

When the office was closed, he could be found at the piano, composing pastiches of John Ireland. On guest nights, when plain girls in the WAAFs and ATS came to drink our spirits, this man deployed a line of insults we all envied.

'Tell me,' he would say, leering at some poor horsey aircraftwoman, 'didn't you win the Derby in 1938?'

After the guests had gone and he was staggering up to bed, I asked him whether he'd made out with her.

'Oh, I threw her a bale of hay. She was quite content.'

In the chapters I sent home are some examples of my efforts to imitate this style – frightened, virginal, Alexander Woollcott wisecracks. We simply didn't know which way to turn. My parents must have worried, though, when they read the last paragraph of my first CSE chapter: 'I'm quite the idol of the intellectuals in my dragon dressing-gown, which I'm wearing as I write. I have vague dreams of filling this room with all manner of dragon-things. It would be too, too utter.'

In fact, I was in no immediate danger from either side. Touring troupes of entertainers were coming back from Burma, Ceylon and Hong Kong, and accommodation was so short that I shared a verandah with a tabby cat and her three kittens.

The arty among the officers was an Australian, Flight-Lieutenant Lawson, who looked like Oscar Wilde in decline and affected Café Royal attitudes.

'Why in Heaven's name do you all want to go back home?' he asked us once. 'The last time I was in London, there were girls walking down Regent Street eating ice-creams!'

His real line was composing light classical pieces like 'Warsaw Concerto'. 'Tobruk Rhapsody', for example, aimed to recapture the sounds of desert warfare – tanks in the brass, bagpipes in the woodwind and gunfire from the timpani.

'What's the piano part stand for?' someone asked Kenneth.

'That's her bit of rough,' he said, 'yerss. She picked up this boy when she was doing the dilly one night. Scots guards, very butch. Got killed in North Africa. So she wrote the concerto to immortalize their love. Don't say a word against it, if you don't want to be RTU'd. She thinks it's better than the Rachmaninoff.'

Soon after my arrival at Nee Soon, Lawson called me to audition a second time. He was taking a rehearsal of some dance satire being sweatily performed by a couple of civilian showgirls and a 'Bohemian-looking man with fair hair and a cigarette-holder'.

In those days, cigarette-holders were worn only by people prepared to flaunt all convention. Bow-ties and suede shoes were bad enough but, at the first sign of a cigarette-holder, decent citizens locked up the silver.

'After some minutes of this vague flitting,' I wrote home – 'vague' was evidently one of our words – 'Lawson asked me to read out some verse. I made a miserable attempt – why I can't say.

'"I suppose you've got more voice than that?" he said.

'"Oh, yes, of course," I replied and he dismissed me.

'I returned to the mess with the spectre of "RTU" staring me in the face. However vague this place may be, it's streets ahead of Paya Lebar Base Signals and Radar Unit, let's face it!'

The odd visit to my friends at Changi fortified my fears. By now three stripes had been sewn to the rolled-up sleeves of my khaki drill.

'Sergeant!' shouted an officer on one of my excursions to the garrison city.

'Me, sir?'

'Yes, you. Tell that airman to get his hair cut.'

'Sorry, sir, I'm not a real sergeant.'

'What?'

'No, sir. Sorry, sir.'

I saluted and made off. He was too surprised to speak, though it could be said that he and his kind have had the last laugh. Lee Kuan Yew's new Singapore is, in Paul Theroux's words, an Aldershot on the equator.

A weekly guide in 1982 from Singapore's Tourist Board has this to say: 'Male visitors are advised to have their hair cut if it reaches below the top of their shirt collar. The authorities frown on long hair. Please note that long-haired persons will be served last at all government departments and offices.'

And again: 'For those presumed to be trafficking in heroin or morphine, the penalty is death.'

And: 'Singapore takes pride in being The Garden City. Littering is an offence that can get you a fine of up to 500 dollars.'

After some weeks, I began to lose touch with my friends at the old units. Letters from Karachi, in envelopes decorated with dragons and snake charmers, I hid from the eyes of Williams, Baxter and Schlesinger. I'd already thought better of my plan to fill the room with 'all manner of dragon things'.

While waiting for the full cast of our play to be recruited, Lawson directed a few of us in a public reading of John Hersey's *Hiroshima*, drawn from eye-witness accounts of the bombing. 'Rehearsals', I wrote, 'have been tedious and uninspiring, not helped any by Lawson's vague insistence on The Drama. . . . We played it to a small but appreciative audience of intellectual soldiers. Quite a success. However, *Not So Much the Heat* is more important.'

An interesting view of world priorities in the two-year-old Atomic Age, but we had hardly begun rehearsing when Major Cotton read us a cable from the War Office cancelling the production. The author had sold his West End option and we were without a play.

'Damn shame! But *nil desperandum*. If nothing else can be found, we'll have you all in a gang show.'

Three concert parties passed through Nee Soon during my first month, though none was strictly a gang show, for they all included women – either from the services or civilians sent from London. One of these girls, a professional dancer, then touring Singapore Island in *Thru the Hoop*, spent her nights in Major Cotton's bed.

'He is a heavy drinker and sadist – in fact, a typical regular officer,' I wrote home, playing on Dad's dread of drunkenness. 'Masochist' had been crossed through and 'sadist' written in its place. I had only just learnt the difference.

The terrible scream that had woken Purdy had come from the Major's quarters and no amount of greasepaint could hide the dancer's bruises when she later appeared bare-legged in the chorus line. The Major had no say in the production of our shows which was, strictly speaking, in the limp hands of Fl-Lieut. Lawson. No one could have expected these two officers, so different in every way, to be at anything but daggers drawn. In fact, they seemed the best of friends and formed a more profound partnership than any of us knew at the time. Now spare and fit for odd jobs, we actors were put on scene-shifting duties for Lawson's latest revue, *Over to You*, part of which I'd seen in rehearsal when I gave my reading. The bohemian-looking blond I referred to then was the star of this production, Barri Chatt, a dancer and drag-artiste who'd lately arrived from England with his female partner. The presence of several girls in the troupe gave Barri no excuse for drag, though his off-stage gear was so androgynous that his costumes in the show looked almost butch. To me he seemed immensely old but was probably in his forties. His hair was dyed peroxide yellow, his eyebrows were plucked and pencilled in and all his other body hair shaved to a baby's smoothness. He wore what he called 'the full slap' (new word) which could be either day or night. After dark the cupid's bow lipstick was more emphatic, the eyeliner a darker blue. Silk scarves flopped at his neck, sandals displayed his painted toe-nails, at the pool his trunks were provocatively laced down the side.

The air of Shaftesbury Avenue sophistication, culled from people he called Binkie, Binnie and Boo, was belied by the accent of his native Yorkshire. The story of his arrival in Singapore has long since entered the Chatt mythology. Some high-ranking officers had met one morning for a top-level briefing in the Victoria Theatre and were waiting for staff cars to take them to chota pegs at Raffles when a taxi drew up and Barri stepped out. Making straight for the astonished generals and air marshals, he waved his cigarette-holder and greeted them: 'Tell them to put the kettle on, loves, your aunty's arrived!'

Barri was put up at Raffles, then the premier hotel, now a haunted house for package-tours. Coward's description of Singapore as a second-rate city for third-rate people was never more apt than in the prompt out-of-bounds on other ranks reintroduced as soon as the war years were over. Had Barri known he would not be allowed to entertain able seamen in his room, he might have stayed elsewhere.

'Luckily my room had a balcony with an easy climb from the garden,' says Terri Dennis in *Privates on Parade*, 'and most naval ratings are very nimble nipping up the rigging after weeks afloat doing the Captain Bligh stint. Well, it didn't say anything in my contract about setting an example. There was no work in England, the panto season was over and life under Clementina Attlee wasn't exactly the Roman Empire. So I signed on for sun and fun.'

Barri got plenty of both, more than most of us get in a lifetime. He was bold (new word – or new nuance) and free to do as he liked among an army, an air force and above all a navy of sex-starved men.

'Oh, doockie,' he said one day beside a swimming-pool, varnishing his toe-nails, 'sex – it's becooming an obsession.'

All the same, he was an artiste and prided himself on Knowing The Business and Being A True Pro. This side of him showed itself at the dress-rehearsal of *Over to You* in the garrison theatre. We were stagehands, Lawson was the director and Major Cotton, with the help of a bottle of Scotch, was working out the lighting-plot. The first rehearsal began at eight and he was drunk by midnight. He blundered about repositioning the spots, floods and gelatines while the rest of us kept our tempers. At last began a run of the first half, starting with the opening chorus, sung to the tune of 'Plenty of money and you'.

> We're all coming over to you-oo-who!
> To make you forget that you're blue-oo-who!
> With plenty of laughter and songs and jokes –
> So sit back and relax and just be happy folks.

This went well enough until Barri's big dance number announced in his best Showbiz Yorkshire: 'Well, you've seen a little of Costa Rica, we've shown you something of a negro's life – its trials and tribulations, its sorrows and its joys – and now we bring you a choreographic fantasia from the much-loved legend of Faust and Marguerite. Thank you!'

A Lawsonesque introduction from the band brought on Barri's partner, dancing her love in tight bolero and full skirt.

'Lift up your skirt, dear,' shouted Lawson from one of the front rows.

She paused, mystified, then went on dancing.

'I said, raise your skirt and show us the petticoats.'

She stopped and stared out, shielding her eyes. The music died away and Barri came on, half into his Faust togs.

'Now, now, doockie, it's not a can-can, it's choreography.'

'I'm not asking to see her legs, only the sumptuous underskirts that have been provided at great public expense.'

'That I never asked for!' Barri snapped.

'The boys want colour, glamour, spectacle!'

'I know very well what the boys want, luv.'

The laughter was interrupted by Cotton lurching down the aisle.

'Look here, Barri, no more argument. She'll show the underskirt – that's an order!'

'It's not that kind of dance.'

Kenneth and I and the rest of our company sat watching from the dim hall while at every window transit personnel craned for a view.

'These costumes have been paid for out of taxpayers' money. I shouldn't need to remind you of that. The boys up-country must be given their money's worth.'

'Nobody told us this was going to be a mannequin parade!'

'Do as I say!' shouted Cotton, stumbling on the steps from hall to stage.

'Right, dear,' said Barri to his partner, 'parade round once with your skirt up, show your undies, then start the music and go into the dance!'

'Wait a minute, wait a minute –'

'Barri, don't be tiresome,' droned Lawson.

But Barri had left the stage.

'Come back here at once!' ordered Cotton, trying again to climb the steps.

'Don't you dare talk to Barri like that,' said his partner through her tears.

'I'll talk to him how I damn well like,' said Cotton, his diction slurred by Scotch, 'I'm his commanding officer.'

He turned to us.

'And you lot – close the shutters!'

At every window were the faces of transit squaddies, finding more entertainment in this rehearsal than they ever did in the shows. Before we'd finished, Barri walked into the darkened house, threw the can-can dress at Lawson and shouted 'Take your bleedin' frock and I hope it suits you.'

Cotton followed him out, then Lawson, slowly, as though honing an epigram. Moments later, the Major returned to announce that the rehearsal was over and we could all go home.

'Parade tomorrow ten hundred hours,' he rapped out in a last attempt at military order, mopping his brow with a white handkerchief.

'Look,' said Kenneth quietly, 'vada the powder-brownish on her hankie.'

'The what?'

'The Leichner brownish. She wears it to make her seem more butch, more the grizzled campaigner.'

'Parade,' shouted Cotton, 'dismiss!'

But before we could, from out of a great shouting backstage came a berserk sergeant electrician.

'Lock me up, sir, please, sir,' he demanded, his mad face close to the Major's ear, 'before I punch you in the face, sir. I've had enough of you and your lighting cues!'

'Now simmer down, sergeant, back to your mess with the others, there's a good lad.'

'No, sir, put me under close arrest, sir,' the man insisted, his fists clenching and spreading with fury.

Baxter had come from backstage too and told us he'd seen the sergeant try to hit the CO once already.

'If you don't put me in the guard-house, sir, under lock and key, sir, I swear I'll smash you in the face, sir, and that would be an offence punishable under King's Regulations and I'm group 56, sir, coming up for release. I want to be on that boat, sir, when it sails, so lock me up, you must, sir.'

'Oh, very well,' said Cotton, and turned to the nearest sergeants, a conjurer and impersonator, 'you two, arrest this sergeant and escort him to the guard-room.'

'They can't,' insisted the frantic sergeant, 'they're not substantive sergeants, they're only privates.'

'Oh, for God's sake – what about Sergeants Moore and Whittle – will they do?'

'No, sir, we can't,' said Whittle, 'we're in civilian clothes.'

An understatement – they were in the frilly blouses of a South American band.

'Well, for God's sake, which of you is a properly dressed substantive sergeant?'

Two volunteers stepped one pace forward.

'Then take charge of this man.'

'This man? This man, sir?' raved the demented Sparks. 'You should call me "sergeant", sir, that's in King's Regulations too.'

He was finally taken off and subdued, we were dismissed and the show opened the next night with Barri doing the number as he wished.

'That's the theatre, doockies,' said Barri later, when we reminded him. 'It's Life, The Drama, let's face it!'

But he wasn't going to face *anything*, least of all Life. Nobody in the Theatre was going to face anything for nearly ten years, nothing but verse drama, *Salad Days* and *The Boy Friend*, until some shouts of anger from the real world began to be heard inside.

The true reason for the fuss over Barri's can-can was that Cotton and Lawson were accomplices of the civilian wardrobe mistress. Half the cash allocation for our costumes was going into their own pockets and Lawson wanted to display what they *had* provided in case some nosy-parker smelt a rat. This was perhaps the only racket Sergeant-Major Marriott did not play a hand in though he knew more about it than anyone and was putting together a dossier of proof so as to blackmail Cotton to drop the case against *him*. One day the CO searched his billet and took away all the evidence to give to the Special Investigation Branch. After this, Marriott drank more heavily. I watched him settle his bar-bill once, calmly shelling out $200 from a roll of notes in his pocket. My own pay was fifteen a week.

At about this time, his American wife apparently shopped him to Cotton, who moved into the house in Orchard Road, kicked out the taxi-dancer and became Mrs Marriott's lover. Hank sat it out at Nee Soon, on a bail of $6,000, playing ping-pong and drinking brandy, while we arties discussed the relative merits of Marx and Sartre. Rae Hammond, a con-jurer then and later a theatre manager, remembers hearing all about the case against Cotton. Marriott told him to hold his tongue about it, then one afternoon appeared in the wash-house behind our mess.

'While I washed my face, he stood there with a fifty-cigarette tin spooning crystals into a tumbler. I can see that tumbler now – it had bright flowers enamelled on it. He was probably mixing some Andrews' Liver Salts, which everyone drank before we had Alka Seltzer.

'I said: "I thought you were going on leave."

'He told me he'd come back to make sure his stuff was safe, only to find it had all been taken – receipts, faked invoices, cheque-stubs – so the case against Cotton was ruined.

'I never liked him much – did anyone? – and wandered away to one of the billet-rooms. Several other men and I sat on the beds discussing a soccer match we'd heard relayed from home when Marriott came in. He too sat on a bed and listened for awhile, then drank from the glass with the enamelled flowers. He lurched forward, looking ghastly. He managed to say to me "Everything I've told you, tell the SIB."

'The MO's billet was next to ours and we got him there in no time. Marriott died as they were carrying him to the ambulance. Cyanide acts that fast.'

'I was in that room at the far end,' said Stanley Baxter, pointing it out on my new photo of the billet. 'I saw the commotion from my balcony and rushed down. He'd tipped this powder from a folded paper into his mouth and washed it down with whisky. He was frothing at the mouth.'

'Rae says he mixed it up like liver salts in a glass of water,' I said.

'Oh, well, he's probably right. I wasn't there. I imagined the whole thing from films I've seen of people taking poison. You know, it seems *dramatically* right.'

'But you do remember the funeral?'

'I was a pall-bearer. They picked me because I was of a height with five other men.'

'Kenneth Williams says none of you wanted to carry him and you were all bending your knees or standing on your toes to avoid looking the same height.'

'Yes, he's very funny doing that. But no, we just obeyed orders.'

'He says when they picked you out, you said "Sorry, sir, I'm Church of Scotland."'

'I know he says that but I had more respect for Cotton than to try it. I do remember we debated some time whether we should fire a rifle salute for a suicide who was about to be done for extortion and theft. It was finally decided we should do the most perfunctory service possible, so the six of us got into this fifteen-hundred-weight on a day when it was pissing down – that Singapore rain that can flood the roads in ten minutes. The first vehicle in the cortège was the hearse, the second was for the sergeant-major's widow and his commanding officer, the third was ours. What's as clear as yesterday is the sight of Mrs Marriott and Cotton giggling and fondling each other all the way to the cemetery. And all the way back.'

'Ken does a very funny imitation of the pall-bearers slipping on the mud at the graveside.'

'Yes, doesn't he? And screaming and clutching each other and one of them falling in. Yes, that wasn't true either.'

The agent who so much admired our sergeant-major later helped run a photographic business in Singapore.

'The dark-room in Orchard Road looked out at the back on to Hank's house and I could stand on the fire escape and watch his widow and Cotton in the bedroom. It blew my mind. I wanted to kill him.'

I learnt of Marriott's death in the *Singapore Free Press*. A week or so into rehearsals for our show, the state of my bowels and my general feebleness had persuaded me to report sick. I had caught a dose of amoebic dysentery and was sent straight to hospital for a medical cure that could take weeks – even months.

'Probably months,' I wrote home, 'it's best to be pessimistic – there are fewer disappointments.' A sentiment more proper to middle-age than youth and one that has shadowed and wasted a great part of my life. What in my experience drew me to it? The natural caution of my puritanical father? A cowardly flinching from pain? An acknowledge-ment that I do not deserve life's treats? An infant experience of paradise lost?

I remember nothing of that spell in hospital. My letters describe visits from Stanley and others, the ward inmates, the nursing staff and, at some length, my dreams, stylistically influenced – it now seems clear – by our Nee Soon immersion in Freud and Salvador Dali. One of the patients was on his third bout of amoebic dysentery, the statutory number to earn repatriation. 'He is fat, unwieldy and uninspiring and sings – at any hour of day or night –

Please take my heart in sweet surrender
And tenderly say that I'm
The one you love and live for
Till the end of time.

The rest of us join him in hoping his boat goes soon.'

At Your Service opened before my discharge came and my visitors reported a great success. I got out in time to join it on its tour of Singapore island. My solo, a cod-dramatic monologue called 'The Con-demned Cell', which Kenneth remembers better than I, had been re-placed by a hefty lad singing and dancing 'Happy Feet', a song that surfaced later in *Joe Egg*. Cotton offered me a choice of waiting at Nee Soon for something to turn up or going on the road as chorus and stagehand. This I quickly took, though I wrote home: 'my talents would be wasted in such a capacity'. Evidently my resentment showed because Lawson told me I was to be Returned to Unit for being truculent. I pleaded with Cotton and watched with relief while the orderly-room sergeant tore up my movement order. From then on, I knuckled under, carting props, operating colour-wheels and appearing in one or two con-certed numbers.

My dim memory of the show has been refreshed by Stanley Baxter, who became a stand-in director during the tour, as Lawson remained at Nee Soon preparing more touring extravaganzas, one so grandiose that it could not be played anywhere but the Victoria Theatre. *At Your Service* began with our full company of ten (or, depending on the size of the stage, nine, eight or less) wearing blue-and-gold uniforms, all no doubt exorbitantly priced, like so many tin soldiers, standing in a line-up and doing square-bashing movements as we sang:

'We're *men* of the service – '

('It had been *boys* at first,' said Stanley, 'but Cotton said it wasn't butch enough.')

'We're at your service entertaining – YOU !

(Ten fingers pointed at audience, ten right feet stamping on the word.)

> We'll bring you songs both old and new –
> Fun and laughter – if you're blue !
> Men of the service,
> We're at your service,
> Snappy, smart and – gay !
> So be happy and bright as we're with you tonight,
> We're at your service now.'

('Salute,' said Stanley, 'smart left turn and march off, ten bodies piling up in whatever we were using for wings or backstage, by which time, of course, the howls of hairy-arsed derision had to be heard to be believed. Luckily Kenneth showed a stroke of genius to save us from disaster. Instead of marching off on the end of the line, he let us go, gave a disgusted gesture and said "Oh, I can't be doing with all that", turned back and went straight into his impersonations.')

These I *do* remember – lightning flashes of Nellie Wallace, Bette Davis, and Felix Aylmer.

'Feel who?' asked bewildered squaddies, already reeling from the rich bouquet, but he whirled them into

> This above all, to thine own self be true
> And it must follow as the night the day
> Thou canst not then be false to any man

and, avoiding applause or mockery, got off pronto with Harry Champion's 'Any Old Iron'.

Somewhere in the first half, the entire company appeared on a blacked-out stage (not easy during matinées), our faces lit by individual torches held beneath chins, to sing a current favourite, 'Pedro the Fisherman'. It told how Pedro had left his sweetheart to find wealth, how she'd been forcibly betrothed to 'swarthy Miguel' and was standing

beside him at the altar, another chance for Kenneth to do his Felix
Aylmer:

> Will you take this maid to be
> Your lawful wife eternallee?

And the rest of us:

> When through the open doorway there
> A sudden sound disturbs the air

and a full chorus whistling the theme should have announced the return of
Pedro, rich and just in time. Kenneth, however, had spent much of the
bridge passage running up and down the two rows goosing us all. You
cannot laugh and whistle at the same time and most nights the pianist
had to bash out the theme without any whistles from the stage. We were
busy laughing or goosing Kenneth in return.

The pianist was our only civilian, Leo Conriche, whom I'd probably
seen in the variety halls of my childhood accompanying people like
Ronald Frankau and Stanley Holloway. He had in his fifties the sour,
tortoise face of the middle-aged Maugham but his air of weary resig-
nation was a relief among so much vitality. 'And now,' he would say,
standing at the piano to announce his own solo, 'I should like to play a
lovely piece you all know and love: "The Swan" by Saint-Saëns.' And, as
he sat, an aside to no one but himself: 'Never 'eard of it.' Unrest would
grow while he played, lifting his right hand high above the keys, until at
the end he stood to the ironic cheers and whistles of the soldiers.

'Are they sending me up?' he would ask himself.

From Rae Hammond's magic act I filched most of the lines for Young-
Love in *Privates on Parade*. 'This is called the Russian shuffle because the
cards are Russian from one hand to the other.' 'You will observe that
during this trick my hand never leaves the end of my arm.' It was Rae, not
I, who remembered being sent to a Burmese unit by mistake with a show
called *Chinese Crackers*. The orchestra-pit was awash with monsoon rain
and no one in the audience understood English. 'And now,' Leo announced
from his piano, 'Saint-Saëns's absolutely adorable "Swan", which will be
much more at home than usual in all this water.'

The item that had come straight from Lawson's heart was a series of
patriotic tableaux, in which tabs were drawn back to show members of
the company posing in Allied uniforms while Leo played a medley of
anthems and Stanley Baxter recited jingo verse.

'I don't remember that at all,' I said when he tried to remind me, 'didn't
they send you up?'

'Through the roof. Can you imagine what your average peacetime conscript thought of lines like 'Britain kneels in pledge to you'? As soon as we

got away from Nee Soon, we dropped it but Lawson would sneak out to see the show in some unlikely spot, there'd be hell to pay and we'd have to put it back in.'

With this anthology of garbage, we toured Singapore. At Paya Lebah, I enjoyed that rare treat of being entertained in the sergeants' mess where only weeks ago I'd been in the cookhouse with the other ranks. Next we were pencilled for Burma but the Prime Minister was shot and, with the country in such a ferment, it was decided that *At Your Service* might be the last straw, so we went instead to mainland Malaya by the causeway that was still the island's lifeline. Going across by train, we took in the huge pipes and remembered how, in 1941, the Japanese had played dirty, dodging the island's defences by coming down the peninsula on bikes and cutting off the water.

I was now one of the wood-hewers who went ahead of the stars to organize props, costumes and kit. I still managed to jot down my impressions: 'Kuala Lumpur is a mass of large civic buildings and small so-called hotels which I believe to be brothels, though I have received no confirmation ... our first date was the Cameron Highlands, Malaya's hill-station and leave-centre. . . .'

On the long lorry-drive through the hot jungly plain to the cool hills, we saw the Sakai, Aboriginal Malayans, hunters with long blow-pipes, their women barebreasted, nursing naked children. In the 1980s I travelled that road again, with a reconnaissance group for the film of *Privates* and it was then that we saw the signs warning them against guerrillas. Their history as scouts for the British during the Emergency makes them a likely target. We waved back from our air-conditioned bus at the new generation of Orang Asli, dressed in jeans and seated on Hondas. What do they hunt now, I wondered, and found the answer later in the shopping arcades of the K. L. Hilton. As well as batik sarongs, crocodile bags and paper parasols, you can buy enormous silk moths or emerald Rajah Brookes, pinned with outstretched wings into a glass-fronted case. Why else would the Sakai have traded in their blowpipes for butterfly-nets?

In 1947 we had stayed two nights in a white stone house with black half-timbering on its first floor and gables. It was at the summit of a green hill up a winding lane, overlooking a vast tract of rolling woodland and tea plantation.

'Clean bathrooms,' I wrote then, 'modern rooms, log fires ... an ecstatic preview of English cold.'

Thirty-five years later I found nothing had changed. En Tong Seng house was still some corner of a foreign field that is forever Surrey. I had described this villa in advance to Michael Blakemore and the others and, as we arrived at the first tea plantations, we came upon an enormous half-timbered rest-house. 'Not that one,' I said, 'ours was far smaller.' The hot six-hour drive from K.L., with the usual punctures and breakdowns, had given us a thirst and we stopped for refreshment at this Tudor tavern before finding our hotel. In the oak-beamed tea-room on chintz armchairs, we browsed through recent *Country Life*s and were served tea and home-made scones with mulberry jam by a po-faced Malayan couple. I asked about En Tong Seng.

'That the oldest house, yes, still there.'

'Older than this?'

'Oh, yes. This only built last year.'

Some other guests arrived for tea from the golf-course or trout-fishing, all of them Malaysian or Chinese. Anglaiserie is chic in this curious resort. Even the brochure of the Hotel Merlin seems a pastiche of my 1940s prose:

Rajah Restaurant: a treasure trove for the gourmet. Malaysian and Chinese cuisine served with *savoir-faire* by our chef.

Greenacres Sidewalk Café: where the cool breeze caresses you as you have your meals.

Rattan Lounge: perfect for a quiet snooze.

Asli Bar: just the place for that relaxing drink and a touch of local history and taboos, provided by the Sakai blowpipes that now decorate the walls.

Visit Sungei Palas Tea Plantations: it cannot be imagined that just a few leaves of an ordinary plant give so much drinking pleasure across the world.

In 1947, 'The show', I wrote, 'was well received in the evening and we left next morning at nine.' From the Hotel Metropole at Ipoh, we watched a funeral 'with mourners chanting and moaning to drive away evil spirits'. At Taiping, we swam in an icy pool in the woods, fed by waterfalls. A ferry took us to Penang, a two-night stand with an infantry battalion of the West Yorkshires – 'an atmosphere thick with militarism'. From Butterworth to Ipoh again, where we were to have played the Town Hall but had arrived on the eve of Indian Independence Day, 15 August 1947. A plan to play the NAAFI was abandoned when no one turned up. Next day we listened on the radio to Mountbatten's speech inaugurating the two new countries – Pakistan, with Jinnah 'as temporary dictator', and the Union of India. 'He praised Gandhi and called him the Architect of Peace. They've been putting him in jail whenever he raised his peaceful voice, yet now they praise him! I am pessimistic about India's future.

115

Even as I write, the masses are rioting in Punjab and Bengal.' Then the quick shift to Movietone: 'Nonetheless the wishes of the world are with the leaders in their job of educating, feeding and clothing the enigmatical peoples of these vast lands.'

Education before food and clothes!

'All along the journey from Ipoh to K. L. next day, the humble bashas of Indian families in the rubber plantations were decked with miniature Taj Mahals, Pakistan and Indian flags and pictures of Jinnah and the Mahatma. I sat in the gharrie looking backwards along the road and over the two years (almost to the day) since I became a conscript.'

Word of mouth went ahead of us and, of two performances planned in K. L., one was cancelled when no one came and the other was given to a captive audience in a hospital ward. Dates at Seremban ('drifting fragrance of nearby latrines, petrol and wet paint') and Tampin completed our tour. 'Slung our mosquito-nets in a library – myself under "Fiction", Les Wilson under "Useful Arts". Spent afternoon in Malacca, oldest of Malayan towns. Air of English seaside resort. Leo bought three postcards. Saw no canes.'

Tampin's performance was a success, a happy send-off for Kenneth Williams, who was to be leaving for England before the tour of Hong Kong. We afterwards took him for a farewell drink at Betty Café, where the menu offered: 'Also, upstairs, Betty Lodging-House – the most comfortable and sanitary in town. If you are not pleased, tell us. If you are pleased, tell your friends.' One of the girls paraded while we ate: 'Absurdly painted and padded, she looked like one of our drag acts.'

'You sleep?' some Indian boys asked us, nodding at the girl. I had not quite finished my jam pancake so I hurled the remains at them. Twenty years of age and still in a sexual funk!

We touched Nee Soon for a few days, picked up clean clothes, heard who'd been returned to unit and read our mail. Cliff was still in Karachi, now c/o Armed Forces, Pakistan, waiting for the boat. I rehearsed Kenneth's parts in the show 'then suddenly he decided to come with us to Hong Kong. A bitter disappointment for it left me without anything to do but the usual thankless backstage work.' Evidently – big surprise! – my Nellie Wallace wasn't up to Kenneth's and he'd been persuaded to stay. Still feeling behind, I reacted to our latest inoculations with a mild attack of cholera and in this state had to supervise the loading of our company's baggage on to ss *Empress of Scotland*. This time, though, we were treated better, eight to a ten-berth cabin. We improvised a cabaret, *All At Sea*, one item of which was my mock-melodramatic monologue for which the only lighting was a candle, kindly lent by the ship's chaplain.

Our arrival in Hong Kong knocked me sideways. 'Everything teems, struggles, rushes for expression. If I can only get through the day without using a string of *Geographic Magazine* or Fitzpatrick travelogue clichés!'

Fat chance.

'Lush green foliage ... blue sky ... white buildings like American skyscrapers left unfinished ... sheer beauty ... at that moment I could almost have believed in God.

'"Here, Jim, can you pick out the NAAFI?" asked a soldier behind me, returning from leave at home, oblivious of so much beauty, aware only of the common round.'

From the ship's mooring on the Kowloon shore of Hong Kong's harbour, we were taken in a launch to the Fleet Club, our 'hotel' for the stay, a tall, dazzling block on the waterfront. Sun-bathing members of the *Over to You* troupe shouted and waved from the roof.

'I know what the Boys want,' Barri had said at the dress rehearsal, though only the ablest-bodied seamen had climbed the Raffles trellis to his room. In Hong Kong there were no such problems, he told us when he came to the Fleet Club to welcome his protégé, Sergeant Denis Parker, the chief drag-artiste in our troupe. Plump, already balding, he'd have been good casting for a gay Friar Tuck. From a Salvationist, small-town background, Denis had, on his arrival at CSE, been a serious, almost priggish, youth who liked nothing better than talking Art and the spiritual side of Drama. Then he'd experienced a Pauline conversion and become a raver overnight.

'No more art for him,' said Stanley, 'no relationships, no love, only as much rough trade as he could get.'

When Barri arrived from England, Denis became his acolyte and now that the older man was sailing home again (on the *Empress of Scotland*, due to leave in two days) Barri handed on the torch. *Over to You*, in fact. While Stanley, Kenneth and I explored the city in tramcars and drank fruit juice in grand cafés, Denis made sure that Barri's last days excelled all he'd known so far. We in our turn waved from the roof of the Fleet Club as Barri and his party made off in their launch, speeding between the junks, sampans, ferries, and yachts towards the liner moored on the far shore with the mountains of mainland China rising gaunt behind. It was on this roof after dark that Denis entertained his many admirers, some picked up on the water-front or in the Fleet Canteen, some passed on by Barri with the best of references. I could never guess what they saw in him – he wasn't an imitation-woman like Barri and, though he was shaved from head to foot, he wore no slap.

Can it have been his warm smile and matronly manner that brought so many sailors to our room asking for 'Sergeant Parker'?

'On the roof.'

'Oh, right, thanks very much, mate.'

In an exchange that was cut before *Privates* reached the stage, Major Flack asked Charles Bishop why there was no hair on his body.

'You know what they say, sir. Grass doesn't grow on a busy street.'

At the end of our first full day, I wrote that it had been 'the most exciting I'd spent since leaving England and, indeed, one of the most thrilling of my whole life'.

What then must it have been for Barri and Denis? For Barri it could only decline after that. Years later Kenneth told me of his return to Attlee's Britain.

'She left Hong Kong with yards of silk and satin to make into drag in rationed London. She was quids in as long as she stayed aboard the boat but the first shock came at Malta. The islanders had seen a lot one way and another – well, they didn't get the George Cross for nothing – but she went *too* far. They slung her off! Two MPs escorted her aboard. "Outrageous!" she was screaming, "I've given my all for the boys. What have I *done*? Press charges if you like! I have no political convictions."'

I transposed this scene to Singapore and used it at the end of *Privates* for Terri's farewell.

'When they reached Liverpool they asked her if she had anything to declare. She was so cocksure by this time she thought she'd brave it out.

'"No, duckie! Only yards of silk and satin bought in Hong Kong and wrapped round my body under my clothes."

'They took her away and searched her and there it all was. They *did* press charges this time and she not only lost the lot but got fined into the bargain.'

Barri soon picked up his transvestite career where he had left it. But how did Denis Parker domesticate himself? Did he go back to beating the bass drum in the Sally Army, his head full of sailors in white drill against the moonlit Chinese hills?

'England, 1948, is a far cry from the Fleet Club, duckie,' I had Terri tell him in *Privates*. 'One lonely night you'll say a few flattering words to some nice chap in a cottage and next you know some cow of a magistrate's giving you three months.'

He is the one none of us heard from afterwards. Even so, what-did-I-call-him? – Denis? – had his moment, which is more than *I* did.

'The women of Hong Kong', I wrote, 'are the most beautiful I've seen anywhere. Beside them, the English women here are dowdy and dull. Even the whores are quite fetching in a gaudy sort of way.'

above Palatine today: a new glass door, all the rendering *eau-de-Nil*. Muller's orphan houses are beyond

below left My father as a young man

below right Nan holding me among the trellis before they built the garage; the apple trees are behind

The Miserable Mirth-Maker

above left With my mother

With Cliff Brown at Palatine,
with wartime windows in the background

Wartime concert party as seen in *Forget-me-not Lane*: Joan Hickson
(as Mother), Ian Gelder (as Author), Stephanie Lawrence (as Miss 1940),
Eddie Molloy (as Mister Magic) and Malcolm McFee (as best friend)

At Your Service, Hong Kong, 1947: CSE

Privates on Parade, London, 1977: RSC

Kenneth Williams

Stanley Baxter in my kimono,
Nee Soon, 1947

COMBINED SERVICES ENTERTAINMENT
presents

"AT
    YOUR
        SERVICE"
A SIDE-SPLITTING REVUE
with

Ken Williams — Stan Baxter
Geoffrey Deakin — Dave Perton
Lawrie Clayton — Rae Hammond
Brian Hargreaves — Les Wilson
Ray Ashley — Colin Maynard
Peter Nichols,
AND
LEO CONRICHE
AT THE PIANO
PRODUCED BY ALBERT ARLEN

AT RAF ... ON ...
TIME ...

As Ananias (centre) in *The Alchemist*, Bristol Old Vic, with James Cairncross as Subtle and John Neville as Face

below left My wife and my father at our wedding reception, 1959

below right Michael Bates as Father, *Forget-me-not Lane*, Greenwich Theatre and Apollo, London, 1971

With my daughter
Abigail, Bristol,
1968

Thelma with
our other chidren,
Daniel, Catherine
and Louise, 1967

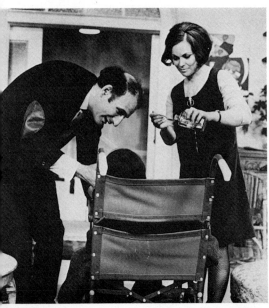

A Day in the Death of Joe Egg: Joe Melia and Zena Walker with the handicapped child, Glasgow Citizens' and Comedy Theatre, London, 1967

The same living room, Brooks Atkinson Theatre, New York, 1968: back row, the producers: Henry Fownes, Michael Medwin, Joe Cates; front row, me, Michael Blakemore and Albert Finney

End of story. My days were spent in sight-seeing, going with an old friend to the Peak on the cable-car, hearing the noonday gun, defining the different moods of the island and the mainland. One of the men went into hospital with food poisoning and I took over his parts in the show until I had to report sick myself and was back in dock with a relapse of amoebic dysentery.

The hospital balcony had a view from the hills over the city and harbour, the food was better, the treatment mild. My four daily injections were given by a sister so sympathetic that she winced and apologized for every jab. A young soldier died of paratyphoid my first night there. 'I wondered what had been achieved by sending him overseas,' says the journal soberly.

One day after one of my injections, the sister looked at my scraggy body.

'Not very fat, are you?'

'No, nor strong.'

'Would you like to go home?'

'Of course.'

'I think you've a very good chance of a medical repat.'

She said so to the medical officer, who later examined me, looked at my records and considered my condition did not merit a home posting. Instead he gave me leave in Hong Kong, which I spent shopping for clothes and a suitcase to carry them in. Back in my ward on the Peak I read *Wuthering Heights* and watched typhoons and cyclones, Nanette and Mary Lou, sweep in from the China Seas. Night temperatures fell as low as seventy degrees and we needed blankets. I have been told I was visited by Kenneth and Stanley, who came in one of those huge Hudson or De Soto taxis, bringing a bagful of carefully chosen cream cakes. I took them, said 'Oh, thanks' and set them aside without another word.

'Baxter was livid,' Kenneth reports. 'As we were going back in the funicular, he kept going on about the trouble we'd taken and you hardly thanking him.'

'Is that what he says I said?' mused Stanley. 'I don't remember that. I *do* remember saying you looked so ill I thought you'd never see the shores of home again. I remember that phrase: the shores of home.'

My journal only records our first excursion into the overwhelming streets and our retreat into an opulent restaurant where, surrounded by rich Chinese eating their way through epic Cantonese meals, we ordered 'three fruit juice' of a head waiter whose inscrutability faltered for a moment before he passed our order to a waitress. She brought us wet flannels and stood by, smiling. Seconds passed. We stared at one another helplessly. What were they *for*? At last Kenneth took his cue from another table and led us in wiping our fingers. The silky waitress turned on an electric fan above our table. Again we smiled apologetically. Our soft drinks came in ice-cold bottles and were poured into ice-cold glasses. Before we could sip them, she topped up each glass with ice-cubes from a bowl. Again we smiled and again she left us. Kenneth handed cigarettes around.

'For Christ's sake hurry up and light them or she'll be back with –' I whispered as sulphur flared in my face and she held a match to my cigarette.

What can explain such boorishness in men of twenty? Puritanical parents? Five years of war? A lower-middle-class fear of losing face? At about this time I was reading Aldous Huxley's *Antic Hay* and remember to this day the shock of recognition at 'people in Lyons' Corner House eating a cherry with a knife and fork'. The passages about wine in *Brideshead Revisited* were as arcane as Sanskrit to someone who had known only Ruby Port and British Tonic. Every sneer at suburban manners was filed away for future reference in a hidden manual of snobberies. We didn't mind being laughed at but it had to be on our terms – on the stage in chosen roles and routines so impeccably armoured that no one could find the chink and hurt us. This is the real malaise of Britain – an urge to classify that runs from Jane Austen through Dickens, Thackeray, Wells, James, Lawrence and Orwell to John Braine, Kingsley Amis and Arnold Wesker.

'Fancy making Ernest Bevin Foreign Secretary,' exclaimed my grandma, 'him what used to drive a mineral-water cart! He speaks in a Bristol accent. What gentry do they think will listen to *him*?'

If getting a drink in a public place gave me such trouble, what would I have done in a brothel? So, for the last few days in Hong Kong, 'I shopped and walked and admired from afar the beauty of the female population.' If only the hearties had frog-marched me to a dance-hall or some sympathetic nurse taken me in hand! I was writing home to a beautiful girl in South Wales, a pen-pal who sent pictures of herself in swimsuits and looked forward to meeting me when I got home. 'Girl I write to,' says a soldier in *Privates*, 'all love and kisses and current affairs but I have the odd wank over her photo.'

Chapter Sixty-Six is 'Bulkhead Revisited', the return journey to Singapore on the troopship *Devonshire*, closely packed with time-expired men of about group sixty. I'd no sooner found my troopdeck than a call came for me on the tannoy. The flight-sergeant I reported to said: 'Aren't you meant to be going home?'

'Don't think so, Chief, I'm Sixty-nine.'

'Well, there's a big Air Ministry enquiry about you. You're to have a Board. Report with this envelope to the MO at Changi as soon as you reach Singapore.'

At the time I thought this the work of the kindly sister on the Peak but it transpired that Dad, alarmed by my laments, had spoken to his MP. I practised my usual pessimism, which wasn't difficult on that ship with its boat-drills, crowded ablutions, cries of housie-housie and regular appeals to the first-class passengers to register their excess baggage. To pass the time, we put on a cabaret. Officers and civilians were given front-row seats on the promenade deck and the troops crowded in behind. So many had to be turned away that we gave a second house. I wrote a Western Brothers song for Kenneth and myself.

Boat-stations in the morning has us lining up in rows,
The yeomen of the first-class lounge behind us sit and doze,
At last we have discovered where the excess baggage goes –
In Devon, in Devon, glorious Devon.'

A squeak of protest that brought rebellious roars from the other ranks, those same men who four years later would vote back the ageing Churchill for another term of Tory rule.

Kenneth stayed on board for the five-week voyage home. Next time we met was in a cinema queue in the early 1950s.

Purdy told us what had happened in our absence – another officer, lately married to a singer in one of the shows, had fallen from a hotel balcony and crushed his skull, Cotton was touring Malaya, RTU had reached epidemic levels and Stanley Baxter's release number had been brought down because he'd been a Bevin boy. I reported at Changi next day with my dossier.

'Had amoebic twice, eh?' the Squadron Leader said.

'Sir.'

'How d'you feel? As weak as you look?'

'I suppose so, yes.'

'It's policy to send a man home in a case like yours and though the Major in Hong Kong didn't think you warrant a repat., I do. If you hang about out here you'll almost certainly get another dose and what good's that?'

Sad to say, he himself went home after I'd been in hospital a few days and handed my fate to a Wing Commander, who grinned at me from behind his desk.

'There's been some doubt about your serving another term overseas. Well, we think you're plenty fit enough.'

'But, sir, the Squadron Leader said –'

'Don't tell me what the Squadron Leader said, sergeant. Go on leave, fatten yourself up, then I'll have another look at you.'

'And if I get dysentery again –'

'Then you'll go home. That's official.'

My education at Nee Soon was now in the hands of Baxter and his friend Edgar Williams, who'd been on Leave In Advance of Python when I first arrived. He'd studied the violin at Trinity before the army and joined CSE as the first member of a symphony orchestra Lawson was recruiting – perhaps to play the Tobruk Rhapsody as well as it deserved. No other musicians were found so Edgar stayed on as an orchestra of one. To avoid RTU, he made himself i/c Make-up and sat all day in a room like a cupboard commanding some sticks of greasepaint and a quantity of crêpe hair.

Long service entitled him to home leave and then he was shipped back to Singapore to sit again in the cupboard with his bottles of spirit-gum and wodges of nose-putty, where I would sometimes join him during my 'leave' to listen to Debussy, Ravel, Delius, Vaughan Williams or Sibelius, all in four-minute bursts on his hand-cranked HMV portable. Short as a schoolboy, he spent most of his army life unseen behind large pieces of furniture. When his college tutors told him to study bassoon because of a dearth of woodwind-players, it seemed some sort of Teutonic Musical Joke, as even standing up he was shorter than his instrument.

Between movements of Rachmaninoff or Brahms, he expounded to me in his Harrow accent (the place, not the school) the advanced ideas of twenty or thirty years earlier. I swallowed them whole – the socialism of the Webbs and Shaw, the atheism of Bradlaugh, the pacifism of Wells and Russell. The notion of Equality burst on me like thunder. It was so obvious – first expounded by Christ as a booby-prize for those who've spent put-upon lives but now defined as a real possibility in the precise blueprints of modern socialism. I had no trouble believing in this at the same time as I described the other patients in the Changi hospital as 'animals ... mousy little clerks, unimportant hearties ... should be killed not cured ....' We read Robert Tressall's *The Ragged-Trousered Philanthropists* and Shaw's *Everybody's Political What's-What*, Orwell's essays, Auden's plays, Waugh, Huxley, Firbank, Strachey.

Sexually we were still in the closet, waiting for Straight Lib. Afraid of the simple act, we mugged up on the fancy stuff. Baxter had bought Frank Harris in Hong Kong and Edgar kept Havelock-Ellis among the wigs. We'd never touched a naked girl but knew all about buggery, bestiality and necrophilia. In London later Edgar took me to Conway

Hall to hear Norman Haire, a renowned sexologist, telling an audience of dirty macs what rustics did to horses (and birds!) or how one unusually choosy patient could only be roused by a wet chest cough. When Edgar eventually brought his pregnant wife to stay with our growing family, I remembered these ghoulish studies with amazement.

Our quarters were being renovated to house married regulars. Chinese builders and decorators laughed and chatted, knocked down wash-houses, threw up scaffolding, painted stairways. We were being shifted to an ordinary billet on the barrack square. We all sensed the end.

'I asked my bearer to clean my shoes,' said Purdy, 'and he said he'd get his bearer to do it.'

Moon-men or zombies arriving from home with chequered pink-and-white skins had been told on the boat that the men they'd be replacing in South-East Asia were tough, barbarous types with communistic, anti-British notions. This was an over-reaction to the RAF strikes of two years before, but it was a marvel we weren't more rebellious when our treatment was so arbitrary.

'A big-eared, red-faced, ginger-haired idiot in the wardrobe department has gone on home leave,' I wrote. 'Dumbo has been in Asia six months, all of it at CSE, is already a paid sergeant while every day I spend here puts my health at risk.' Dumbo, being a regular, got preference over my dysentery.

Baxter promised me a part in the show he was now producing but one day told me he couldn't use me after all.

'You've had it, Peter, they've already arranged your RTU. If I'd known it was happening, I'd have asked for you sooner.'

Neither Cotton nor Lawson had ever taken to me, I'd not had the sense to hide in the woodwork like Edgar and Dumbo and it seems to me now that only Stanley's backing had kept me there so long. 'I think it's very likely,' he said when I asked him recently, 'but you were a terrible health hazard.'

Towards Christmas, torrents of rain swept the square by our new quarters. We found we'd all been spoiled for dormitory life, the midnight rumpus of drunken hearties, the grisly food of a transit sergeants' mess. Nights out in Hokkien Street, eating Fried Mee and Hokkien Mee Soup, Nasi Goreng, prawn, crab and octopus, where Edgar and I learnt to handle chopsticks, were little consolation for the wash-rooms of our billet being flooded with a brown swill. I squeezed the last inch of toothpaste from the tube and told myself there was nothing to stay for.

For which to stay, boy, for which to stay. My father, reading the maudlin passages I sent home, had taken to correcting my syntax and changing words that frightened him. 'The next few days will be the last I spend at this home of eccentrics in the middle of an army. I have learned a lot by this intimacy with interesting people.' The word 'intimacy' is bracketed and 'association' written above. I suppose he thought I'd gone gay. Understandably. 'Very soon a whole gang will be leaving' (he suggested 'crowd' for 'gang'). 'Stanley Baxter, a severe critic of any work I care (suggested "have") to show him, is one. Edgar, one of the finest people (persons?) I have met will follow soon. So will Denis Parker, ladylike young man in coloured shirts, who hopes to join a rep. Purdy, from Bristol, has signed on for another stretch. We all knew he was doolali and he's now drinking like a drain.'

It fell to Purdy, now Company Sergeant-Major since Marriott had taken cyanide, to propose the loyal toast at Christmas dinner.

'Gentlemen, the King!' he managed to get out, sipping his wine and sniggering at the same time. We all stood up, many openly laughing.

'The King!'

'God bless him!' said Purdy towards the ceiling.

'Amen!' and 'Bless him' the rest of us responded and fell back into our chairs.

Cotton, who still spent most nights at Orchard Road with Mrs Marriott, helped the other officers serve our soup, pork, ham, plum pudding, nuts and fruit.

Purdy rose again.

'Now be upstanding, and drink the health of our Commanding Officer.'

'Well, chaps, this is something of a farewell party for most of us. We've had some pretty bad times here but I'm sure you'll agree with me we've also had some damn good ones. When once we're out of this army racket' – for him a nice choice of words – 'we may look back on all this and think these months at Nee Soon were some of the best of our lives.'

He raised his glass.

'Good luck to you all!'

'Wouldn't it be awful if that turned out to be true?' Stanley said to me when we'd drunk the toast. In the event, no one I knew looked back on that time as anything but source material and on Nee Soon as a meeting-place for future friends, but for Cotton it may well have been the high point.

Rae Hammond, our conjurer, remembers hearing him a year or two later in a Children's Hour broadcast from the North. He was playing Third Frog.

And in the late 1950s, Stanley Baxter and Evelyn Laye, on the pre-London tour of a West End comedy, stayed at some digs just outside Leeds.

The landlady was a charming woman with two grown-up daughters. One
night she asked him: 'Didn't you serve under my husband in the Far
East?'

'Major Cotton?' Stanley said.

'Yes, I thought so.'

She said no more but he afterwards learnt that Cotton had gone into
Leeds one night, taken a room at the Queen's Hotel and killed himself
with an overdose.

The rain had passed and we spent Christmas in equatorial heat. After
the midday meal, a few of the bandsmen – three trumpeters, a trombone
novice, a guitarist and some drummers – formed a scratch group, joined
by a comedian on ukelele and a tap-dancer on cymbals.

'We prepared to view all this with the tolerance usually accorded the
efforts of children but the noise they made was original and refreshing,
like the brass band of a madhouse. An audience gathered on the square.
New arrivals at the transit camp, with pink faces, hands and knees,
white legs and arms, began taking photographs. A drum-major appeared
and with his baton led us into a ragged march. Edgar, Stanley, Denis and
I followed the band.'

Other men poured from the great white blocks around the square, all
wearing paper hats and carrying bottles. Three of us left the parade and
made for CSE's wardrobe. When we fell in again, Edgar was wearing a
bush-hat and carrying a candelabra, I had a tiny trilby and a blunderbuss
and Denis was in drag. By this time, the procession had left the square
and was heading for the main guard-room, where the sentry presented
arms and raised the barrier. In the afternoon sun, nearly all of us had
stripped to shirts and paper hats. The Indian and Chinese shopkeepers of
Nee Soon village applauded and children tagged on behind. Buses halted
to let us by, drinkers came from cafés and young Chinese let off firecrackers. Our circuit of the village done, we marched back into camp.
From the direction of our theatre – sure enough, the Gaiety – came an
officer's jeep driven by Purdy in overdone drag. It hardly mattered that
he was too drunk to keep a straight course. At first I thought his ATS
girl-friend sat beside him but, as they came closer, we saw that it was
Cotton in another of Denis's show costumes. The jeep led our parade back
into the square, where by now the salmon-pink new boys had mustered as
though for a passing-out. We did a final lap of honour while they cheered
us on. They were straight from basic training and a major and CSM in
drag can't have met their eyes before.

'Yes, here we are,' said Stanley, 'the sergeants of the Far East –
anti-social, anti-British, anti-colonial red perils. What d'you make of us?'

With a dead cigar stuck in his mouth, he had the look of an academic on a bender.

We sent a request up to the band for 'The Red Flag' but they only knew 'Keep the Home Fires Burning' and that served for a travesty salute, Cotton in the shade of a billet, flashing battery-powered lamps in the huge tits of Denis's ATS tunic. With a final linking of hands and a refrain of 'Auld Lang Syne', we dismissed to our billets. Only an impromptu Rag Week lark, a Last-Night-of-the-Proms, You-don't-have-to-be-mad-to-work-here-but-it-helps caper. Somehow, though, a fitting finale for CSE, so right that, when Michael Blakemore needed a curtain-call for *Privates on Parade*, he – without knowing of our Christmas Day parade – had Denis Quilley reappear in ATS drag. A nice case of art imitating life.

One day I had the sew-sew woman remove the stripes from my shirt-sleeves.

The last three months in Singapore were a long pause and more of the same. Two weeks in hospital – this time with worms, two on leave in the Union Jack Club, where I went canoeing and with parties of men and women on picnics. 'Left the club with six voluntary women, a packet of sandwiches, a banana and a copy of Plato's *Republic* for Katong swimming club, where the sun lit a quiet sea and we swam, sunned, drank, talked, played records, wondered whether the Office Blonde's costume would stick or bust, lay in a wicker-chair in the midwinter tropic sun reading the Socratic dialogues and sipping NAAFI tea.'

I was in the city for the start of Thaipusam, the Hindu festival where masochists walk miles wearing kavadis, or decorated frames of steel, their spikes resting on the naked flesh.

News came of Gandhi's murder. I gave it less column-inches than my American-type beach-shirt with a pattern of swirls, shellfish and wire-netting, sold to me by Purdy who was too shy to wear it. One of the few thrills I could afford was flaunting it in service canteens where hearties jeered and said 'Spiv!' I saw myself as the newly bearded Gumbril in *Antic Hay*, delighted when boys shouted 'Beaver!' in the street.

Nineteen inches of rain fell in January, the most for twenty-three years. I earned $10 for a story published in an air-force magazine under my pseudonym Gene Maxwell, I broadcast sketches on Changi radio and joined the cast of an amateur production of a light comedy with French windows in which I played the father of a pretty wing-commander's wife. At one point in the action she had to sit on my lap and can't have failed to feel my erection through my khaki drill and her cotton dress. During weeks of rehearsals and several shows, this hard-on never failed to happen and, though noblesse obliged her to ignore it, this may have been another lost chance. Les Wilson and I were allowed into Raffles Hotel as 'Singapore's Premier Light Comedy Team'. The manager offered us $30 for a try-out cabaret.

'Don't be too subtle for them,' he said, 'they're none too bright.'

'From what we saw of the Palm Court,' I wrote, 'the cream of Singapore society seems to have been left out too long. We got five laughs in five minutes and the manager felt we might have finished with a song.'

There was no cabaret when I went back last year – only a trio of young Chinese playing selections from *The White Horse Inn*.

'During the last seven days, which have lasted just over a year, nothing has happened, except my renewed friendship with Percy (David) Allford. . . .

'Hair like lemon candy-floss,' I wrote in Chapter Seventy-Seven, 'somehow manages to look immaculate, even in k.d. Has other virtues – a modicum of intelligence and a talent for mimicry.'

What made me so ungenerous? Why this pose of premature senility? David was, after all, one of the first people to direct me towards better books. On *Dunera*, Forster and Saroyan. Later, in Bristol, he'd point out the skyline I'd never noticed.

'You've grown up in a very interesting city, full of marvellous buildings. Coming from Sheffield, I can envy that. You take it for granted or don't even know. Why the bloody hell have you never stepped inside the Lord Mayor's Chapel?'

He was 'Percy' at the time, a Mandarin pseudonym, as my 'Gene Maxwell' was all-American – Eugene O'Neill, Gene Krupa, Maxwell Anderson, Elsa Maxwell. By the time I got to Changi for the second time, I'd bought a pair of rimless glasses and tried to look like Glenn Miller.

'Percy' didn't long survive the air force. The slim youth in neat k.d. spread in no time into the large senior partner of the practice that designed Gatwick and Kuwait airports, Warwick University and St Thomas's Hospital facing Parliament.

My education continued now, under David's tuition. *A Portrait of the Artist as a Young Man*, *To the Lighthouse*, *A Room of One's Own*, *Howard's End*, *Animal Farm*, *Brighton Rock* – I swallowed them all among the mosquito-nets, lost to the cries of 'sew-sew', the farting contests and the hammering, as boys of twenty made wooden crates to protect the tin trunks full of tatty treasures, not wanted on voyage, that would prove such an embarrassment when they got home some weeks after the man himself. Now that our release was close, Mespots or Dear Johns arrived more often. An erk who'd been saving himself for some

Brenda in the Midlands had asked an earlier demobbed friend to deliver silk and lace to his fiancée so that she could make a start on her wedding dress. A Dear John came soon after and in the same mail an apology from the friend for stealing the girl. 'We couldn't help ourselves,' he wrote.

'Looks to me as though he's helped himself to quite a tidy slice,' says one of the men when this is read out in *Privates*. Eric Young-Love, who receives that letter in the play, is based on a Clerk General Duties in my Changi billet but his reality has been blurred by several attempts to write him down. The real man came from Wimbledon and spoke with a plummy accent, standard-issue Young Conservative, whose double-barrelled name and better background made him believe he must get down to our level by peppering his speech with the sort of thing he thought we understood. It was an unforgettable patois – somewhere between public school, public house and Battle of Britain. His immense head, almost hydrocephalic, moved in abrupt jerks like a hen's while he strode forward, bouncing on the balls of his feet, his arms hanging in curves like the handles of a vase. His k.d. and white shirts, dangling from his mosquito wire, had the shape of their owner too. Every morning he was up and doing an hour before anyone else.

'Come along, you scroungers!' he shouted, mixing condescension with bullying, 'out of your pits! It's a wizard day, maties, one nearer that ruddy old boat. Get mobile!'

'And you get fucked and all!' groaned the others from their beds and off he'd go to shave; a long and often gory business, as he scraped away not only at his face but up to several inches above the ears. His early rising never helped – he took so long to do everything that by the time we were on our way to breakfast, he was still struggling with his shirt, calling the bearer for his shoes. 'Come along there, Johnnie, finger out, *juldi-juldi*,' and imploring 'Wait for me, my old mates, I'm just coming.' The bearer always left his shoes to last, no one ever waited. He was last for breakfast, usually going without, and last to fall in and march to the offices where we spent our working days as cut-price clerks.

David and I would turn aside from my tutorials – 'The Waste Land' perhaps or whether socialism could replace God – to watch Young-Love's disasters. Even to me, his bedspace was chaos. To someone as fastidious as David, the sight of such a muddle raised fundamental questions.

'We must ask ourselves how can we establish some form of order without tyranny. How to help even those we cannot like. What place can be found in our New World for a man who's perpetually mislaying his caps? Has Corbusier made any provision in his *Unité d'Habitation* for someone who sweats that much? Every day he's on a charge for dirty bedspace

128

but, if his punishment is extra guard-duty, this may endanger the whole unit.' He had been on guard one night when a Chinese civilian had stolen the CO staff car. Eric hadn't challenged the driver but raised the barrier, saluting the car as it passed out, thinking he'd earned a pat on the back. To try and make up for this, he'd volunteered for permanent Saturday night guard-duty but been refused. If anyone ribbed him about it, he thrust out a fist and offered a bunch of fives.

Only two other men at Changi were known as greater disasters – a pair of corporal cooks i/c Catering. Lugubrious Brums, they provided food so foul that we spent all our pay on canteen egg-and-chips or, whenever we could, in Singapore on Hokkien Mee. On one occasion they mistakenly ordered several tons of prunes when they'd meant potatoes and for months we had prunes for breakfast, tiffin and high tea. Chinese boys ladling paste from a vat (Banana Cream, said the blackboard) would always manage to give each man a prune or two. After every meal, the swill-bins were full of uneaten prunes. It was natural that Eric should befriend these two. No one else would speak to them. One wet day I was billet orderly, sitting beside my bed enjoying the prim disgust of Eliot's choruses from 'The Rock' ('And daughters ride away on casual pillions') when Eric blundered in with a great cylindrical tin, which he thumped down on the floor of his bedspace.

'What the hell have you got there, Young-Love?'

'Wizard skive, mate. Bang-on scrounge. Made a couple of oppos in the cookhouse –'

'I've seen them, yes. What's in the tin?'

'Lemonade powder.'

He sat on the bed, the armpits of his shirt dark with sweat, and wiped his head with a towel.

'That's enough to keep the whole billet in lemonade for a year. We'll all be home by then.'

'Shouldn't bank on that, chiefey. The latest gen says demob's slowing down.'

'Where d'you hear that?'

'Never you mind,' and he tapped his nose to indicate news from high places.

'Piss off! I've read the nominal rolls. I'm going by air.'

'Right-i-oh, my old mucker, but don't come whining to me for lemonade when you're still here in six months' time.'

He never managed to open the tin and had to hide it under his bedroll, in his home trunk, anywhere, while he sought a knife or marlin-spike that would pierce the top.

He had to report sick with prickly heat and was found to have the worst case in the whole of South-East Asia. Proudly, he told us he'd been photographed for medical records. The only remedy, he said, was standing in the tropic rain bollock-naked. He did that several days running and went down with a cold.

David had spent a year in this billet, crossing off the days, a clerk in the office of the Church of England padre, making friends of the Indian civilians and observing Young-Love's disasters. What surprises me now is how much time we let slip by. We did so little, only looked on like visitors at an asylum. Nowadays, as time begins to run out, I am afraid to waste a moment; then we dreamt all day, talked half the night and slept the rest. In middle age I have written fifty scripts, kept a diary, helped bring up a family, bought or rented a dozen flats or houses, owned ten cars, employed accountants, agents, gardeners, cleaners, builders and architects and still had sex more often than the *Guardian*'s national average. But in my youth we waited and watched. Was that what the times had led us to expect? We'd watched all through the war and it didn't yet occur to us that now it was our turn.

So David asked me what I'd seen at Nee Soon and I asked him what he could see in our future. A new white world, he thought, as it had been when the cathedrals were new. And together we watched Young-Love.

'I like your glasses, Nick,' he called across one evening, as David and I were discussing the symmetry of the Tootsie-Fruitsie ice-cream sequence in the Marx Brothers' *Day at the Races*.

'What's that, Love?'

'I say, I like those rimless glasses of yours. Feel like getting a pair myself. Look bang-on with my mufti.'

'D'you think so?'

His mufti was a Harris Tweed sports coat that now hung with his shirts, arms curved, turning in the breeze of the electric fans. It was part of the costume he was preparing for civvie street to impress his bint who was waiting in Wimbledon. He took the name of the optician and had rimless glasses made, but the first time he tried them on, strutting about in his tweed coat, they fell on to the stone floor and broke in pieces.

Some of my last letters home survive and show my state of mind better than the stilted chapters. To my mother I wrote:

It was lovely to hear you talking about my career in that way. I have always had a great sympathy with you over your lost chances – crushed, frustrated ambition is a dreadful thing. I must either go on the stage or write or else die mentally. I'm perfectly serious! Every minute I spend in the office here is an abject misery, bored and humiliated, ordered about by morons, counting the seconds till four-thirty when I can leave this hell – except of course that I may be on guard, in which case it starts all over again. This treadmill is simply not me – let's face it! Have heard nothing yet from the Bristol Old Vic School though have applied for an audition. I'd prefer to try for a school or rep company in the London area. Let me know if there's anything you want – I'm getting Tich a wallet – is that okay? What do you and Dad and Nan want? Not too big or too dear. Enclosed photo of me in one of my coloured shirts.

PS Did I tell you that a subhuman Warrant Officer ordered me to have what he calls a haircut, which means having my head cropped to the same length as his. An Indian barber's shaved my scalp! I thought you should be warned in case it hasn't grown by the time I'm home. Roll on the boat!

She replied that the house was being made ready for my return: 'spring cleaning and decorating – but none of your old stuff being touched, the back room's just as it was. Cliff was here to tea on Sunday. He was painfully thin when he first got home but his Mum's fattening him up now.'

Dad saw my letter and sympathized.

Yours of 7th inst. to hand. Can readily understand your resentment re haircut. Often wish I'd been in one of the services and able to tell such so-called Big Cheeses that talking so big only makes them look very small. Had he tried any of his old buck with me, I should have walked off and left him standing. They don't put it over the Old Man, boy, though must say a well-cut barnet can be a thing of beauty and a joy forever. Who said that? I'll give him a kick in the pants – boom! Long hair looks poverty-stricken, as do beards and unpolished shoes. They are among my anathema and could make a list of these to set against my likes.

Viz:

DISLIKES	LIKES
Filth in all its forms:	Cleanliness of thought and deed
filthy fingernails	Clean nails
filthy talk	Good talk of a good kind
dog's soil on footpath	Ideals of Co-operative Movement
Creepers (esp. Masonic)	Stewed apple and custard
Those who talk about the	A nice fire
Good Olde Days	
Bartok	Dvorak, Mendelssohn.

Must close now, as Violet Annie Ladysmith is calling me to move carpets, put up curtains, get behind jolly old vacuum-cleaner, all pending imminent return of Elder Son, young Buzfuz. Gertcha!

Edgar wrote from home too: 'Today had letters from Stanley Baxter and you, to remind me I was once at Nee Soon. He's depressed in Glasgow and finds everything grey and normal. Well, it's not grey here, the sun's shining, there's blossom on the trees. Yes, there's enough to get suicidal about but if you want you can enjoy life. Whatever's wrong here, at least we can *do* something about it.'

The lottery was in my favour for once – I was chosen to go home by air. Quite at random, it seemed, several names came out of the hat, including mine and Young-Love's. In driving rain, we walked about the camp getting our clearance chitties signed. Young-Love was intolerable, he had so much gen.

'Heard the latest, my old mucker? Our kite's leaving Good Friday. First hop Hawaii, then Los Angeles, two days in New York and one more takes us to dear old Blighty. Bang-on!'

'Piss off, Love! That's the wrong foocking way. You go Ceylon, Pakistan, Iraq.'

'Not this time, mate. We've struck lucky. We're going to be in the lifeboat, chum, asbestos. We're laughing.'

But not for long, in his case. The cholera and typhoid they pumped into our bloodstream made him feverish. The sweat aggravated his prickly heat and he caused open sores by scratching, but somehow organized the dispatch of his tin trunk containing the Harris tweed coat, drew the blue serge uniform he'd need in England and answered smartly when the CO asked him if he'd enjoyed his service: 'Yes, *sah*!'

A few days before Easter, David and I went with a Tamil friend of his to see *Kismet*, the most successful Indian film ever made, and afterwards walked back into the billet to find that Young-Love's bedspace had been cleared of kit, shirts, belongings, photos of the girl who was waiting in Wimbledon, even his bedding. The others told us that two military police had taken him off to be detained as witness in the court-martial of his friends the cooks, who were charged with flogging army stores – sugar, tea, cigarettes and tins of lemonade powder. He'd gone off threatening a bunch of fives all round.

'What can be done with him?' said David. 'The grit in the machine. The human factor.'

He too was staying for awhile – in the housie-housie he'd drawn the troopship, SS *Dunera*, where he and I had first met.

The morning of 1 April, high winds slammed open the doors of our dormitory and threw squalls of rain across the beds. I said good-bye and invited David to my twenty-first party in Bristol. In torrential rain we drove to Tebrau, twenty miles up-country, nervous and excitable. We felt we were walking on knives. No three-on-a-match that day but a few prayers that it wasn't an April Fool joke. We were housed in a wooden basha at the heart of a rubber plantation and I was put on guard the first night.

'Patrolling the rubber trees,' I wrote, 'thinking that in ten days' time we may be walking in St James's Park.'

Either the crash course in Mod. Eng. Lit. had improved the style or the long-awaited day had concentrated my mind. The last pages of the journal read better.

'The Commanding Officer is said to be mad: he blows up rubber-trees, keeps ducks in the mess and shoots dogs, for which he has an armoury in his room . . . tonight a home-bound type showed us Mickey Mouse films on a projector . . . last night I dreamt I saw a long snake climbing a wall. My father and I killed it with a hatchet. Woke, remembering it had been his birthday . . . I've been reading Graham Greene's account of his travels in Mexico, *The Lawless Roads*, which David gave me before I left. As the Russians refused to co-operate in Berlin, we confided our doubts of Communism or any totalitarianism. Well, what is next in the usual sequence of beliefs?

'"We must all have something," David had said, "for some it's Communism – but sooner or later its too smooth logic grows indigestible. What then?"

'"Existentialism?" I suggested.

'"Or Roman Catholicism," he said.

'David doesn't know whether there's a God but wishes there were. I suppose he's right. We must have something. Greene writes: "Even if it were all untrue and there were no God, surely life was happier with the enormous supernatural promise than with the petty social fulfilment, the tiny pension and the machine-made furniture."

'The papers report "the Russian menace", the squabbling over Europe, which must directly concern me as I sit here in a Malayan rubber plantation. When "something happens", as it must, I may be called upon to fight Communism, about which I'm still in doubt. I oscillate between Marx and God, Bristol and Singapore. And here in Singapore the Communists are already causing riot, killing civilians . . . as long as bright sunlight pours between the tall trees, this place is beautiful – almost empty now, though at times it's housed as many as six hundred . . . has the quiet air of a jungle rest-home . . . my mind's in transit too. . . . I fear England and the future. . . . I started out being sympathetic to the East; that turned to hatred, then slowly to understanding. The Asians have something important to teach us – but they won't bother and I don't blame them. Burma's just gone independent, Malaya's got a new constitution. . . . On guard again last night I was struck by how old the young men looked. One said: "I see so many pictures nowadays I don't know one from another. Something to pass the time." They all seem to be passing the time till demob – and when that's a failure they pass the time till death. One of David's friends wrote from home, recently released, 'there's no group number now . . . roll on death. . . ."

'On the guard roster, all these young-old men – the pompous clerk, the Northern lout practising for home with his swear-box. . . . I could not shake off the impression of those faces in the field-kitchen. A young Malay girl came walking sedately from tree to tree, tapping the bark, emptying latex from the half-coconut shells. . . . I borrowed someone's camera and went out to her. "Picture?" I asked. She looked away quickly and went on with her work. I took the picture but felt a fool, retreated to the basha, went on watching her graceful movement from tree to tree while from behind me came the monotonous obscenities of the Northern lout, like ugly punctuation. . . .'

Greene's journal reflected my fears precisely. I quoted from it at length: 'The dysentery was as bad as ever. I watched anxiously for the blood which would mean hospital and no escape for weeks from this country which I hated.' And, after his return to England: 'I wondered why I had hated Mexico so much. This was home. One always expects something different.'

He in turn approved W. B. Yeats's diagnosis in 'The Circle':

Through summertime we call on spring
And through the spring on summer call
And when abounding hedges ring
Declare that winter's best of all;
And after that there's nothing good
Because the springtime has not come –
Nor know that what disturbs the blood
Is but its longing for the tomb.

I think now that what disturbed mine was its longing to be born.

We flew home in a York in five daily hops – Ceylon, Karachi, the Gulf, Malta and Wiltshire, a pleasant and uneventful flight. A Wing Commander protested at having to share his compartment with other ranks but the crew ignored him and when he got airsick we felt perhaps there might be God.

Karachi was in a new country. I asked a man who'd known Cliff if the murals he'd painted in the cinema were still there (dragons, goblins, girls in undies?) but he said it had been repainted for the Pakistan air force. 'That seemed to be the story: of the air force we knew, nothing left. Otherwise it was still India – the wooden charpoys, the call of "char-wallah!", the shining bodies of bullock-drivers, the way you could find the lavatory with your eyes shut.' We took a liberty-truck into the city. 'Sacred cows crossing busy streets, a camel chewing a young tree, meagre horses pulling ancient tongas, the Anglos doing their best to ape the few English, who will soon be gone – still in their unnecessary Bomber Bowlers. I left the main roads. A group of young men chewing betel before a shut-up shop called "Union Jack Stores", kids playing hockey watched by an old man smoking his hookah. A twisted freak lies in the road and when someone offers him two annas, he smiles and refuses – he's not a beggar, just someone resting. A pretty little girl grasps my arm and begs for "baksheesh". I lift her along with my arm, she hangs on for a ride and laughs but a passing babu clouts her with his briefcase. She drops off but doesn't cry. Except for the absence of Hindus and the new shop names – Pakistan Shoes, Pakistan Dyeing and Cleaning – not much had changed. A country so easy to hate but now I didn't. *I* had changed and understood how they felt towards us, a resentment born of agony and vile treatment.'

While writing *Privates* in the 1970s, I came across this passage in a letter from 1890:

I waxed indignant as I listened to my ... fellow travellers upbraiding the English for their exploitation of the natives. Yes, thought I, the Englishman exploits Chinese, sepoys, Hindus, but then he gives them roads, aqueducts, museums, Christianity; you too exploit but what do you give?

Not Kipling or some other sahib, but Anton Chekov.

In Habbaniyah on the Persian Gulf, I had a hot shower and put on a blue uniform for the first time in two years. At night we slept under three blankets. The RAF station was immense and totally British.

We followed the pipeline across the desert, flew over the river Jordan, with to starboard the Sea of Galilee, then the Mediterranean and Malta. In Valetta we were astonished by the European-ness, the dark clothes, the English money.

'Overcoats!' I wrote, 'and hats! Stone cold to the touch. Priests! Bomb

135

damage. It was almost embarrassing to be served in a café by European waiters. When the main streets closed at eight-thirty, a kind of life continued in back alleys.

'"Hullo, air force, come upstairs?" – how pathetic those whores, the weariness of standing in a vestibule lined with Victorian furniture and aspidistras saying day in, day out, "Hullo, navy, come upstairs?"! In a dance-hall, music came from an odd trio sitting under a large banner "Straight from Harlem, New York", a fat pianist, a one-legged drummer and a negro who screamed into a microphone "When Irish Eyes Are Smiling". My mates were robbed by hostesses who drank coloured water that cost twelve bob a time.'

A last chance at debauchery – and what did *I* spend *my* money on? A taxi back to camp.

Awoken to high winds at five by a boy who said 'Wakey, wakey, sign here' and thrust a book into my face. Sardinia was like a graveyard of dinosaurs, across their backs the snail's trail of a mountain road. France, its brown fields, occasional towns, clouds low on the land. We dropped through the clouds to water. The next land we saw was England, the first food we ate was rabbit, a fire burning in the grate under a pseudo-Tudor ceiling. I revelled in everything, quoted Hardy, forgot to protest when we drove in a coach towards London instead of west towards home. Telephoned home from Baker Street station, heard the Bristol accents of my mother, the actor-laddy tones of Dad. Next day to Blackpool, where we were examined for syphilis and t.b. One boy was told he could go on leave but mustn't kiss. They issued us with civilian clothes, gave us pay and railway warrants. We had to pay our own cab to the station. I changed at Crewe.

'It wasn't like I'd expected,' I wrote. The cold, dark compartment. From my taxi through Bristol, I saw an empty city. When we reached Palatine, it was three in the morning.

'Looks as though no one's up,' said the driver.

'It's my first time home in two years.'

'Oh, ah. That'll be five bob.'

I pulled the brass knob and set the bell bouncing on its spring. Beside me stood the fibre suitcase I'd bought in Nee Soon village. My name had been painted on the side in Roman lettering by Kenneth Williams. The house was still. Dad wasn't there, I knew that. On the phone he'd told me he'd be visiting the Great Society in Newton Abbott. So it would be Vi or Tich or Nan who'd answer. I heard someone, saw the forty-watt bulb go on in the hall and the door was opened by Cliff.

The rooms were boxes. Had I really grown up here? Somehow Mum,

Nan, Cliff and I squeezed into the tiny dining-room but when Tich at last came down from bed, it seemed the walls would burst. He was a sixteen-year-old giant. I decided I had better call him Geoff. It was, as I had always hoped, the same. On the mantelpiece were the clock with its Westminster chime, a black cat mascot with bushy tail, a metal vase with one Remembrance Poppy kept year after year, the bevelled mirror that had reflected my face as my growing body pushed it from the bottom of the frame and out at the top. Next day I walked up Ashley Down Road and ticked off the houses, our same grey-faced neighbours still queueing for the 21 bus, and our local shops – Tilley the cobbler who had that rarity, a private telephone, which he allowed favoured customers to use; the dairy with its sunny smells of butter and cream; the cake shop where Mum never went, since she'd seen an assistant fondle a sore before serving scones; the wet-fishmonger in rubber boots; and Wong Poey the launderer, whose children looked like Charlie Chan's but spoke with thick Bristol accents. Cliff played me some of our old seventy-eights in the back room, still papered with pin-up girls from GI magazines. Now that I'd seen it, I wanted it all changed. It embarrassed me.

'For two days Cliff inflicted himself. He meant so well. That was the trouble, they all meant so well and did so badly. On Friday Dad came home and told me to take my elbows off the table. After a week I said I was going to London to stay a few days with Edgar. Of course they didn't like my rushing off so soon but they were kind and pretended everything was all right. Dad drove me to the station in the Green Goddess.

'"Have a good time," he told me, through the train window. "Feel free to do exactly as you like."

'As though he still had the power to stop me!

'"We were all waiting for you to come home," says my wife when we remember these times. "Your brother kept telling us it would all brighten up when you got home. Then Cliff came and said the same. We counted the days. But when you arrived you hardly looked at us. I felt as though I wasn't there."'

7 Late Comer

At this time Thelma, my future wife, was just sixteen. She'd spent her childhood in a suburban village on Swansea Bay between the town and Mumbles. Across the coast road and the tracks of the Mumbles tram was the pebbled beach, where her father took her hunting for shellfish.

> Cocks from Kidwelly
> Good for the belly!

sounds like a rugby song but was only the market-cry of South Wales cocklewomen.

The reader may remember that she had met the Emperor of Abyssinia and Dick Nichols in Glynderwen Crescent, Blackpill many years before her family came to live in Ashley Down. Dad never failed to delight in the coincidence.

'Your good lady – what's-her-name? – Stella, Zelda, Velma – had the great good fortune while still a nipper to meet Yours Truly. Sad to say, I had by that time already donned the old Ball and Chain but young Bella knew a good thing when she saw one and, on arriving in Bristol many moons later, tried to get her hands on your young brother Geoffrey. He, alas, preferred young whosit – Mary? – so Velma turned as a last resort to the only unmarried Nichols male, to wit Piecan. A booby prize, what, boy?'

But this, of course, was in the later, more benign mood of his retirement years. All the same it was roughly true. Thelma and Geoffrey met at the local youth club, played ping-pong and no doubt shared the odd Ovaltine tablet. She was a day-girl at Colston's School and her closest friend at that time was a blonde Geordie called Mary, who took her to her own youth club at Avonmouth, where her father was chief of the docks police.

'If our youth club was boring – and it was! – theirs was like a bus-stop at the end of the world. I mean, we at least had a tennis table.'

The only interesting people there were Mary and Robert Stephens, then seventeen, with George Dillon and Atahuelpa still a long way off. Thelma was scornful of this provincial scene and took Mary to *her* youth club, where the first person they saw was my brother.

'Who's that terrific-looking boy?' Mary asked.

'Oh, that's only old Geoff Nichols.'

'Fantastic! What does he do?'

'He drums a lot.'

'Plays the drums?'

'No, the table. You know, with his fingers. But he's learning the trumpet.'

'The trumpet?'

In those days that was like saying he was an air ace who ran a chain of casinos. Mary and Geoff were soon a pair and Thelma was gooseberry until the arrival home of Cliff, who became her date for visits to the club and the Scala cinema. Even this mad round began to pall and then 'When Pete gets here' got to be like When-the-war's-over, when-the-boat-comes, when-we-leave-school. This veteran of exotic debauch would sail in on a wave of jazz-crazed sex and tropical splendour. Instead came a cadaver with specs, talking in a Noël Coward accent and saying 'Let's face it'. I, of course, was thrown by Cliff's appearance at the door of 192. In Singapore I had decided he and his goblins belonged to a distant past. Walt Disney and Muggsy Spanier had no place in a future of Henry Moore and Delius. I later described it in *Forget-me-not Lane*: 'He tried to warm the embers for a few days but I went off to London to stay with one of my new service friends – discussing E.M. Forster and personal relationships.'

Had Cliff not been with them, I may have been more friendly to my brother and his girl-friends, though they *were* only sixteen and I was nearly twenty-one. It was almost a generation gap. There is no mention of Thelma in my diaries until over ten years later, though we often met in our student days when she was at art college and I at drama school. We gate-crashed parties in Georgian terraces, smuggled ourselves into Arts Balls in long dragons Cliff had spent a year making and once, she remembers, met at a fair. 'I'd been on the Moon Rocket and was white with the fear of it. You were with David Allford or some other snooty friend but you said the only tender words I heard from you till after we were married. You said: "If I had any blood, I'd give you some."'

But she was always with a hard-drinking crowd who wore beards and laughed in pubs. Her world of painters and wild characters frightened me. They made a point of speaking Bristolian just as I was learning Posh.

'When that I wuz a little tiny boy,' I sang, as Feste in our drama school production of *Twelfth Night*.

'Woz!' said the principal.

'Sorry?'

'When that I *woz* a little tiny boy.'

'Isn't that what I said?'

'Say it.'

'When that I *wuz* a little tiny boy.'

The Bristol Old Vic School certainly taught me 'good talk of a good kind'. Apart from that and country dancing, a little ballet, some fencing and a madrigal or two, I learnt to tell a screwdriver from a chisel. I remember the teacher's astonishment as he watched me put a screw in.

'That's a chisel. You'll blunt the blade. How old are you? Twenty-one and haven't learnt the difference?'

He was a socialist and must have wondered what the world was coming to. We were all socialists of some sort then. I was the sort with clean hands. I had little time for workers and even less for work, but was crammed full of Future. For me Bristol was something of a return-to-Go but it wasn't the *same* Bristol. Externally, yes – the streets near Bristol Bridge were still in ruins, St Nicholas Church was a shell and austerity had become a habit of mind, rationing a way of life.

'It makes you wonder who won the war,' says the mother in *Forget-me-not Lane*, 'I blame the Labour government.'

But, for me, once I had got over the shock, the new life was like finding a hidden quarter in an old town. Our drama classes took place in the upstairs room of a fruit warehouse in Bristol's Covent Garden. Across the road was the stage door of the Royal, the oldest working theatre building in Britain, then almost intact, with its hand-operated traps, gantries, gallery benches, and a nineteenth-century thunder run over the stalls, a wooden trough along which cannonballs were sent rolling like skittles. In the 1970s this was all spoiled by a vandal-architect – the friendly dressing-rooms of my day were replaced by concrete cubby-holes and the makeshift lobby by a split-level foyer that's a cross between Barclays Bank and a carpet showroom.

The front of the theatre was in King Street, then undiscovered by tourists, a cobbled way a few hundred yards long, running to the waterfront at Welsh Back. Apart from the theatre, it had alms-houses, the Cooper's Hall, and – more important – about half a dozen pubs, from the spit-and-sawdust Naval Volunteer to the half-timbered Llandoger Trow. You could eat or get drunk for very little, if you weren't fussy. If you were, halfway up the steps to the covered fruit market, there was Marco's restaurant where we ate Italian in the back room for ninepence. The theatre pub was the Old Duke, where the landlord was from the North and asked for Time in a mock-pathetic appeal that began: 'Ladies and gentlemen, I'm well after the time ordained by statute law for the closing of these licensed premises . . .'

Since those days King Street has been tarted up. The Llandoger is a steak bar, words like quiche and chili are on blackboard menus, there's an art gallery, a studio theatre and trad jazz is everywhere.

Geoffrey was first in the field, forming his eight-piece band in the 1940s. 'Terrific,' I wrote on my first hearing, 'quite stunning, startlingly good. The setting perfect – arty lighting, slow-moving couples, odd artists sketching the band in action.' That was at the architectural college hall, near which, in a condemned ruin, lived the city's early beatniks or hippies, then called – for want of those coming words – bohemians. I drank rough cider with them, listened to their tirades and wrote a play about them called *Underneath the Bough*. There was yet no literature of hedonism and we had to make do with Fitzgerald's *Omar Khayyam*, which I dare say no one reads these days. Cliff married a drop-out arty girl and fell in with this crowd for awhile. Once I'd started at drama-school, we seldom met. My new friends snubbed him. He was neither Theatre nor Art but always found his own Cliff-like version of what the rest of us did. Though he never played a real jazz instrument, he blew into a jug and formed a band of other jug-blowers.

But all this was for me the penumbra. The light of my life was the Theatre. 'It's life, doockie,' I often said, echoing Barri Chatt, and might have added what he'd said about sex, 'It's becoming an obsession.'

My first months at the Old Vic School were the happiest of my life so far. My gratuity and grant took care of the fees and my expenses and I scrounged on my father's generosity and called him Scrooge. It seems clear now I should have left after the first term. By then the treats were over and nobody there could help me become a playwright. They never thought much of my acting chances, though I stuck it longer than most of the other students for whom the Old Vic was a finishing school. The girls mostly married and one can sometimes spot one or two of the men of my year carrying spears or beers in television plays. The instructors included an old dear who used to come from Bath on the bus and an ex-RAF bursar who left under a cloud. In retrospect I admire their sauce but not much else. We played them up when we could but I was getting too old for that. Union rules were looser then and we played walk-ons and even small speaking parts in such lavish productions as *Julius Caesar* and *The Admirable Crichton*. We hoped to be noticed by the director and offered a contract.

'Who's that boy third from the end? Ask him if he'd like to do Mercutio.'

Just to pass through the stage door was thrilling. To step on to the stage before a live audience was all we asked of life. To speak lines – that would come in time. For now, it was enough to enter the temple and approach the altar with the other devotees. That thrill has entirely gone these days and once that's happened it's best to leave by the nearest exit. Being stage-struck was, I suspect, an aspect of my extended puberty (which would last a few years yet). Another was the way I started falling in love with every girl who wasn't already spoken for. Had I taken to Thelma sooner, she might have saved me from the sequence of flirts and virgins who looked to me for a lead I couldn't give. One lived with her mother above a china-shop and late at night, by the light from the street, we would wrestle among the fragile goods. Sometimes whole dinner-sets tinkled as I dropped to my knees to kiss her breasts. Another lived in a posh resort on the Bristol Channel, her father a timber-merchant who thought me far beneath her. A third saw herself as plain and once said, when I made to kiss her, 'Oh, dear, here we go again.'

The two most interesting men were both from Hollywood. The student Garry Thorne had been brought up in Beverly Hills, his parents the film-writers William Cowen and Lenore Coffee. They were well known at the time as the authors of a favourite drama-school play about the home life of Christ called *Family Portrait*. It was forbidden to depict Him on the stage and a good deal of contrivance was called on to explain His absence so the play became known as 'He just stepped out for a moment'. Garry hadn't grown up, like the rest of us, seeing film-stars in films; he'd dated them. One day, I was told, the doorbell rang and his mother wasn't quite ready.

'Garry,' she said, 'be a good boy and run downstairs, apologize to Miss Garbo and entertain her till I get there.'

He was unaffected by all this, a handsome, likeable and modest young man whom everybody liked. None of us envied his MG, his motorbike, his cashmere sweaters or his social ease, perhaps because none of us envied his acting ability. He became one of my closest friends for the next ten years. His eldest son will be surprised to hear I am his godfather. Garry's mother joined the growing number of characters I keep trying and failing to write.

Garry had left Hollywood for the backwater of post-war Bristol. He'd taken Grace Kelly to drive-in movies and poured drinks for Bette Davis. Garry grew up with film-stars but – for me – George Coulouris *was* one. The first I'd spoken to, a man still glowing with the glory of his work with Orson Welles. As the lawyer Thatcher, he'd come to tell the young Kane of his inheritance and got pushed into the snow by Rosebud, the sledge. Throughout the 1930s he'd appeared with Welles's Mercury Company but now he'd returned to his native country as leading man of the Bristol Vic, a Manchester Greek who had more the look of an Indian chief.

'Well, what d'you make of us?' he demanded of me after our first re-hearsal with the new company. And when I hesitated, 'Come on, come on, don't tell me you've not been sizing us up, seeing if you think we're any good. Well?'

Once, when I'd been away with a cold, he said 'You must expect to get sick if you read books like *The God That Failed*. Poison your system! All those lily-livered Trotskyists – Koestler, Spender, Silone! What a gang of turncoats! As bad as Clifford Odets. Didn't I see you reading *The Fervent Years* as well?'

Devouring was more like it. Clurman's story of the American Group Theatre was for me a book about heaven on earth.

'Poor bloody Odets! Starts out writing great plays like *Awake and Sing* and *Golden Boy* and ends up writing a tragedy about a man with a Hollywood contract! And that *is* a tragedy, believe me!'

It was another thirty years before I learnt of Coulouris's own Hollywood days, as seen by the future Mrs Hal Prince, then a child.

'He always rode round Beverly Hills on a bike. He used to tell us kids we were filling our minds with television crap and he was going to put something decent in there too. He'd round us up in someone's house and sit us down and read *Hard Times* to us. Can you imagine – in lotus-land, that ghastly place where books were something put in by interior decorators! D'you *know* what we owe that man?'

During his Bristol season, Coulouris was an alarming Tartuffe, put on drag for *The Provok'd Wife* and was (a born Cassius) miscast as Brutus; his lack of interest in the part disinclined him to learn the lines. To us members of the crowd, his improvisations were always fresh, never the same twice. 'As Caesar loved me, I weep for him. As he was long-winded, I hated him. As he was drunk, I wished him well. As he was soon to die, I envied him. But as he was lily-livered, I slew him.'

Not long ago he passed me on a Hampstead pavement arguing with a friend. 'What you don't seem to understand about your blessed bour-geoisie . . .' he was saying.

Since writing the last paragraph, I've been upstairs for some lunch and told Thelma what I'd been remembering.

'Well, of course, he must have left because of McCarthy,' she said, 'and naturally he'd say Odets was pathetic – he ratted on them all.'

'Of course!' I said, but it had never occurred to me.

On my twenty-first birthday I was given, apart from the right to vote, a wristwatch, a week in Paris and £500 in National Savings Certificates Dad had started buying the day I was born. Being the man he was, he never actually *gave* them to me. He *showed* them to me and said he'd look after them. He got far more fun from them than I did. Over the next few years they were doled out one by one whenever I needed shoes mending or a railway fare. It was like pulling teeth. I went on my first visit to Paris with my mother. We stayed in one of those *neuf-heures* hotels on the rue de Rivoli and the only naked girls I saw were on the stage of the Folies Bergères.

One sentence remained from my French orals of four years before: *Je désire devenir un écrivain*. It was no use for ordering meals and the wish was no closer to being realized. A writer needs a subject, and some sort of world view, but for two years I took almost no notice of what was going on outside – the Berlin airlift, Jinnah's death, Mao's China, Titoism, the State of Israel, a new term for Truman, the start of wars in Korea and Malaya. At least sweets, clothes and petrol came one by one off ration. Yet all this went as unnoticed in the theatre as it did in church. The drama of the day was poetic, the hot playwright was Christopher Fry ('as great as Shakespeare' said Olivier) and the stories were set in Merrie Englande or Ancient Greece. This movement now puts me in mind of ragtime, with its catchy tunes, brief life-span and in the way both succumbed after ten years to something a lot more vigorous. It's been said that every advance in art is a return to reality.

I could find no perspective on my own family life. My brother and I were separated by five years and Dad was nearing retirement. Geoffrey suddenly surprised us all by deciding to run away to sea. His best friend of the moment had become a merchant seaman and he was going to do the same. Dad's week-ends with Brahms and Haydn were soured by this – if the young piecan had to do something as barmy as going to sea, at least let it be with the *Royal* Navy. Why not Dartmouth Naval College, become an officer, get a decent pension?

'Well, 'is Dad and Mum, they'm worried stiff,' said Nan, reporting all this to Thelma, 'but 'e'm as stubborn as a h'ox. I'd give him such a good 'iding. After his Dad been and promised to send him to Dartmoor!'

This crisis, like the ones in Europe, blew over and Geoffrey continued a scholastic career as mediocre as my own. In some ways though he was already my senior – at rugby and cricket and jazz and the lifelong relationship he now began with Mary, as well as putting on a leopardskin to bang the bass drum in the OTC. When he left school, he took the first job he was offered – in blood transfusion.

My first short play was included in the end-of-the-year show on the stage of the Theatre Royal. 'Scintillating and barbed,' said the *Evening Post*, 'the cocktail-party playwright and his actors bore the brunt of this delightful satire.' My first notice.

David Allford became a regular guest, enjoying Bristol, showing me the beauties of Bath and pointing out Dad's eccentricities as he had done Young-Love's. When he needed a sticking-plaster, I opened the cabinet between our beds and began rummaging among the bottles and jars of medicine.

'What's all that?' he exclaimed.

'Medicine.'

'It's enough to stock a branch of Boots.'

'Not Boots,' I said, 'the Co-op.'

The two shelves stacked with Dad's old chemical samples had never impressed me as odd – not the tins of Vapour Rub, wintergreen, cold cream, sun lotion; nor the jars of jellies for ear, nose and throat, emulsions of our infancy, cod-liver oil and malt, Fixolene for the hair; the tubes of Golden Eye Ointment; the drums of aspirin, cascara and bisurated magnesia tablets; the bottles of Friar's balsam, cough cure, castor oil or gentian violet; nor, perched on them for lack of room, the Swiss rolls of cotton wool between blue sheets, mysterious rubber tubes or bulbs and sinister suppositories. Few bottles were full, most had only a drain left. Nothing was thrown away.

'Mister Nichols,' David said later in the scullery, 'why is one tomato-sauce bottle standing upside down on top of another?'

'Sensible to ask, Donald. If the Old Man's doing it, there must be a reason.'

'I'm sure.'

'You may have noticed how sauce adheres to the wall of the bottle, sauce you can't get at even with a long-necked spoon. Now with the consumption of ketchup attained in Palatine Lodge we are talking in the nature of a quarter-bottle every five years. Waste is anathema to me, Donald, so I add malt vinegar to the old bottle, swill it round and pour it into the new. However even this may not entirely drain it. Thus the last stage of the process – one bottle standing on another to catch the last few drops. What's there to laugh at? What's he laughing at, Vi?'

'Well, he's not laughing at *me*.'

'He's as bad as Buzfuz. Another noodle.'

Later he began diluting the sauce when the bottle was only half-used. Someone unaware would bang the end to releases a plodge of the stuff and instead a jet of pink vinegar would cover not only the plate but most of the table too. Mum said it was a false economy and Nan called him a great mad-gaming looby but he was still doing it the day he died.

David never tired of monitoring Dad's foibles.

'Peter,' he called from the bathroom one day, 'come here a moment.'

I found him staring into a mirror hung on the wall behind the lavatory.

'D'you realize', he said, 'all you can see in there is a reflection of your cock?'

'I suppose so, yes.'

'If you're standing having a pee, you can watch yourself. Why?'

I'd never questioned it. Next day we discovered that Dad, after stropping the blade of his cut-throat, sat on the toilet-seat to shave, twisting round to see his chin in the looking-glass.

'Peter,' David called one day from the bedroom window, 'd'you know what Dick's doing now? He's got on a white overall like a grocer and he's sweeping the gutter.'

'That's nothing. He always does that. He doesn't trust the council workers.'

'And look now! Come and see!'

'What?'

'He's pinning a notice to the trunk of that tree.'

I joined him and saw the postcard, two feet above the pavement. I opened the window and called, 'What does that say?'

He paused in his sweeping.

'What d'you *think* it says? "It would be appreciated if dogs did not foul the public footpath."'

'A lot of the dogs round here can't read.'

'Don't talk so big, you make yourself look small.'

But he later raised the card to owner's eye-level.

He had long ago tired of conducting records with rulers or pokers and had had a Proper Man run him up several batons, which he kept on the albums of his 500-odd classical discs. David enjoyed watching him bring in the various string and woodwind sections of the NBC on some Rossini overture.

'Don't talk to me about Bartok, Denis. *Now* what's he laughing at, Buzfuz?'

He and Nan never got on. She still insisted on drinking her glass of stout in his living-room. Not simply drinking it either but peering through it at the light to check its purity. The air-raids had left her nervous about loud noises.

'Is that them coming back?' she asked of thunder or test-planes from Filton. 'Them damn buggers!'

Otherwise she was capable and hardy till one day in 1950 she took to her feather-bed at the end of the passage.

'There's a little fellow on the mantelpiece, Vi. He keeps popping out and making faces.'

'I'll tell him to go away.'

'Little bugger. I'd give him such a hiding if I had the use of my lagues.'

Cliff still came on occasion to Palatine and I am ashamed to admit that he behaved better towards my grandma than I did, sitting with her in the tiny room full of cheap furniture, humouring her demands to get that monkey off the wardrobe or those mad-gaming loobies away from the window.

I remember nothing of her death or funeral but her living presence remains. I must have been no more than an infant when we stood listening to the Sunday speakers at the top of Blackboy Hill. An extremist ranted and Nan led me away.

'Come on, we don't want our house burned down.'

A mystifying incident. Lights flashed in the dark. Huge people shouted. She saw political action as a threat to the home. Why do I recall that when everything else has gone?

It was about this time that I boarded a bus and sat on the long seat at the back. Sitting opposite was Purdy from Nee Soon, still grinning, now in the neat clothes of a Bristol accountant.

'Hullo,' he said and we stared at one another. I suppose we said more but it would be more apt if we just sat staring, laughing.

The two years as a student done, I began looking for acting jobs, writing to the rep companies, trying to get an agent to take me on. Every day my diary of that time starts with such an entry as: 'Wrote Hayes, Colchester, Dartford and Eastbourne; refusals from Ipswich, Birmingham and Salisbury.' The principal of the school, tired of my weekly visits, finally fixed me a job with a fit-up company at Exmouth. Two days before rehearsals, I was trying to finish writing a play when Cliff came to show us his first baby 'which has grown obscenely during the last few months. I pointedly tried to continue with my work while mother said she had "a lot to do" but he withstood the lot. I thought he would drive me mad.'

By what he always called 'a remarkable coincidence', Dad was driving to Exmouth Society on the right day. I had lunch with him and some Co-op managers.

'Amazing (or amusing?) to see how obsequious he was in their presence. His usually pompous and dogmatic assertions became polite suggestions and he visibly shrank in stature. So men all down the scale take it out on their families who know them only as head of the house. His boasts of how he ticks off his employers will seem even emptier now . . . in the evening a furious gale sent the fairy-lights swinging dizzily along the esplanade. A fishing-boat from Brixham was wrecked on the rocks.'

This was the first of many similar jobs over the next five years, in

Falmouth, Yarmouth, Frinton, Coventry, Swindon, Henley, Aberdeen, Glasgow and Edinburgh. My starting salary was £5 a week (£4 10s. 0d. for rehearsals), which after some years rose to £12. In the touring companies we all helped with the set-up. 'Rehearsal at ten in the nissen-hut, until twelve-thirty; call at two-thirty for the journey to towns and villages in Devon, Dorset or Somerset; arrive and set up; perform play in evening; strike the scenery and stage; load the truck; journey back till perhaps two a.m., learning lines for morning rehearsal. No wonder the shows are uninspired.'

Exmouth was exceptional in two respects. The landlord left the house at dawn to fish for sea-bass, mackerel and salmon, and we often ate his catch for breakfast. He told me of chasing a salmon among porpoises so lively they almost leapt into the boat.

'Talking of porpoises, I am reading *Moby Dick*.'

And it was here that I met Samuel and Wilfred Avery, the Twins, as they were usually known, friends of David's who were soon friends of mine. Later in London it was around their firm partnership that my new friends clustered. I introduced them to Garry and his wife, Kenneth Williams and Maggie Smith, Roger Gage and his first wife Joan Plowright, and they drew into the charmed circle the Robert Bolts, the Alfred Burkes, a glass designer from Helsinki, teachers from the suburbs, relatives from their family home in North Devon. Some entered the group, liked what they saw and stayed; others never took to the orderly, sexless, affable and intense air they lived in. I was a member till marriage gave me a home of my own to go to.

Throughout my twenties the Twins made us all welcome, asking nothing in return, except perhaps that you should not hurt them. Though they were painters, you never met artists at the flats or studios they shared. Teachers and theatre people couldn't penetrate their critical battlements. For the most part we knew nothing about art nor even what we liked; those who did and spoke out didn't come twice. This was the Twins' weakness. In most ways they were strong, amusing and generous hosts. Sam cooked like an angel, Wilfred could cure warts. The first night in their basement flat on Exmouth front, the vegetable was seaweed, boiled with lemon and vinegar. They were art teachers in primary schools at Exeter and Teignmouth. I talked too much and knew it was because I never spoke in the theatre company.

'Conversation in the dressing-room is highly intellectual – Sartre and Koestler,' said Diary, 'I am left behind; they're too advanced for me. One of them will now and then say something to me in a condescending way but for the most part I am tongue-tied.'

The Twins had round heads with hair cut short, bucolic faces and their voices bumped along in the way all Devonians speak – as though in a state of passionate indignation. Their memories were mostly of South Molton, the sheep-market town where they grew up. They'd scarcely ever been apart since birth and their recitals were like Thomas Hardy re-told by Murray and Mooney.

'That must have been old Ockie Norris.'

'Ockie Norris?'

'Why not?'

'That weren't ever Ockie Norris, Wilfred.'

'Bugger me, Sam, it bloody was! I'll swear t'was Ockie ate live frogs.'

'Never was!'

'You'll be telling me next you don't even remember what he said before he ate them.'

'Ah bloody don't so now then.'

'He used to eat them in the public bar of the pub our parents had.'

'Ah know *that*.'

'But Peter don't.'

'T'wasn't Ockie Norris though.'

'Well, whoever t'was, he used to ask the people there if they wanted 'im to swallow the frog head first or feet first.'

'Go on.'

'And someone always asked what difference it made.'

'And what difference *did* it make?'

'Well, Ockie used to say, if he goes down head first you see the last kick of his lagues. If he goes down feet first you see the look of terror in his eyes.'

'Oh, bugger off, Wilfred. He never did.'

Baxter had started me reading, Edgar made me listen to music, David to look with a fresh eye at my home town and my father. The Twins opened my eyes to painting. My first art lessons were in Exmouth pubs.

'Let's be precise,' I said, and pointed to a horsey print, 'that's a picture I like.'

'You like the horse. But look at the painting.'

Anything bad in art was 'literary' – there was no worse term of abuse than that. Subjects were of no importance – horses, nudes, oceans, houses, fields, Christ and his mother, Rembrandt's face – irrelevant! All that mattered was the actual paint, the brushstroke, the design. At first I argued. Did they mean that Ingres didn't enjoy the sight of a naked woman? He may well have done but that's not why *we* enjoy his pictures. Isn't it? Even partly? No, or he might as well have taken snaps. Well,

Gainsborough couldn't have taken snaps and he painted subjects all the time – ladies and grooms and trees. Because he was *paid* to paint ladies – they were his patrons. Then why did he paint his own children? No, Peter, you will insist on this literary approach . . .

Throughout my twenties I tried to rid myself of this heretical interest in depiction but never quite pulled the abstract wool over my own eyes. It was Thelma, with her academic training, who showed me that the denial of subject was itself a heresy, that model and manner weren't mutually exclusive. And years after that Tom Wolfe sent it up by saying abstract art needs such a wealth of words to explain it that it is itself a by-product of literature. In fact, literary.

All the same I might never have taken to painting without the Twins' encouragement. Wilfred's lectures were often long-winded and quirky but could also be down-to-earth. Facing a virtuoso Rubens, all writhing bodies and drama: 'You bugger, Peter Paul!'

Another time, after solemnly telling me ''Tis not as though I want a Van Gogh role to be forced on me,' he went on to praise the courage of Cézanne, 'hoping his apples would rise to the occasion'.

'They were trying to provoke us,' said David Allford after we'd both married. 'Perhaps we should have fought more. Or perhaps they were part of our extended puberty.'

My first part as a paid actor was Sebastian in *Twelfth Night*. No one has ever made their name with this role and in a blond wig and blue breeches it was no wonder I was sent up whenever we played a children's matinée. I made no friends in the cast but was able to go along to Bournemouth one weekend to visit Edgar Williams, now playing bassoon in the Symphony. We talked about Korea and being called up again. He said he wouldn't go, it would be the end for him. He'd now achieved happiness and was going to hold on for dear life. War would not take him from the place he'd found in the sun. One morning I sat in the empty auditorium of the Winter Gardens watching the orchestra as they concentrated on a Mozart adagio. The mood was broken by the sound of a jet-plane screaming across the bay and the Austrian conductor Rudolf Schwarz shouted with rage and threw down his baton.

'I wondered if you noticed', Edgar said to me afterwards, 'that when he reached to pick it up again, his sleeve moved back and you could see the concentration camp brand on his forearm.'

To get more work I had to stay in London and the only Londoners I knew were my Uncle Bert and Aunt Hattie in Stratford East. Two of the pages describing them have been roughly torn out and I remember a scene with Dad who was still reading and censoring my diary. He would sometimes 'mark' my entries with comments in the margin. 'Ungrateful and rude remarks about the family of a father who has shown you every generosity, e.g. wristwatch, good schooling, £500 in National Savings.' I took to answering: 'Not only generous but so nosy he can't resist reading private diaries!'

But those pages are no great loss – my visits to Gurney Road were much the same from childhood to the 1970s. If I arrived as much as ten minutes late after the train journey from Bristol and the hour-long bus-ride from Paddington, Hattie would snap as she opened the door: 'I thought you were never coming. Your dinner's ruined. It's been keeping hot all this time. I've got you a nice egg custard. I made it for you.'

Perhaps at four years old I had praised her egg custard.

'Give him a chance to get inside the door, Harriet,' brother Bert would say from the dark hall of the tiny house.

'There you are,' my aunt always came back, 'Auntie's done the wrong thing again.'

While I ate my way through the custard, Hattie would sit watching me, singing snatches from current musicals. 'I'm the hostess with the mostest on the ball!' and Bert would growl 'Shut the row, Hats!'

The other brother Rob had died by now, leaving the baby grand to fill the front parlour in silence, except when Hattie ran a duster up and down its keyboard. Bert had retired from the pepper factory and spent his mornings walking to the public library to follow the fortunes of his stocks and shares in a free copy of the *Daily Telegraph*. He borrowed a novel and a history per week and read them in their back room, smoking St Bruno's Flake and spitting into the coal-fire, lighting the gas-mantles when evening came, and he and Hats listened to the news on Redif-fusion, for the house had no electricity. Cold running water came to the outside lavatory and one tap over the kitchen sink. In wintry weather, Hats used a commode in the house and once a week they filled a hip-bath with kettles of water heated on the gas-stove. They were so unused to anything modern that, when I took a fountain-pen from my pocket, Bert laughed and Hattie shrieked with excitement. One Monday evening he took me on my first visit to the Theatre Royal, to see a marvellous performance of O'Neill's *Anna Christie* with Freda Jackson and Frederick Valk. This was pre-Littlewood, the trendies hadn't started coming out on the Central Line and the house was only half-full of local people.

Despite my praise, Hattie was glad she hadn't come.

'No fear! Walk up Angel Lane. Filthy hole! You can't expect decent people to come to a place like Stratford! I mean, if you lived in Ilford, Peter, would you like walking up Angel Lane to see a play?'

'You wouldn't have liked it anyway, Hats,' Bert said, 'it was all about what-you-might-call in-a-manner-of-speaking a Loose Woman.'

'Oo-er! Don't tell Dick your uncle took you to see that. He'd have a fit.'

Bert laughed and spat in the fire and his sister rounded on me.

'Somerset Maugham!' she snapped, 'he reads Somerset Maugham! He tried to make me read one. I said: no fear.'

Bert shrugged indulgently.

'He's a bit too smutty at times, I grant you, but he makes a good screw so he can't be that bad.'

'Oh, yes, I expect I'm wrong again. I generally am.'

During the day I tramped the streets around Shaftesbury Avenue, asking the agents for acting work. I learned to take off my glasses before climbing the stairs to their offices and how to pick up the scent of jobs in the spit-and-sawdust of the Salisbury. I got six weeks' assistant stage-manager and play-as-cast in another fit-up company, starting Monday, Coventry. Of course there was no phone at Stratford so the London agent had to phone Bristol and Mum had to wire me to phone her back.

'Well done, Peter. They want you to play Caesar.'

'Caesar? No, only a flunkey.'

'What?'

'A manservant. In *The School for Scandal*. You sure it didn't say he wanted me to play season?'

'Was that it? Oh, Lord. I've told all your friends down here you're playing Caesar. I phoned the Old Vic. They all think you're playing Caesar.'

When I left, Bert and Hattie saw me to the front gate. I looked up the road. Some houses had been bombed and others were being demolished leaving gaps like lost teeth in an ageing mouth.

'You won't be sorry to see the last of this,' my aunt said.

At eighty she'd be the same and when I suggested they might have a colour television piped in she snapped: 'No fear! I hate it. You look at the picture, there's all that glamour, you switch it off and what have you got? Stratford!' She offered her cold thin lips to be kissed. 'Don't catch my cold. I'm going inside for fear it worsens.'

She went inside singing from *Oklahoma*.

Bert shook my hand and palmed me £2. 'You've had good luck here, in a way of speaking. Use this for your fare. And mind you wave at Harriet through the window.'

* * *

I searched for digs in a steady drizzle. Coventry was all scaffolding and makeshift markets, bombed ruins and shell-shocked people. After ten years? The night Shaw died we set up *Pygmalion* in Netherton. There'd been a fuel cut all afternoon and we had to work by candlelight. I found digs with another flunkey, an Australian who told me, over our midnight suppers back at the digs, how the Aboriginals mesmerize a kangaroo by waving emu feathers and how in spring the bush rings with the cry of the bower-bird. He and I hated the fit-ups at Nuneaton and Loughborough and I decided not to work in these 'posh' companies again but try to get a real acting job without scene-shifting. 'How much can you learn by watching? At last, one has to try oneself. My only contribution to the performance of Shaw's play tonight was rolling dried peas around a cardboard-box during the rainstorm. The Australian's monologue moved on from bower-birds to Buddhism. He'd come under the influence of a mystic or guru who could contact him wherever he was, simply by bringing his mind to bear.

'"My greatest sin was ambition, striving," he told me, "if one deserved eminence it would be granted."'

My diary shows that in those days I listened more than talked and pages of it are filled with my room-mate's stories of his quasi-religious and pantheist experiences. It seems not to have amused me at all that his guru's name was Bruce. He lent me Isherwood's translation of the *Bhagavad-Gita* and I struggled with it on the company bus or at home while he was out 'trying to clear up the sadness and indecision within him'.

One Tuesday the rest of the cast went to the Mayor's parlour for a drinks party but my shyness made me so miserable that I avoided them as much as possible and didn't go. The Australian had left our digs after lunch to change his ration-card, he said, but didn't catch the coach at five and that night we did the show without him. He was already in bed and asleep when I got back and had gone by the time I woke next morning. I assumed he had decided to leave the show halfway through the run but that evening's local paper, brought in by the landlady, reported that he'd been charged with soliciting a plain-clothes policeman in a public lavatory. He was remanded in custody but had been bailed out for the night by the producer.

'I'm innocent and childish still!' my journal rants. 'My virginity, my idealism! What a sad joke! I'm a sort of Candide, forever believing the best.... It was miserable that evening – all conversation kept stopping as I entered the dressing-room. I suppose they all thought I was queer too.

'Our landlady is a decent godless woman who loves her sons and hates the Jews. She was disgusted. "Don't get me wrong," she says, "I feel sorry for him, he can't help it, can he? Our parson was the same, married with two beautiful kiddies. So nicely spoken too."'

The show rolled on round the market-towns of the East Midlands.

'At our bus-stop every morning I try to chat up a pretty girl called Julie Andrews who's playing in panto at the New ... Coventry's statue of Lady Godiva is a strapping young girl clothed, in Tennyson's words, "only in her own chastity". In fact when she made this ride she was fifty-three ... surely even *I* shan't be chaste at that age.'

My fellow flunkey appeared in court a few days later. When I arrived in the small room in St Mary's crypt, they were dealing with some muddled business about licences. Suddenly that was over, a clerk called the Australian's name and he came in between two great policemen, a cowed figure whose hands worked tensely behind his back as he faced the bench. The arresting officer read his evidence to the woman magistrate.

'As I was proceeding on plain-clothes duty in Bird Street public convenience, I was accosted by the accused who requested me to show him my thing. In due course I identified myself, informed him that he was under arrest and duly cautioned him.'

The accused made a grovelling apology in a more Australian accent than usual. 'I don't know what came over me, I must have lost my head ... if I can get treatment' and so on. The woman on the bench listened politely.

'I'm sorry,' she said at last, 'I'm afraid you must go to prison for three months.'

I went to see him afterwards. He was in a cell behind a barred grill and told me that if his mother found out, it would kill her. I offered my home address as a buffer but he was too dazed to grasp the point so the policeman guarding him offered to explain it later. He would, in any case, only be allowed one letter a fortnight. When our time was up, he was taken to the cell and I stepped back into the streets of pre-Wolfenden, pre-Orton England, 'vowing to write a play about this primitive arm of British justice'.

Every so often in the years that followed I sketched unreadable outlines of plays I tried and usually failed to write. There seems to be an annual average of six, and now and then a note will say 'finished the last play, started a new one' or 'gave up the schoolmaster play in despair'.

At the end of 1950 Garry, the American, was drafted into the infantry and finally went as aide-de-camp to a field general in Korea. His father turned up in Bristol and gave me his tuxedo, a grey suit, a flying-jacket, a pair of jeans and some ties.

'Well, you know, he had so much stuff. Fifteen suits, would you believe it?'

Garry had earmarked this wardrobe for me, knowing that anyone taking an acting job in those days had to have (in Equity's standard contract) a dinner-jacket and one lounge suit, to wear as he wandered through countless French windows to drink cold tea (for whisky). In fact, I never stayed long enough in any company to make much use of Garry's, with its Hollywood label, and it spent more time at the pawnbroker's than on the stage.

For my first few acting parts the companies provided the clothes: a monk's habit (*Saint Joan*, Bristol), doublet and hose (*Richard of Bordeaux*, Guildford) and Ruritanian gypsy gear (*Bohemian Girl*, Covent Garden). The Guildford job came through Kenneth Williams, whom I met by chance in a queue. He took me to meet his parents in the barber's shop they ran in Marchmont Street, near Russell Square. Theirs was a fresh side of London life that thrilled me with its bawdy humour, warmth and candour. There were no holds barred in the salon where his dad gave short back-and-sides and his mother supervised the perms. Their living-quarters were now on the first floor but had been in the basement till one night Mr Williams had complained through the front window to a noise-maker on the pavement above and got his face pissed on. The only phone was beside the shop and Charlie would answer, then yell up the stairwell, his mouth by the receiver: 'Kenny – another of your pouffy friends on the blower – Blinkie Beaumont or something.'

I was shown Kenneth's bedroom, as orderly as his billet had been at Nee Soon, its bookshelves lined with lyric poetry, Boswell's *Johnson* and anthologies of devotional sermons.

'Sit here for a minute and read some Wordsworth. I'm lancing a boil on Looie's bum.'

That done, he took me on the Metropolitan Line to the Queen's, Poplar, to see a show called *Boys Will Be Girls*. Posters outside offered £100 to anyone who could spot a girl. Had I not been apprenticed in Nee Soon, this would have been an esoteric performance in an arcane language. Barri Chatt was the star and led the cries of 'Vada' and 'Bona'. Barri was still in dockland but there weren't many sailors now, mostly couples with a few children.

'Good family stuff this,' said the manager, standing in the aisle in a bowler-hat. Time has proved him right, of course, though neither the Queen's nor Barri survived into the age of Danny La Rue, drag shows in the local or *Privates on Parade* at the Royal Shakespeare.

Kenneth's onstage behaviour was as lively as when he'd goosed us all in

'Pedro the Fisherman'. At Guildford, after giving the king some fustian advice, he'd turn upstage and corpse us bystanders with a crazed face or lolling tongue. We took our revenge one night when, the other nobles having died or defected, he was left alone on stage with Richard. They were expecting the enemy force and the king asked his friend what he could see from the castle window. Kenneth had to stare into the wings and this night the half-dozen men in the cast were there with cloaks pulled up and trousers down, flashing our assorted genitalia.

'What do you see?' asked the king.

We watched Kenneth's silent struggle.

'What?' repeated the poor king, 'tell me.'

'Points of light among the trees,' he got out somehow, with his eyes shut. Perhaps the one occasion he's not been heard distinctly.

The play ended soon after, we pulled up our trousers and lowered our cloaks and lined up to take the curtain. We underdressed in that way to give ourselves a good start in the rush down the dark main street to the station and the last train back to town. The night the mayor of Guildford made a speech afterwards was a very close-run thing. No one, of course, had cars. Once I missed a midday train to Henley-on-Thames and Sweeney Todd got one less victim that matinée.

One decisive day I took an emblematic single ticket to Paddington from Bristol and eventually fell in with several other young men who needed a place to stay – an English graduate down from Oxford, also wanting to write, a couple of actors and a student venereologist who ran a sideline with a pick-up lorry. We rented a flatlet near Portobello Road – one enormous front room and a kitchen behind. Dad drove to town one day bringing me a lot of needed gear and was dismayed by the squalor.

'How could you leave a lovely house like Palatine Lodge for such a dump?' he asked, but I thought of it as paradise regained. We gave a house-warming party after some weeks, decorating the room with gladioli and chrysanthemums from the nearby market. Forty people came and stayed till four in the morning. There were so many complaints that the landlord gave us notice to be out by the following week.

To earn his rent we'd taken work as film extras, first applying at offices in Poland Street where secretaries shouted 'Anyone here Green on Robin Hood yesterday?' or 'Who was Brown on Tuesday Island?' These colours were grades of priority. First call on crowd work was for the regulars, pathetic and genteel, resentful of the casual element that was spoiling the profession. Once some of them had been actors themselves but now they only did Crowds. Amongst themselves they were all on first-name terms with the stars.

'Alec Guinness? Oh, Alec's charming, always a pleasant word, no side to him, but keeps apart just enough to tell you who he is.'

Every day was spent waiting for perhaps ten hours to do ten minutes' shooting, for a plane to go over, a star to be dressed or the light to improve.

'Waiting all their lives', I wrote, 'for the sun to come out.'

When cheap labour or government hand-outs lured the Americans to make films here, work was available to all. Street-traders, students, artists, ponces, all signed on for a few days' well-paid idleness. We caught the first tubes before sunrise, walking to the stations through streets where only cats and constables moved. At Walton or Uxbridge, coaches met us and took us to the studios past waking villages beside pools where swans glided in the dawn mist. At Pinewood, among shabby and neglected meadows, they'd built the main street of a potteries town of fifty years before. I'd been chosen to lead a platoon in the parade of helmeted troops and during a rehearsal I blushed to hear our drill-sergeant shout: 'That Officer, sir, get in step!'

An animal-trainer told me he could earn £75 a day with his kicking mule.

On a sound stage in another suburb, we lay as survivors on the deck of a cargo ship in the Pacific. When this came under attack, maroons deafened us and stunt-men plunged through sheets of flame. We were paid special action bonuses but the men nearly mutinied when it was found we weren't getting wet money.

'When they turned on the hoses,' said an older man, 'we all got wet. But my son comes out with five quid and I only get facking three! Not facking right!'

One day, walking to Holland Park tube, I saw a familiar figure on the far pavement – a huge head, shaved well above the ears, hair gleaming on the sweaty scalp, eyes popping with umbrage – it was Young-Love from Changi, become a businessman! In a pin-stripe suit too hot for the day, a briefcase held under one gently curving arm, he strode towards some new disaster. I followed to find what it was. He led me well off course and I was about to let him go when he left-turned smartly off the pavement and marched into a police station. I went on, imagining the rest. 'Officer, I wish to report the theft of a bowler-hat and rolled umbrella,' or 'Let me assure you, sergeant, that I *have* paid my wireless licence.'

Our new flat was beside Earl's Court stadium but during the week of the Royal Tournament, explosions and brass bands were such a pest that we flitted without paying rent and four of us shared the top floor of an otherwise empty house in South Kensington. We stayed a year, much of which I spent elsewhere on acting jobs. In Liverpool, for instance, where they held a mini-Festival of Britain, I walked on in Balfe's opera *The Bohemian Girl*, revived by Thomas Beecham largely, it seemed, to set off his much-loved petulance. Dad's claim that he was like Bert Orritt didn't stand up. He wasn't as jaunty as Bert and was less likeable altogether. Ten of us augmented the chorus as soldiers and gypsies and had, at one point, to seize a veteran bass.

''Ere, boys, 'ang on,' he told us in his offstage voice, 'it's only actin', don't grab 'old.'

So we laid hands on him lightly, shuddering like cartoon characters from the resonance as he sang. The diva and principal tenor were American and chewed gum throughout, somehow parking it in some corner of their mouths when they came to an aria. At Covent Garden twenty of us shared a room on the third floor and I was impressed by the immense fly-space, the bewigged flunkeys and the stage-manager, who wore a dinner-jacket and red carnation.

My luck as an actor improved a bit, though my memory of these years is a murky void lit by sudden flashes. Real Life was London now. Work was usually elsewhere. At Yarmouth in winter I played leads in the Aquarium, a weekly rep doing A. A. Milne and Benn Levy to houses of thirty pensioners. The larger hall of the same building had been converted to Cinemascope for *The Robe* and we had to shout above the Roman chariot-race. Warm days we sunbathed on the roof and watched seals basking on a sand-bar some way offshore. A statue of Britannia had been set the wrong way, blessing East Anglia. In the main street a looped recording repeated all day: 'You can buy a box of Yarmouth bloaters as sold to the Duke of Edinburgh and Philip Harben, the television cook ... you can buy a box ... etc. ...'

One night I went to sleep with this running in my mind and was woken by the landlady saying, 'The pier's on fire and all the instruments is burning.' We joined the rest of the town's population in pyjamas watching the blaze fanned by the north wind, the beach below us alive with rats.

When I arrived at Frinton-on-Sea, they were doing a comedy about debutantes and the director told me she thought the butler badly cast. Did I agree that he should be sacked before the next play? I said no. There was a sort-of natural authority about him. They kept him on for an Agatha Christie – *Ten Little Niggers*, which later became *Ten Little Indians* and for all I know *Ten Little Coloureds*, *Ten Little Blacks* and *Ten Little Members of an Ethnic Minority*. In a farce called *See How They Run*, this same actor and I lost our trousers. I have the programme still with our names thus:

Lance-Corporal Winton	...	PETER NICHOLS
The Intruder	...	JOHN OSBORNE

My diary makes no mention of him because we hardly spoke. Of Frinton it says only: 'caught a plague of boils and contrived somehow to intrigue a virgin.' These were weekly reps, standards were low, houses small. We blocked the first act Tuesday morning, learnt it in the afternoon or after that night's show; the second act Wednesday, third Thursday, ran the whole thing Friday and again Saturday morning before the matinée. Monday afternoon we dress-rehearsed and opened that night. A tight schedule, but luxurious to those in twice-weekly rep, where they put on a play in three days flat. In Scotland I reached the affluence of fortnightly runs, playing leads in Rattigan, Ian Hay and *Dracula*. His Majesty's, Aberdeen, was like the city – a tight ship. We rehearsed behind the safety-curtain while an army of cleaners Hoovered the plush and shone the brass. As Dracula, I wore a greenish make-up and before going on had to stand over a smoke-box with my cloak held out as you hold a towel over a bowl of inhalant. I arrived onstage smouldering as though I'd put a lighted cigar in my pocket. In Glasgow this was seen by a girl-friend who began laughing even before I made my entrance. I knew this because I could hear her on my dressing-room tannoy. Next morning's headline put it nicely: 'Count Dracula no longer so fearsome.'

After my Bela Lugosi, Scotland saw me as Louis Hayward in *Ten Little Niggers* (again! – no lines to learn), William Holden in *Born Yesterday*, and in *The Seventh Veil* I tried to recreate James Mason's success as a cruel impresario with a gammy leg. On the first night, I entered down a grand staircase, missed my footing, dropped my stick and stumbled headlong the rest of the flight. Later, left alone onstage, I sought solace in a little Mozart, limping towards the grand piano which began playing the sonata when I was still nowhere near it. Strangely, though, Glasgow looked elsewhere for its comedy – mostly to the huge Alhambra, where Stanley Baxter now played revues and pantomimes, was married, owned a large house and was a national celebrity. Over tea in Fuller's he was sympathetic and said he thought I should stick to writing.

The Bristol Old Vic was usually good for a small part in some classic. As the soldier Michael Williams, I went with *Henry V* to London and for a gluttonous week in Zurich. But it was as Ananias in *The Alchemist* that I scored my first genuine success, local but indisputable. There was a lot of me in the zealous Puritan of Jacobean London – and a good deal of my father – but the papers saw me as a palsied crow, a spectre from a St Trinian's cupboard. 'Good casting,' said the director, ungenerously taking the credit but I revelled in the brief sunshine, learning late that fame is an aphrodisiac.

At a party given by some medical students, a blonde German nurse sat on my lap and only left me to fetch more wine. She took me back to the flat she shared with two other nurses and there, on a put-u-up, I lost my long-preserved virginity. She wanted me to stay but in the small hours I walked home through the empty streets as I had so often, more relieved than ecstatic. It wasn't heaven I'd entered so much as the human race. And so easily! There was nothing to it, after all. You just relaxed, as if in the sea. I'm sure my performance (like the one I was giving onstage) was selfish but the girl appeared content and asked me back the next night. For some reason I stayed away but went the night after and then remembered to ask her name. So began a fitful affaire that lasted on and off for the next four years. Frieda was a Berliner of seventeen, her father a Lutheran or Calvinist theologian and some shadow over her family had driven her to England, she claimed, to learn the language and continue her music lessons. Her conversation was an excited muddle of Bach, coffee-bars, jazz, Goethe and money. I never discovered what she believed, if anything, or what pleased her. Her music was like her life, taken up and dropped. She would sit at the keyboard, frowning at the score, and launch into a sonata, but at the first slip on some tricky arpeggio, she'd say 'Pee, pee, pee,' slam down the lid, move away and ask me 'Hey, listen, d'you like Marlon Brando? I think he's a bit silly, yes? . . . Now you're looking at me in that very English way, as much as to say she's only a baby, she knows nothing.'

There were times when we seemed to be doing an updated *Seventh Veil*, a parody of a parody, with Frieda a nymphet concert pianist and myself a callous James Mason ready to bring my stick down on her hands with an angry 'If you won't play for me you'll play for nobody else!' This was even more apt later when I became aware of her many other lovers. In London, living at a nurses' hostel, she became a typical 1950s figure – the Bardot au-pair girl in black leather skirt, cruising the Espresso bars on her Vespa scooter, 'mein phut-phut'. She was forever closing doors on her past.

'Oh, listen, that crazy kind of life in Bristol – I'm not like that any more.'

In the same way she dismissed my jibes about the Nazis. 'Those silly old men – nobody thinks about them any more.'

Yet when I mentioned *The Diary of Anne Frank* she told me it was Jewish propaganda. 'Everyone knows that, you silly boy.'

In *The Merchant of Venice*, I played one of the Salads, as those attendant lords are known whose names all begin with 'Sal'. In *The Winter's Tale* I was the old Antigonus, eaten by a bear, and that unnamed gentleman on whom Shakespeare bestows a long and elegiac description of Perdita's return. Whether this was a relic of the messenger tradition or a gift to a fancied boy, I neither knew nor cared, only wallowed, dressing up like a Michelin man in padded hose and doublet, the tights held up by old pennies twisted into the waist. One day, between matinée and evening, I cleared a space in a far-off prop room, took out the pennies, dropped my tights and there – among helmets and candelabra, masks and samovars – had Frieda on a table.

I wish I could claim that the flood-gates were opened, the lost years made up. But though my diary hints at more ('the wonder and flattery of women's admiration'), there were only a few – the daughter of a college principal, a Bovril demonstrator at Olympia and my future wife. 'I threw myself at you all those years,' she says now when I tell her what I'm writing. 'At the time of *The Alchemist* and when you asked me to tea on the houseboat. I was shameless. All you did was scoff.'

'I didn't realize.'

The houseboat was a converted barge moored between Bristol and Bath. The artistic lady owner – once married to T. C. Worsley – wintered in Clifton and needed a caretaker during the cold months. I was woken early on frosty mornings by the long-boat stretching and creaking in the first warmth. What with pumping out the bilges, drawing well-water, shopping, cooking, and acting at night, there wasn't much time left to write. Girls came for tea and Thelma was willing. We were alone on a bend of the Avon, lust hung heavy in the cabin, the bunk was firm but all I did was scoff. I had nothing to fear but fear itself.

The first bed we shared was the one I'd grown up in. Mum was in Canada, Dad in London, Geoff was at teachers' training college. Thelma took the morning off from her studies of Sickert and the London Group and walked up the road to Palatine Lodge. After that we went our separate ways again. Lust and gratification are as hard to remember as hunger and warmth. Even yesterday's climax has already gone so what hope of recalling those of thirty years ago? Pornography is to sex what anecdotes are to life – unsatisfactory images of the thing itself, mnemonics that come to be confused with real pleasure and pain. I remember places – borrowed bachelor flats in Chelsea, the bedroom of a principal's house while a students' sherry-party rumbled below – but I never lived with a woman till marriage and love-making in those days was literally hole-in-the-corner. I often shared flats with homosexuals who found the sounds we made distasteful. Once I was interrupted at an advanced state of the game, could think of nothing but to take the girl to the pictures but found the cinema reeling, and staggered up the aisle to swoon of anti-climax as I'd swooned of laughter in the choir.

For a time I acted in television – live, of course, and black-and-white. In an early police series I played a West Country constable for six episodes. This led to a corner in West Country parts. Television directors then were mostly Londoners – anything west of Staines was the Amazon to them and my Mummerzet served for a Devon postman and a railway-porter in *Tess*.

Between acting jobs, I packed parcels or sold socks in Selfridge's and hose in Harrods or stood as a uniformed doorman outside the New Gallery in Regent Street before it got religion. My friends, all now in London – Garry and his new wife, the Twins, David Allford and his wife – often asked each other and sometimes me why I couldn't make sense of my life, find a regular girl or a well-paid job that would give me the time to write the plays I was always describing. My girls asked me why I knew so many queers. I wandered the streets and asked myself but found no answers.

I made up my mind to change everything – employment, country, friends, my whole way of life. I had no strings, no allegiances, my possessions would go into a suitcase. London didn't know of my existence. There was nothing to keep me.

8 The Life They Lead

James Joyce, Wilfred Owen and I have something in common. We all taught English in Berlitz schools – Joyce in Trieste, Owen in Bordeaux and I got a list from the Oxford Street branch and wrote to Florence. A reply from the Italian HQ in Milan told me they would take me on for the Florence branch but I'd have to pay my own rail-fare and would get £8 a week for teaching eight hours a day.

Before leaving I bought for sixpence a secondhand book of *Colloquial Italian*. I spent a fortnight in Milan learning how to teach the Berlitz method. To begin with, I lodged with a young student's family, but after only a few days was asked to leave. No reason is given in my diary but I believe it was because I shat in the bidet. Gennaro was embarrassed and tried to make a case for me but I was ashamed to tell them I'd never seen an object my own children later called a bottom-washer. I took a room in the Casa dello Studente, a vast place with neutral rooms and corridors lit by blue lamps. There was some prejudice against the British, Gennaro said, justifying his parents. I told him of the stranger on the Piazza del Duomo who'd told me Englishmen were friends of Tito, tyrants of India and – the crowning insult – eaters of bad food. The typical English, he said, was the man Christie who wore a *bombetta* (miming a bowler-hat), killed women and had sex with them afterwards. I found all this amusing but Gennaro was apologetic. In Mussolini's time, he said, the English language was forbidden and words derived from it – such as bar and cinema – were taboo. The Fascists went to a lot of trouble to make Italians hate us. The message had stayed in thicker skulls and many of his fellow-students hoped for the appearance of a new Mussolini.

'You know he was killed not far from here and hung with his mistress, upside down, from lamp-posts.' We were on the roof of the cathedral, near the golden Virgin among the weird spires and pinnacles of that astounding church. Gennaro took me to Santa Maria della Grazie to see what he called the Last Dinner, barely surviving the ravages of Napoleonic troops and British bombing. I found it disappointing and was more taken with the Teatro Gerolamo, a child-size theatre for marionettes.

The teaching staff of the Milan Berlitz were mostly middle-aged and old women. I set down the conversation of an Australian and a Cockney.

'Don't ask me what countries I've seen, dear,' said the Australian, 'much easier to say which I *haven't*.'

Despite their wandering, they loved gossip more than life itself. Their targets were the other teachers.

'A detestable person but interesting. Says he's a Dane, but German-Jew sticks out a mile. I hate German-Jews even when they're nice. Saw too much of them in South Africa.'

'Madame Mouse reckons he's in love with her,' the Cockney said.

'She reckons every man's in love with her. Old enough to be their grandma.'

'And look at her face. That beard – '

'The body's not bad.'

'Quite a good body, I grant you that – but that face on top of it !'

'Well, you don't have to look at the mantelpiece.'

'Finished me when I saw her with her teeth out during the earthquake. Everyone out in the street in their nighties and she'd been so scared she forgot to pop them in. Jesus !'

'There's always a second tremor,' the Cockney told me, 'you have to wait for the second tremor.'

'In Japan we used to get an average of three a day.'

'Well, give old Mouse her due, she's always got a good-looking bloke on the go.'

'Only by giving them free lessons. We could all do that.'

The direct method was a way of teaching by imitation. Teachers were supposed not to use the students' tongue at all, only their own. A good idea but only so far.

'Is this a spoon ?' the teacher asks the students, showing them a spoon. He slowly nods his head, 'Yes, this is a spoon.'

'Is this a spoon ?' he asks, showing a knife, shakes his head, 'No, this is not a spoon. What is this ? This is a knife.'

But – with classes of twelve or more – that may take an hour to accomplish. My practice classes in Milan soon showed me it could only work in private lessons, one to one, and then only if both agreed to break with the method as soon as possible. I was dazzled by the beautiful people who came to learn. 'To see them struggling for a word, frowning, prompting each other, finally bringing it out like a gift, is more rewarding than any method.'

I saw what Milan had to offer – the great cruciform shopping arcade, La Scala, the Piccolo Teatro, Sforza Castle, Brera gallery and the ghoulish chapel of San Bernardino alle Osse. The bones of the name are from a cemetery that was here before the Church of the Blessed Virgin of the Sorrows was built. Skulls arranged in crosses glare from three walls, penned in by wire netting, and thousands of other bones, variously decomposed, fill the spaces. On the fourth wall is a lurid picture of bleeding Jesus with his weeping mother. An old woman sells candles, which give the only light to shrines bedecked with gaudy hearts and garlands. Devotees come, genuflect, touch the skulls with holy water and make the sign of the Cross. Some innate Protestantism made my gorge rise at this death worship. It rose too in the Church of St Ambrose as Gennaro and I filed past the saint's pickled remains in a queue of smart Milanese.

'I do not profess the faith,' he had said to me earlier but now he crossed himself.

Everyone who came from Florence told of gorgeous women, palaces, paintings, Tuscan wine, cypress-wooded hills and towering streets. I arrived by train in sunshine, left my bag at the elegant Fascist station and walked to the school. Turning a corner I was taken unawares by Giotto's campanile, white, pink and green, cassata-coloured, beside the cathedral.

'Wouldn't it be wonderful', I heard an American tourist exclaim some days later, 'if they could go all over this and get it back to its original colour?'

At our nearby school, the young principal fixed me a place for the night by phone and his secretary walked me through the streets, across the Arno and up the Via Belvedere to a villa behind a high wall, where I was to stay the night on a sofa. Signora Comberti was an elderly Florentine widow and was entertaining an English married couple and a German woman – not only with food and wine but with a monologue of the kind I'd only heard from the entertainer Ruth Draper. 'I so envy you, seeing Florence for the first time! There's less now, of course, than there was. The war destroyed a lot, you know. The Germans retreating had to shoot their guns at the Allies and the Allies naturally had to shoot guns at them. They always kept a move away – it was like draughts – first one, then the other. A lot of damage.'

'They left the Ponte Vecchio,' the English woman said.

'Yes, out of sentimentality they left us this old bridge. Blew up the houses and all the other bridges and left us this quite unremarkable old bridge. The Germans weren't at all brutal – very nice, in fact. They warned the people to leave their houses but most of the old ones didn't understand, they were very frightened of the bombing and so on, so they hid in the cellars or upstairs in the attics. And when the houses seemed to be empty, they were blown to smithereens. The old people died, which was probably just as well. The others who'd got out had nowhere to go so my out-houses were full of refugees. I'd been told to prepare rooms for the British officers who were further up the hill by San Miniato watching the German retreat. There was a total blackout, of course, and I came into this very room with a candle and saw that the shutter had been opened. I closed it but too late because not long after a British paratrooper came, covered with those pretty leaves they used to wear. I said "I'll show you the rooms", but he hadn't come for rooms. He said I'd been giving signals, flashing lights. I could hardly follow what they said, poor boys, I believe they were from Somerset. I was taken miles in the pouring rain – but I must say they were charming, they gave me a nice towel to dry my hair. They thought we'd been signalling but it was only the refugees answering the calls of nature. "Oh, Signora, I was so careful with the match!" Yes, really, my dear young man, I envy you the first sight of so many beautiful things. The *David*, the Baptistry door, Botticelli's *Primavera*. I had an old Englishman staying here once, couldn't get enough, his deafness made him more responsive to all there was to see. He came home one day, clapping his hands for joy. He'd seen the most beautiful thing in Florence – a girl.'

'They certainly are', I said, 'amazing.'

'Of course! They think of nothing else but being pretty. Italian men don't like bright girls. For company, they like men or clever women but wives must be beautiful and stupid.'

The English couple discovered they had seen me not so long before in some weekly rep. I was dizzy from too much wine and excused myself early and they went on talking while I dozed on the sofa, slapping at mosquitoes.

I'd been reading one of Lawrence's travel-books – *Etruscan Places* or *Sea and Sardinia* – and noted his description of 'stepping into a night so beautiful he wanted to shout'. For me it was the next morning, when I was woken by warm sunshine on my face and rose to a view of the city, Brunelleschi's dome, rising to Piazzale Michelangelo and San Miniato al Monte. The Signora brought me coffee and we sipped it together.

'I try to remind myself of poverty and all the terrible realities of life but this beauty keeps flooding back.'

The beauty often caught me unawares during the first weeks – I was hoarse with suppressed shouts. Not that I could see any from my first lodging. The window had a view of three brick walls and, to find if the sun was shining, I had to thrust my head through and look upwards to a square of sky. So most of my time was spent on the streets or taking classes. Sometimes it seemed to me a dozen Lollobrigidas or Manganos had gathered outside my classroom, lilting on one hip, turning their heads with accomplished scorn or standing boldly with legs apart, chatting in husky voices.

'*Buongiorno, professore.*'

'Good afternoon.'

To them I seemed a stern English professor but while I asked them if a knife was a spoon or a door a window or an eye a mouth, I was planning my own conversational approaches for the moment the lesson ended. My phrase-book never had what I wanted. '*Voglio dormire con lei, per favore*' – '*Io sono inammorato di lei*'? Was '*lei*' too familiar? '*Voi*' perhaps? '*Penso che voi avete una bella figura.*' When it came to the point, I could never say it. My landlady had a voice like a man. She threw canasta parties with her friends and they all shouted. One day she had a spectacular heart-attack and I had to carry her to bed. A doctor came and while the old woman lay there moaning '*Sono malatta ... moro ... subito morta ...*' he kept saying to me '*Tutta saluta ...* quite healthy. ...'

I found another place with a better view and, over my bed, an immense oil-painting of the rape of the Sabine women. I had a desk at which to write but got nothing down. Even my journal was neglected for weeks. I was reading *War and Peace* and discussed its heroes with a Russian woman at Berlitz as though Pierre and Natasha were people we knew in life. October passed, the air freshened, the nights drew in. Sometimes there was the odd thrill of pleasure, after wine or walking in the hills or discovering an unknown artist – Masaccio or Donatello – but more common were those old moods of fear at the way time was passing with nothing done, 'staring grimly into what Swinburne called "the golden Arno", which is in fact dirty yellow. I have been poor for some weeks, unable to take a tram to work, planning meals of soup and bread at the Ristorante Communale, though a young English woman at the school gave me the occasional meal. She liked me, she said, because with me she could enjoy discussions.' I usually had my mouth too full of her pasta to add much to the discussion but she seemed happy, rabbitting on about art ancient and modern, the theatre, Tuscan speech, People She Had Got The Better Of, Oxford, the poor, sex.

'If an Italian man speaks to a girl, she can be sure he wants to sleep with her, which is all very well but I like discussions too.'

She began to follow me around, holding my hand, finding me private lessons, loitering with intent. Once she found me chatting to a student in the hall and told me in rapid English that I mustn't ever talk to these girls; if you were seen talking to an Italian girl, it meant you were sleeping with her and then I'd get the sack.

It nearly came anyway – but for another reason. The students began to play me up, giggling when I asked them if a glass was a fork or, as time went on and boredom set in, if a pencil was an elephant. I used these classes as much to learn Italian as to teach English and, when the young men seemed to make fun of me to amuse the girls, I rounded on them, using the few broken phrases I could find.

'*Stupido! Come bambini, lei!*'

They were so affronted that they went in a body to the Principal and refused to be taught by me again.

'Whatever did you say to them?' he asked me later.

'Only that they were being stupid and behaving like children.'

'The worst thing you could possibly tell a class of young Italians.'

He was Italian himself and understood.

'You destroyed their *bella figura*. Please never say that again, however stupid they are.'

Berlitz got away with murder. The simple catch in their agreement was that, though you only taught for eight hours in any one day, the lessons could come at any time between eight a.m. and ten at night. From Monday to Saturday you were theirs. I struggled on for some weeks but evolved, as everyone did, my own method to replace the cutlery. One evening the Principal came in to find me leading my class of gorgeous Florentines in a chorus of 'I do like to be beside the seaside' and it was not long after that he posted me back to Milan. It was cold now in the Australian's flat and she could only afford a feeble fire. The Cockney coughed painfully over her cigarette.

'Hear that?' said her friend. 'We're dying on our feet. This filthy place. Time I was moving on. Have you seen the slogans chalked on the walls – "*Elisabetta Vacca! Porci Inglese*"!'

'Well, of course, I agree about Elizabeth. She is a cow. I don't trust her. And that Philip she's got hold of. He's nothing but a German. Probably a Nazi.'

'They ought not to say so,' said the Cockney loyally, 'after all, they're only a lot of greasy little Eye-ties.'

'Oh, Christ, I agree with you, dear,' said her friend. 'I won't have any Eyetalian insult our queen, cow or no.'

The Italian notes give out mid-sentence at the end of a page, as though I had no more paper. Whether I went back to Florence I cannot now remember. My next visit to the city was in 1981 with my wife and grown-up family. We stayed above the Via Belvedere and I told the hotel proprietor's wife about my visit in the 1950s. She asked me the exact year and, when I told her, said she'd probably been among my students. She spoke excellent English so maybe 'I do like to be beside the seaside' is a better method than

Berlitz. The jet age and container-trucks have done their best to destroy the city. Michelangelo's *Pietà* has gone from the cathedral, where I used to spend my lunch-hours, but perhaps in winter when the back-packers and guitarists have gone back to Uppsala and Minneapolis, Florence becomes itself again.

Out of the forgotten time that followed emerges the clear decision to quit acting and find a job that would pay the rent and give me time to write. The Twins had always been teachers of art in state schools – first in Devon, now in London. They taught half a week each in a junior school, two Mister Averys, so similar many of the kids must have thought they were one man. They lived in a pleasant studio hard by the walls of Fulham football ground and, while we discussed my future, the vast crowd roared above us. Teaching, they told me, gave them time to paint. It could give me time to write. No other job carried three months' paid holiday. It had never occurred to me. I'd scarcely set foot in a school since leaving the Bristol Grammar and had long since given up my old faith in education. I knew so little about it, in fact, that the people who interviewed me were stunned when I asked them what the letters GCE stood for. Luckily they were stepping up college intakes to cope with the post-war bulge, now filling secondary schools, so I was accepted as a mature student for two years' training, with a grant that covered the course, my keep and more pocket-money than I'd had since Dick's saving certificates had run out years before.

The college was at Cockfosters, the last station on the Piccadilly line, which I knew only from Max Miller's joke (Is this Cockfosters? No, my name's Robinson), and my first digs were in a nearby semi-det. in a street of identical semi-dets. The husband left in the morning with his *Telegraph*, leaving his childless wife alone but for her budgerigar, Henry. At last I lived in a house with French windows on to the lawn! They could only be opened when Henry was in his cage, which was not often enough. Much of the time he flew about, perching on my head as I ate, or hopping around on the table, pecking at the food. Conversation was impossible. When Henry tweeted, she listened to him. And answered too! When hubby came home prompt at six, he'd get a daily bulletin of all Henry had done and said. He feigned interest with a grim smile but I could feel him raging behind the *Evening News*. One day the bird flew off – to be eaten, I hope, by some strapping tom-cat. At any rate, it never came back. Wifey cried and hubby sympathized but I knew *I* hadn't left the window open.

After this place of quiet desperation, I found a noisier family in a street of Japanese cherry-trees near Southgate Green. The father worked as a printer in another suburb and had been to London only twice. His wife supervised dinners at a school where their daughter taught English. She was engaged to a previous lodger, an Iraqi, which gave just cause for the family to share the general anti-semitism of these otherwise amiable streets. The son of the house was studying something but spent hours with the radiogram playing Mahler and Bruckner symphonies. I shared the back bedroom with another student teacher who practised scales on his violin. To escape the tiny house full of noise I took the bus from the Green, with its decorative wooden stocks, to the main gate of Trent Park and walked from there the mile-long avenue to college. At the turn of the century, Sir Philip Sassoon had replaced the old Georgian manor with a heavy piece of red-brick Edwardiana and, between mansion and orangery, he'd put in a decent swimming-pool. Otherwise what he found was left – mellow stables, a pergola where wistaria climbed on marble columns, and the great park with its farms and forests. Down a sward from the mansion is the artfully natural lake, among the farm-buildings is the hangar he built to house his early aeroplanes. In spring the Gainsborough landscape erupts with daffodils. There were worse places to waste two years.

The teaching instruction was useless – not only unrealistic but based on the thinking of an educationalist called Burt, who was later exposed as a fraud. But there was a library and I made good use of it, to judge from a formidable reading list that ranges from the Book of Joshua to Nigel Dennis's *Cards of Identity*. A class called Hygiene appealed to my natural hypochondria. In History we studied Plato, Rousseau, Montessori and Pestalozzi. There was even a class to improve our diction, which some needed more than others. A Mister Hines, who was always suggesting a crafty snout and held his cigarette secretly in a cupped hand, was heard to snarl as he came from the class: 'Facking Speech Troinin'!'

I fell for a series of girls – one Welsh with marvellous breasts, another Portuguese-African – but made one lasting friend. We hated each other at first sight – me with my disgusting fur-lined jacket, him with his Davy Crockett hat – but I soon saw what he had to teach me: wit and style. Bernie Cooper was cool. Not quite as cool as his friend Gordon because Bernie had ginger hair and a ruddy complexion. The Davy Crockett hats were a temporary lapse – the usual scene was Italian. I had my hair cut Roman-style, combed forward, and bought myself library-style glasses, and later on bum-freezer jackets and point-toed shoes. He put me in touch with jazz again – but Dave Brubeck and the MJQ. He and Gordon had come to this place much as I had. A friend had told them: 'Hey, man, there's this very good thing. Teaching. Really cool. Free college for two years then these very long hols, man.'

Several members of the college staff asked the Principal to send Bernie and Gordon packing, saying they were skivers, lounge lizards, more bothered with the cut of a collar than the conduct of a class. The Principal refused. When Gordon took his first class in some Paddington secondary modern, they shouted him down. He shrugged and told them that if they didn't want to be taught, he wasn't bothered. He walked out after forty minutes and worked in a shop for several years. He finally came back to teaching, and is now a headmaster. Bernie is a natural educator. His latest letter to me came yesterday from Bangkok, where he is living with and helping a community of slum-dwellers, expressing his state of mind at reaching fifty: 'still cool, still ambivalent', or – as I described him as the hero of my play *Ben Spray* – the oldest teenager in the business.

Many of the lectures were so boring that we doubted whether we could bear much more. Bernie suggested sending along a balloon with his face painted on to stand – or sit – in for him. We saw this would appeal to everyone and the day would come when the lecturer faced a hall full of balloons. If he had any sense, thought Bernie, he'd send along his own balloon too. A nice picture – all those silent balloons, gently swaying while their owners lay beside the lake.

I studied the teachers and pilloried them in an end-of-term revue. Next term they were as boring as ever. Bernie and I sought broader targets and wrote a revue that anticipated *Beyond the Fringe* by several years. The Principal, whom we all liked, asked me why I hated everything so much. His distress confused me. I'd imagined he would share our scepticism or at least admire it but he needed to *believe* in something – even the theories of Professor Burt. The line in *Joe Egg*, 'I'd rather have nothing than a lot of lies', probably comes from some such moment. Bernie's scepticism was more a pose than mine. His romanticism drives him headlong from one belief to another. Hungary was invaded by Soviet tanks during our time at college and he joined a group which, led by a Czech emigré, intended going by train to Budapest to 'do something about it'. They were dissuaded by the Principal and sent some blankets instead. Neither this nor the British invasion of Suez meant much to me, they only confirmed what I already knew about monolithic communism and last-ditch imperialism. My memories of the Egyptians were of stolen pens and whiting on my shoes.

I should have been more upset and shared the general unrest that led to the staging of *Look Back in Anger*. If world events hardly touched me, this surely might have. I remember standing in the living-room of Palatine Lodge reading a sour review in *The Stage* and, as the play opened in May 1956, I take it I was home for Easter. The author's name rang a distant bell. From the publess putting-greens of Frinton came an echo of that snarling voice advising me that the virgin I was chasing at the time was not my type. Was it the same John Osborne? I wasn't interested enough to see the play for some months. Like everyone then I read the posh Sundays, the week's homework, only giving them up for good in 1974, as seriously damaging to the health, so I must have seen Ken Tynan's notice. If so, it didn't persuade me to go. A friend did that, much later – and I was amazed, entranced and infuriated by the fearless selfishness.

'Is this how people behave?' asked a middle-aged woman in the row behind.

'These aren't people, they're animals!' growled her husband.

I glowed with a new awareness – they were old and I was young. It had taken that long for my generation to raise our voices – ten years since the war ended and now suddenly there were Amis and Wain and the rest giving the boot to Georgian houses and the Arts Council and our dreary monarchs. The Queen Mother had visited a Sassoon relative who lived on at Trent and had agreed to inspect the college.

'We were in the workshop pretending to be a class in stagecraft, saving our nails for half-an-hour for her arrival. And there she was at last – so middle-class, so obstinately powder-blue. She paused at every bench, said "How interesting! What a lot of work! And this is a hammer, isn't it? Yes", until we finally made parodies of bows and curtseys and she was gone, poor soul!'

Another college friend was president of the Kenneth Griffith Appreciation Society of Gravesend. One Saturday the actor, now better known as TV's favourite lay-preacher, came to Kent to meet his fans, who gathered in the small front room of a semi-det. I chatted to a young man hiding in a corner and he said he'd driven Griffith down from town. He was an actor too, he said, called O'Toole.

I was turning out short stories now – after V.S.Pritchett, William Sansom and Penguin New Writing – but at least they were about a life I knew. One about the real Young-Love described the billet at Changi; one remembered the day Toby Wainwright had refused to fight the rough boys in our woodpile; one was about Nan's family, one about our local barber, another about the woman who owned the houseboat. They still read well but are spoilt by rhetoric and soppiness. At the time I thought them good enough to ask the opinion of the travel-writer and essayist, Patrick Anderson, who had come to Trent to teach Eng. Lit. He offered to submit them to John Lehmann but I lost my nerve and told him I'd do some better ones. My urge was still to write for performance so my next pieces were monologues, one of which (about an American relative) I did in our college show.

Vacation jobs were Post Office sorting at Christmas and Trees In

Streets, a branch of Bristol Corporation. Bernie joined me for this, climbing high with a tree-saw while I trimmed the verges below. The summer between college and my first teaching-post I worked as a labourer in Hyde Park.

'Those who are so free', says my diary, 'with generalizations about the working man should see him as he really is: slow, suspicious, ignorant as a child, eager for routine, fawning to authority and respectful to gentlemen. He believes in kindness to animals, cruel revenge and respects good fighters, especially the Germans.'

I did show some awareness that the Hyde Park casuals weren't true working-class, not at all the grass-roots of Transport House, more the flotsam of Rowton House.

'Their low adventures always happen in Bedford, Cambridge and Norfolk. Behind the castles, colleges and market days lies a seam of vagrant obscenity, thriving on the smallness of the towns, moving by forced retreat to London, where it often languishes in the stiffer competition and Jock or Lofty become cooks in the park-keepers' cabins.'

'I been with the Parks Department,' says Loach in *The National Health*, 'in my trade of catering. Well, I looked after the chalet while the rangers were out on patrol picking up the soiled French letters . . . Custodian of the Chalet . . . making the breakfast. This was in Hyde Park I'm talking about. The tarts used to do their business in the spinneys . . . overnight this was . . . and leave this muck laying about. We tried putting barbed-wire round but the ponces must have had cutters. Next day the rangers'd find this way cut through and all the used French letters again.'

My diary notes that the minimum charge for short time was £2 and that there were industrial disputes if any blackleg tried to undercut. The girls sat one to a bench along the road near Knightsbridge and got up when a Rolls or Daimler pulled up at the kerb. They usually sat in the car to strike a deal and more often than not returned to the bench without getting their price. I was mystified by the way park labourers looked at the ground when they walked the whores' beat and was told superstition would not allow the girls to keep coppers and the grass around them was always good for a handful of discarded small change.

David Allford also watched the tarts – from the first-floor window of his drawing-office on Bayswater Road, then the best-known pick-up street in town. Sometimes I'd walk across the park for a lunchtime pint with him. One Saturday, he drove me down to see his design for Gatwick Airport rising from a messy site and pointed out the glass 'fingers' stretching to meet the planes. 'It's the first in the world where airways, railways and roadways meet.' Now and then I spotted an acquaintance by the Serpentine or walking by Rotten Row. As long as I had a brush or barrow, they never saw me until I spoke. Most of us don't notice menials.

I lived in a hostel in Sussex Gardens, run by Gordon's father, a major in the Salvation Army. The other lodgers were mostly ex-service officers, now lowly civil servants in Whitehall. They were still fighting the last war and, like the labourers in Hyde Park, respected the Germans.

'The Suez fiasco', I wrote at the time, 'has its party line – well, what's the army for? Not to reason why, that's certain.

'"Love to see a wog flying one of those Russian Migs. Ever seen a wog flying anything? Ever dealt with wog mechanics? Oh, you'll find the police force and post office in Egypt are pretty good, yes. That's because we built it up for them years back. This business broke up Eden's health, you know. Who can bloody wonder? With half his countrymen against him. Should have acted faster, stronger. Anyway we were all behind him, all those who'd had any truck with wogs."

'After dinner, they take their cups of tea upstairs to what they variously call the Magic Box or the Evil Eye. Gordon relates how one of them, by his own report, finishes the evening. At ten, whatever he's watching on the jolly old flickergraph, he says goodnight, goes to his room with a cup of Bournvita, drinks it while reading his *Evening Standard*, changes into dressing-gown and pyjamas, washes and, before cleaning teeth, eats one bar of milk chocolate bought that evening on the way home. He folds the wrapping, throws it into a basket, and turns back the sheets for sleep.'

I escaped this living death by spending my evenings with the Twins or Bernie, now in a basement with some hairy members of a Victorian jazz band, or with Garry at Blackheath or his parents at Albany.

Mr and Mrs Cowen were still my only contact with wealth. Their addresses had all been grand – Curzon Street, Wigmore Street or one of those leafy lanes behind the Brompton Oratory. There were always real hunting oils and leather-bound volumes and discreet servants. A butler would open the door and take my threadbare raincoat, almost openly winking at the dotty game we were both playing. It was only in their houses I felt my poverty, not by any hint of theirs but in my reflection in the antique mirrors – frayed shirt, cheap tweed jacket and Fixolened hair. In those days I was Rastignac or Julien Sorel. My diary scoffs at their Mrs Miniver view of England, but the cashmere sweaters, jewels and furs showed what money could buy.

Lenore talked haut-Americain, a fast anglicized gabble which lit on one word now and then for emphasis. In the Brompton house she'd said to me: 'It's so PEACEFUL here. D'you know, Peeder, for many years we stayed at

Brown's Hotel because it's so ENGLISH. Then, after we'd sold our home in California, we decided to put down ROOTS and moved to NORTH London – to be precise it was WIGMORE STREET. But it felt so far OUT. I was so doobious when Bill suggested we get a place out here beyond Knightsbridge. Should we feel CUT OFF? Well, I'm happy to tell you, nothing of THE KIND. Right around the corner there's Harrods store if you want to buy a CHEESE or a BUTTON. And I looked from this very window this morning and there right on the street was a man on a HORSE talking to a GIRL and I said to Bill "It's like a VILLAGE!" I can thoroughly recommend it, when you get around to looking for BACHELOR ROOMS. But perhaps you'd prefer to be IN TOWN?'

'I couldn't afford to live *here*.'

'Peeder' – and this would be with a smile, queenly but firm – 'let me give you some advice. Never admit to being POOR. I've never been poor. BROKE, yes, NEVER poor.'

But the rustic peace and quiet began to pall and soon they moved to Albany, which had often intrigued me as I walked down Piccadilly, with its discreet and elegant façade. I took the bus from Paddington to join Garry and his wife Patty for drinks after dinner. 'This is such a GOOD address, don't you think so, Peeder? Close to the Cavalry Club for my husband and Fortnum's the local store. And such nice neighbours – Mr Priestley, Mr Rattigan and Mr Greene, to mention but a FEW. They may drop in for a drink, by the way, so – GARRY – are you listening? – make sure there's plenty of ICE.'

She'd advised her son on his choice of a flat. 'See here, Garry, Paddy, here's one – only five hundred a YEAR. Two reception, two bed, bath and kitchen, fridge and TV, sounds CHARMING! Oh – BAYSwater – the wrong side of the PARK! NOBODY lives there. That's why it's so inexpensive. Will someone freshen this drink?'

Garry and Patty fixed on a garden flat in Blackheath, two houses away from our first London house, where we'd spend our happiest and most successful years in the 1960s and 1970s.

'Paddy,' said Lenore, after the first shock had worn off, 'let me tell you what I FEEL – I could live here mySELF. REALLY!'

'Praise indeed,' said her husband, winking at his daughter-in-law.

'I mean it, Bill. If only it weren't so EXPENSIVE!'

'It's not, Mother, it's cheap as hell.'

'No need to use vulgar expressions, Garry. I don't mean your RENT, I mean how much it costs your father to hire a CAR for the evening with a driver – most of which is spent in some PUB while he waits to take us home to ALBANY.'

'You could take the train to Lewisham,' Patty said. She had been born to a modest family in some hick Canadian town. 'You could take a cab to Charing Cross, get the train and Garry could meet you here.'

But Lenore, for all that she seemed a non-stop talking machine, had sensitive antennae and was on to that. She gave her icy smile. 'I hope you don't mean to say we're not used to living ROUGH, Paddy. Because, let me ASSURE you, dear, we've had our SHARE of being BROKE. Before you were even BORN we had something in America they called the DEPRESSION. Fellahs used to knock at our door in Beverly HILLS – fifty steps up from the main road, so it wasn't a CASUAL CALL. And I don't mean BUMS, Paddy dear. I mean very pleasant men, well-MANnered men but down on their LUCK. I said to my Japanese COOK, "Give these men a good hot meal, thirty cents and a pack of cigarettes." And I asked one of them what was their greatest PROBLEM on the road. "Well, madam," he said, "you'll be SURPRISED. It's finding CLEAN SOCKS." So I said to Miss Hunter, our children's NANNY: "Turn out my husband's DRAWER that's full of old socks, darn them and give one pair to EACH MAN who comes begging." So, you see, Paddy, I really do have some idea what poverty IS.'

In a book of recollections Lenore wrote in the 1970s, she described these lean years in detail, and how she and Bill kept on their two servants at the same salary on condition they'd run the house economically.

'Anyone coming to the house would see the door opened by Kishi in his spotless white coat and, if the children were brought down, Hunter would be in her fresh uniform and both children beautifully clean and properly clad. No one knew that we were in any financial difficulties, where, as a matter of fact, we were wondering if we'd have enough money to pay the doctor! ... I only mention this because life is so capricious these days that some reader may have a similar problem and solve it as we did, because it worked like a charm.'

She couldn't afford the hospital bills so had the baby at home – 'a son, whom we named Garry, after his father's regiment, the Fort Garry Horse'.

Within a few years their luck improved. By 1937 they were building a large house in Mandeville Canyon. 'The stables were my husband's pride and joy. In addition to the four box-stalls there was a tack-room, with the beautifully polished saddles hung on pegs, covered with cloths. We had, altogether, an odd establishment: a Welsh groom, an English gardener, a Mexican under-gardener, a Filipino butler-chauffeur, an English Nanny and, later, an English nursery governess ... plus two secretaries, male and female.'

One Bank Holiday week, with a pointed stick and a basket, I cleared up rubbish in the park. Crossing Rotten Row I waited for two horses to canter by and noticed that the riders were Bill and Lenore. 'Although I started late,' she wrote, 'and never developed a good knee-grip, eventually I even went stag-hunting down in Somerset.'

St John's Gospel, reporting one of the several occasions when Jesus catered for large parties, reads: 'He said to His disciples: Gather up the fragments that remain, that nothing be lost. Therefore they gathered them together and filled twelve baskets with the remains.' Which makes the Apostles the first recorded refuse-collectors. August in the park, 1957, still had its loaves and fishes but now in paper and polythene, and cigarettes and ice-cream packets and Lyons' individual fruit-pie cartons far outnumbered them. Nothing gives you a lower view of the human species than clearing up its muck and I prodded my way among them like some frowning figure of retribution.

I also learnt the madness of overtime, going slow on Friday, leaning on my broom or spike or barrow till five o'clock so there'd be some work left to do on Sunday, when we rose at six, clocked in at seven, stood about for a few hours and claimed time-and-a-half. This Lewis Carroll barminess still goes on. I see the street-cleaners checking their watches all Sunday morning. How can you found an effective party on a membership prepared to stomach such lunacy?

The job gave me some interesting reportage and enough cash for a modest week with Sam in Paris. This time we stayed at the Hôtel Taranne beside the Deux Magots facing Café Flore and the church of St Germain, where we heard much American spoken and some Japanese. The French were out of town.

Back in London, with nowhere to live, I put up for a fortnight at Garry's place. One night Bill and Lenore came to dinner.

'My dear Peeder, if you'd told me you were going to PARIS, I'd have given you some good addresses. Olivia de Havilland would have been THRILLED to entertain you – she lives QUIETLY just off the Champs Elysées. Did you dine at Maxim's? I understand it's impossible now to live there on less than £25 a DAY!'

Hearing I was about to begin a teaching career, Bill gave me some useful tips on discipline, learnt when he was instructing his cavalry in the use of the Mills bomb. I told Lenore I had no home and she promised to ring me if she saw any useful box numbers in *The Times*. My salary, with London allowance, would be £12 a week and luckily I found a basement room, sub-let from an elderly woman who taught Middle English at London University. It was in Bloomsbury, facing Coram's Fields, a quarter I called 'half-literature, half-lodgings' – not unpleasant, though Wilfred shuddered and rushed back to Fulham. The lecturer and I were each on trial for three months, which would see me through the first school term. In fact, I stayed a year and a half, sharing bathroom and a sort-of kitchen and paying Miss Daunt £3 10s. 0d. and listening to her advice on the girls I brought home.

Garry took me to school the first morning in his Fiat. St John's was a cosy, old-fashioned secondary church-school, one of several in the Ladbroke Grove area that were going to be swallowed by the great new Holland Park Comprehensive then being built. It had been written off as having no future and, to the local education authority, that meant no present either.

I climbed the front steps, hoping I wouldn't trip under the scrutiny of an assembly of alarming roughs. 'Blimey – look 'ere,' one shouted, 'Lonnie Donegan wiv glasses!'

I was not the only newcomer. The other was a woman who'd already taught a year elsewhere. The headmaster, a weary man who was about to retire but looked more fit for the knacker's yard, took us to our form-rooms. Mine was a science laboratory with benches for desks and a row of sinks with taps down one side. There were cases full of glass retorts, crucibles, stuffed beasts and jars of chemicals. Every desk had a bunsen burner on a gas jet. My desk was on a dais and behind me hung, on a metal frame, a human skeleton. The head told me that my teacher-pupil ratio was unusually low, which meant in English that the class was small – only sixteen instead of the usual thirty or forty. He did not mention that every one was either criminal, delinquent, or both. Or, as the jargon has it, 'encountering difficulties'. Nor did he discuss the curriculum, nor show me any books, nor even issue such basic tools as pens, pencils or rulers. Had I understood at the time, the message was clear: I was not expected to teach 3C, only keep them quiet from nine till four and prevent them setting fire to the classroom. They came in quietly enough, watching me – I know now – for signs of weakness, like a prize-fighter in the early rounds. I took the register and tried to put a face to each name. Now it's mostly the names I remember – and only the boys at that. In a world of physical assault, the girls were bound to come second best. They seemed middle-aged drabs to me already, combing each other's hair or gossiping, faced with a life behind a Woolworths' counter or married to some brute like Marsh, the form bully. At fourteen he was as tall as I and far heavier. When he wasn't intimidating me, he was bullying McKenzie, Harris, Hanlon or Wadsworth.

My policy was to be reasonable but strict. I ushered them to assembly and back and did not notice the gradual increase in noise. By the time mid-morning break came I was shouting. The wisdom that had given the two new teachers the two worst classes also put us on playground duty our first morning. The head turned up to stand with us as we watched the thuggery of the exercise yard. A trustie brought us cups of tea and we sipped them in the safety of a covered way under an overhanging classroom. A drop of liquid plopped into my tea. I looked up. It was dull but not yet raining. In any case we were sheltered. The head got a drop on his ear.

'That's coming through the ceiling,' he said. 'Your room, I think, Mister Nichols. Did you lock the door?'

'Yes.'

'Make sure they were all out first?'

'I thought so.'

We climbed to my room, opened the door and found that all the sinks had been plugged, the taps turned on and the floor flooded.

By that time Gordon had already walked out of his school. At the end of the day the girl who began with me went to the divisional office to give notice. I followed her at the end of the first week. The inspector was sympathetic, seemed used to complaints about St John's and asked me to try a little longer to make sure I hadn't been hasty. After another week I gave the shortest notice I could, which meant staying a term. This was the lowest point of my adult life, the only job to give me nightmares.

'Individually,' I wrote after two weeks, 'they are amiable, untidy, thickheaded cry-babies. Together they're a donkey. Their refusal to budge one step towards work reminds me of the unrideable mule at a fair. Only because it's Friday night and they're out of my sight till Monday can I muster the facetiousness to crack a few jokes over their absent heads.'

Whenever an A class used our room for science, I had to trudge from one building to another, leading my sixteen rejects, like some tone-deaf Pied Piper, looking for somewhere to sit, or subduing them in the gym, keeping Marsh from the girls' bog, giving up hope on the 'reccy'. Each time I returned to our class I expected to see the skeleton detached from his frame, a pile of boñes on the floor. 'That's our *last* teacher, sir,' they were always telling me. 'How much d'*you* weigh at the moment?'

Sam Avery recognized one of my children by name. He'd taught him in Junior School and thought him one of the most difficult boys he'd ever dealt with, not brutal or ill-natured, despite appearances, but a victim, a case of chronic beating by a criminal father. He ran away from home but crept back at night to sleep on the balcony of the family flat, leaving again before anyone was up. The mother was now dead and the father gone. The boy was in some kind of fosterage.

'The first drawing he did for me', said Sam,' told me all I needed to know. He began from the centre of the page, working outwards towards the corners, slowly covering the whole page in black paint. There was some improvement by the time he left me but I dare say that's been lost again.'

No one at training college had told us we'd be doing psychiatric social work. I had my own problems of this kind and felt I was only equipped to teach them to read and write and take in some rudimentary history and geography.

To this end I tried to pass on the meaning of Liberty, Equality and Fraternity. We were reading our only text-book, a garish comic-strip version of the French Revolution. The girl reader faltered on the French names. 'Robespierre, Danton and Marat,' I told them, with an overripe flourish I knew they'd enjoy, for I was already falling back on comedy.

'Marrer?' said Harris, balancing as always on one leg of the chair, 'there's millions of them down the church.'

Two days before there'd been a harvest festival at the parish church, to which our school was nominally attached. A few of the posher kids had brought fruit and vegetables, some in brown paper-bags off the nearest stall, but most in tins from Heinz's factory. How else were they to come by anything that grew? Their parents were mostly totters, scrap-merchants, villains, menials, bargees, urban debris. Some had allotments and their children brought marrows.

'That's not the same as Marat, Harris.'

Some moments later I tried to revise our lesson.

'Now tell me, McKenzie, how did Louis XVIII die?'

'Ooo, sir!'

'All right – Harris?'

'Sir – from eating too many marrers.'

They haunted my basement room and loomed in my dreams. Into the sleepless nights I was trying to fill with shameless women, McKenzie burst with his curly hair, long neck and face in a state of constant umbrage. One day, when I was helping them look up the meanings of naming-words, doing-words and describing-words, McKenzie suddenly demanded: 'Who *wrote* this dictionary, sir?'

'A lot of people, I expect. I don't know. I know who wrote the first one of all. Doctor Johnson.'

'Where'd he get all them words from?'

'He didn't invent them. They were there already.'

'*Who* was it, sir?'

'Doctor Johnson. You can see his face on the beer adverts. Wore a wig.'

'Iron!' jeered Marsh.

'What's that, Marsh?'

'Iron hoof! Pouffe. Queer!'

'Not at all. Everyone wore wigs in those days. Just as we wear collars and ties.'

'*Who* was it again, sir?'

'Doctor Johnson, McKenzie.'

A ritual evolved: at the end of the day, after checking the gas-jets and water-taps, I'd look at my watch just before the bell.

'McKenzie, who wrote the dictionary?'

'Oo, sir, Doctor Johnson.'

It was during these months that I at last touched bottom. Since then, however falteringly, the graph of my life has shown an upward trend. I was thirty, shared a basement with an old lady, hated my work and had no lover. Not that I didn't lust after every pretty girl I met. My sex life was on ice again. All I had instead was a platonic promiscuity. The African girl from college wrote to tell me she was engaged so I fell at once for Garry's Swedish au-pair. Once or twice I stayed the weekend in their spare room and one night she appeared at midnight beside my bed carrying a lighted candle and singing 'Santa Lucia'. She gave me a slice of cake and explained that it was an old Norse custom. I could hear Garry stifling his laughter in the hall. Frieda returned and we spent many hours in recrimination. My balls ached but she talked of marriage and of my unkindness to her in the past. She told me she'd nearly had my child and had never troubled me for help or money, knowing she'd get neither. But *was* it mine? How could even she be sure when I was only one in 'a dotty series of masochistic amours'. That was Diary again – where the last phase of our affaire is buried and where it had better stay.

In the following spring she came to Palatine for another family wedding and endeared herself to Dad by playing 'Für Elise' on the baby grand that had been inherited from the gaslit house at Stratford East. My mother seldom played but still gave lessons on her upright in what Dad called 'the breakfast-room'.

That was still some way off. The present was St John's.

'I have met my Waterloo', says Diary smiling through its tears, 'on the playing-fields of Putney.

'Every Thursday afternoon, two luxury coaches carry the boys of two classes, another teacher and me to what is known as "sports". They fill the bus with orange-peel, toffee-wrappers and skiffle songs, pester the driver and laugh at dwarfs in the street. At the grounds, the weaklings discover mysterious headaches, weak bladders and a variety of limps. The bullies yelp up and down the pitch playing what they call "games" which have no regard for FA rules. The other teacher referees with a whistle and I take the sick parade. On neighbouring grounds, neat crocodiles of junior boys file on in spotless kit or sit in cross-legged circles for coaching. Girls with hockey sticks practise from the touchline in orderly rows.'

The referee teacher was Welsh, formidable, strict. He taught me more one rainy afternoon than all the college lecturers had in years. The rain cancelled outdoor games so he and I were given the indoor gym and the entire third and fourth forms to contain till the bell at four-thirty, when parents would line up outside to collect their children on carts full of old fridges and bikes, pulled by derelict nags. The Welshman and I entered the hall to the sort of sound you'd expect if lions and tigers got into the parrot-house. He at once blew a deafening blast on his whistle. Immediate and astonished silence. Before the noise could start again, he shouted: 'Right! Everybody! Sit on the floor in silence!' – and they did! He walked to the centre of the hall and swung round as someone muttered.

'Who was that?' he growled. 'You, boy? Stand up!' He pointed at random and a boy stood up.

'Hands on head!' he shouted.

The boy obeyed. The sitting mob stared at him and someone sniggered.

'Find it funny?' said the Welshman and pointed his finger. 'You up too then! Hands on head.'

A girl stood. There was silence again. The Welshman prowled between the cross-legged youths, his demeanour challenging them to talk. I stood at the side, lost in admiration. At last a teacher I could respect! For the best part of an hour he held them there in silence while rain beat on the roof. By the time the bell rang, about a dozen were standing with hands on heads.

'Who said move? You will go *quietly* – class by class, girls first, boys next, starting with 3C. And I said *quietly*!'

Marsh and McKenzie and the rest filed out in silence. In an orderly manner, school dismissed. I told the Welshman that, while there were educators like him about, you could keep your Rousseau and Montessori. He smiled and shrugged but I saw that he was sweating. Next morning he didn't arrive and his wife rang to say he'd been admitted to hospital with total nervous collapse.

So it was that I tried to take the football while a woman tended the sick parade. It soon became clear I could not tell a corner from a goal-kick.

'You meant to be reffing, mate?' said one boy, after a vicious sequence of unreprimanded fouls.

'Is this meant to be football, is it?' pleaded another.

Some Teddy-boys from another class joined the fun and, when I tried to control the game, called me 'Steamer!' which meant I was a steam-hammer or killjoy.

'Ain't you going to do nothing?' Marsh asked me.

'Such as what?' I said.

'Say you'll chiv 'em.'

'What's that mean?'

'Do 'em wiv your razor.'

'Right. Get in the coach, we're going back.'

But they refused to go. I involved myself in arguments I could only lose and after that there was nothing to do but leave. During the next week I visited a junior school in Brixton, where the head offered me a mixed class of eight-year-olds, starting next term. At St John's, trying to assert authority, I was learning their level, had given up the French Revolution and was teaching folk-poetry. For my first example I took 'Knocked 'em in the Old Kent Road'.

'How d'you get this job, sir, anyway?' asked Harris.

'Influence,' I said. 'Now look at the words –'

'Shan't!'

I had had enough and clouted him.

'You can't 'it 'im like that,' called Wadsworth, 'I saw it on telly. You can cane us but you can't just 'it us. I could get you chucked out.'

'You never cane us, do you?' said Marsh. 'Why's that?'

'He's scared.'

'We'd be afraid of you if you caned us.'

'Speak for yourself, mate.'

'Our last teacher, sir, he was the best caner in the school.'

'Well, he certainly made a good job of you lot.'

'Tell you what,' said Marsh, 'how about coming down the gym wiv me? I'd give you a right bloody pasting.'

'Take your feet off the desk, Marsh.'

'I asked old Wilkins to come down the gym. Next day he'd left. When you leaving, sir?'

'I'm just settling in. Now – back to work.'

'That's all we get is work. We don't like it.'

'I haven't seen you do a scrap since I arrived, Marsh.'

'You won't neither.'

'We never do noffink in this class, never go nowhere.'

'I wonder why, Harris.'

'Cos we're Free C. Tain't fair.'

'Yer,' said Marsh, 'we wanna see the statues in 'olland Park – all women wiv bloody great knockers.'

'You wouldn't enjoy Reg Butler.'

'Never get the chance.'

'Dere's de bell, sir.'

'Nobody move!' I said but Marsh made off. I beat him to the door and began driving him back to his desk, jabbing his chest with my finger to emphasize my words.

'When I SAY don't MOVE, Marsh, I MEAN don't MOVE, got me? Now SIT down and WAIT till I TELL you.'

To my relief, he did as I said. Quickly I followed up my advantage. 'Everyone – face front!' I made to the door again. 'Read what's written on the board, all together – one-two-three!'

And the chant went up:

> Last week down our alley came a toff,
> Nice old geyser with a nasty cough . . .

When they'd finished, I said 'Very good. But wait for the word "go", Wadsworth. Before you do – McKenzie!'

'Sir?'

'Who wrote the first English dictionary?'

'Oo, sir, Doctor Johnson.'

One Saturday, in a Mayfair church, I promised to teach Garry's son the Creed (which I had yet to learn myself), to see that a high moral tone prevailed in his home and that he grew up a good Christian. At Albany afterwards, the Swedish au-pair was wearing a coat trimmed with ermine from her father's farm. We drank champagne which, Lenore told us several times, had been laid down in Coronation Year, and ate a buffet lunch from Fortnum's.

'This Rocquefort is VERY good,' she said, 'though I say it mySELF. Oh, Heavens! Look at the way this fellow's mixed the FRUIT!'

Garry, embarrassed and slightly drunk, rolled pellets from the paper napkins and flicked them at Patty.

'Stop that, son,' said Mr Cowen. 'Really, it's too sophomore for words.'

Lenore pretended not to notice.

'Peeder, did I ever tell you about the day David SELZNICK said to me, "Only two things matter in motion pictures – sex and MONEY!" I said, "Mister Selznick, I prefer to say AFFECTION and SECURITY – it sounds so much NICER."'

As Christmas approached, it was clear that my class's complaints were justified: every class but 3 and 4C went on visits to exhibitions and museums. The burly man who ran 4C like a kennel of guard-dogs mentioned it in the staff room.

'Never you mind, Nick, we'll take our lot on a journey, agreed? Leave me to sort it out.'

I saw him buttonhole the headmaster after a staff meeting that had concerned the school-fund money raised by the sale of biscuits during the break and whether to hire a conjurer for the Christmas party rather than repeat the fiasco of the film which ruined it last year. The poor man had the look of Captain Queeg measuring the strawberries while mutiny brewed below. It was agreed that we should take our forms to the Pool of London to see the Russian ships the burly teacher knew were moored there.

'On a coach?' I asked.

'On the tube. Be all right, Nick. Do it out the petty cash.'

The day of our visit, the Thames was hidden by dense fog. We stood on London Bridge with our twenty prize pupils – the worst had been weeded out.

'What now?' I said.

'Take 'em to see St Paul's.'

We traipsed up Cannon Street, the pavements clearing ahead of us as before an army. On the cathedral steps, he looked at his watch.

'Tell you what, Nick. I got to see my tailor a few minutes – just round the corner. You take 'em in the church. It's all free. See you out here again – shall we say half an hour?'

He made off before I could speak and I led the boys and girls through one of the great doors. Their awe lasted till they heard the echo. Then followed the acoustic experiments they usually made in tunnels. Some of the riskier elements had separated from the main body and I made off to find them as vergers hurried down the aisles to shush the others. Wadsworth and McKenzie were nowhere to be seen. The crypt and Whispering Gallery both cost money to enter so I turned from them but, while I peered into the darker corners, the man at the desk asked if I was looking for some boys.

'They told me they had no money so I let them into the crypt for nothing. They said they'd come all this way to see it and hadn't realized they'd have to pay. It seemed –'

'Yes, well, it's time we went, so can I go and find them?'

Before I could, a mother and her daughter ran from the crypt in terror, saying some thugs had insulted them. I ran down and rounded them up. They were playing monsters around Wren's tomb. 'If you seek his monument, look about you.' I grabbed their arms and hustled them to the West Door, through the nave that was now alive with the yells of our classes and the pleas of vergers. With the fag-end of my strength, I somehow mustered this mob on the steps. The other teacher came towards us.

'All right, Nick?'

'They're all yours. I'm going home.'

That was almost the end.

3C seemed almost sorry to hear I was leaving them. Of six form-teachers they'd had that year, I'd survived longest. I had grown fond of one or two and felt sorry for them all – except Marsh, whom no one could like or pity. They used to say that, if Marsh told you he was doing a job you never knew whether it was a house in Clarendon Road or a girl called Sheila Watkins.

On the last day, McKenzie came and dropped a packet of twenty Senior Service onto my desk.

'Happy Christmas, sir.'

'Thank you, McKenzie. Where d'you nick these?'

'Sir, I never.'

This once, I thought, it was the thought that counted, not the tobacco.

'Who wrote the dictionary, McKenzie?'

'Sir – Doctor Johnson!'

Home for Christmas – seeing my brother's growing family of girl and baby boy, Dad now in a pottering retirement, my mother a grandma, still only admitting to twenty-one. Dad had one night driven the Green Goddess into a bollard and promptly quit driving, handing the twenty-year-old car over to Geoffrey. Of our generation, no one else but Garry drove a car. Cars were for old people, except that more of my friends had children now and began needing cars to carry them about.

I went to work on the bus, waking early, making my own breakfast, catching the southbound double-decker in Holborn, empty till the office-cleaners got on after their morning's work, for the half-hour journey to Brixton. The work was hard but the younger children were inclined to learn and we had the security of a form-room. At midday, if not sharing dinner-duty, I explored the market near the Town Hall, beside the elevated railway on its massive steel columns. 'In the arcades, butchers in blue-striped aprons and blood-stained boaters auction the meat, throwing joints and chops from one hand to the other as though it were too hot to hold. Some hack at the carcases of horses. In pet-shops, birds sing in cages, fish ogle and children prod the tortoises. A middle-aged furrier stalks and creeps among her stock like a trapper. Curtains of sausages, walls of cheese – there's nothing by halves in this part of town. I wonder British films haven't taken it, castrated it and sold it to America.'

By the final bell, my class had their homework set for that night (and most would do it) and I caught the bus back into town, always going against the tide. Settled on the empty upper-deck, I slept off the day's labour, not seeing the churches and Bingo cinemas, Festival Hall, Waterloo Bridge, Aldwych or Kingsway, but never oversleeping Lamb's Conduit Street, where I bought two cakes for tea, which I usually had alone but sometimes with Miss Daunt in one of our rooms. Early evening I wrote and by March, half-term, I'd finished a television play for a BBC competition. Later I'd go to friends or a girl would come – Frieda, forever turning over a new leaf, or the African, bored with marriage, wishing I'd been more positive.

Garry was working on a film of his mother's starring Lana Turner and one of his jobs was entertaining her fourteen-year-old daughter. He brought her to my room, took us for hamburgers and a movie and Cheryl was amazed to be out with a teacher. In her school in California, she told me, they took no notice of teachers. Her favourite classes were the mock-marriages and mock-divorces, which Diary wittily notes 'probably go on the prospectus as pre-vocational training'. A few days after this came news that she'd killed her mother's gangster lover with a carving-knife. She went into a remand home and the matron told the press that they have 1,100 children there whose parents never visit them 'but now she's here they might come out of curiosity'.

Patrick Anderson took Bernie and me to the Fitzroy, where the pianist struck up 'Mad About the Boy', his theme song. Patrick described his new novel and I afterwards visited Kenneth Williams in his dressing-room at the Garrick, where he was starring in revue.

'His incurable sadness matched my own and comforted me. One can't always bear it alone. At school, a young woman teacher must leave her job to care for a mother with cancer and a blind grandmother. So what have we to complain of? Well, her consolation is her simplicity. We carry the disorders of our character with us like chronic diseases.'

'Selfishness, I suppose,' Kenneth said, then recalled a friend's remark when Ken had said he didn't care about Chinese earthquakes because they didn't concern him: 'That's the road direct to ulcers. Watch it.'

'I follow Voltaire,' Ken had answered. 'We must dig in our garden.'

'You haven't got a garden!' said his friend, 'you live in a drawer in the sky with the minimum of responsibility.'

A few times Ken brought his co-star Maggie Smith to Lyons' Corner House and amused us with his stories of digs and landladies, the Actors' Church Union lists where LSF meant Lavatory Same Floor and LTD meant London Telephone Directory – or, as Kenneth saw it, Landlady Takes Dick. 'LTD?' he would ask, when he rang for lodgings. 'Definitely,' would come the answer.

I enjoyed watching Maggie's evident affection for him and her regard for his high camp skills. Later that year she and I went about a bit and held hands in cinemas. I introduced her to the Twins' circle but it was all too pi for her and, during one of their shared lectures after a play, she suddenly said 'Jesus!' and marched off up the centre of Charing Cross Road through the oncoming traffic.

Once, leaving a theatre with her, we were approached by the legendary Kenneth Tynan. He greeted her and walked beside her.

'Who's this chap?' I heard him whisper.

'Oh, he's no one,' Maggie said.

It was the sort of response Tynan prompted. In his world Anyone who wasn't Someone was No one. This was, after all, his *métier*. Though often called a critic, I think of him as a publicist, a mandarin PR man. For wasn't it he who said it would be a conversational necessity for the next year to have seen *Waiting for Godot*? Tynan tarted up the theatre, gave the old thing a tuck in the tits. While he was around, it had the glamour of a gossip column, scandalous and sexy. It was *news*. Not any more. He's sorely missed.

Maggie and I drifted apart again, she eventually to marry Robert Stephens, last seen at ping-pong in Avonmouth Youth Club.

I was now writing and performing solo turns at the Twins' social evenings. Without money, they tried to bring back the salon, offering coffee and a studio and hoping for gifts of wine. The guests ranged from Angus Wilson to the Finnish ambassador. My best solo was based on the horrors of St John's. It later – minus the jokes – became the opening scene of *Joe Egg*.

'I wore', says Diary, 'my Italian suit, French tie, Swiss shirt and pointed shoes – the perfect European of the 1950s, an era when girls show their milky knees in the new short skirts and wear invisible make-up and strut in dangerous dresses on half-heels, their Welfare-State figures plump with school milk and chocolates. I'd love them all, if they'd let me.'

But they wouldn't – all Spring held for me was the long-awaited school journey to the Isle of Wight with thirty-six mixed juniors and the sour-faced, saw-voiced Miss Parsons, whose pep-talks at prayers had kept me amused for weeks.

'Hands up those children who haven't planted their nasturtiums yet ... eight! Eight slow-coaches whose seeds should be in the pot but are still in the paper packet! That's what Miss Mulcock was afraid of. What's the good of seeds in a paper packet when they might be showing a littawl green shoot? Hands up those who *have* got a littawl green shoot ... well done, those people! Littawl green shoots are what we expect from Sudbury children – not paper packets.'

My preparation for the trip was meagre – I browsed through a few guide-books from the school library.

'Not enough facts,' said Diary. 'I'd have done better to ignore all that and let my imagination rip, which the writers certainly had. "Ventnor – aptly named the Madeira of England", "Sandown, the island's Bay of Naples", "Gurnard has a fascinating putting-green", "The view from the summit of Shanklin Down baffles description – especially if the day is clear", "Nature busy with her hand of healing has clad the ruins in a garment of beauty". I know this style through Dad's letters, but it does suit the island, it's musty with Victorian relics of all kinds – the Queen even managed to die here. I'm sorry we're not seeing Osborne House, which promises a wall-painting by Dyce, "Neptune entrusting the command of the sea to Britannia" and "an excellent mosaic pavement, now for the most part covered in linoleum".'

We arrived at Ryde, England's Istanbul, in a rainstorm. Under a dome two Union Jacks hung like washing and we assembled in an empty cafeteria near an electric organ that waited for the real season to start some weeks hence. This early, only schools and pensioners came to Wight on cut-price deals. We entrained to Shanklin and there, while unloading luggage into a cab, I was suddenly bawled at by a party from across the street. Miss Parsons, lining up our kids, gave a look that was meant to kill. I looked too and saw the more respectable members of the thirds and fourths from St John's.

'Sir! Don't you know us, sir? We often talk about you. Where've ya bin? This your new school? Ain't they littawl?'

Their teacher was a High Church divinity student who'd been sent down from King's for burning the bishop's effigy. I'd forgotten his second name.

'Hullo, Larry,' I called.

'Oh, I say!' shouted Lizzie Chambers and McKenzie, 'Hullo, Larry, dear boy.'

Larry told me on the phone later that Miss Parsons's face had been a picture. That was nothing new. It was always a picture – usually of umbrage or scorn. She scarified the children, the Isle of Wight and any attempt to open the minds of the young. They nonetheless enjoyed themselves – even at tame Shanklin, with its Keats Green, denoted by an unkind picture of the poet, painted perhaps in several varieties of Brown Windsor: with its Olde Worlde village, thatched cottages and sad pier, a placard proclaiming to beach and cliffs the single word 'Hilarity'. The days crept by in a crocodile of uniforms, to the sound of slamming bedroom doors, pillow fights, soprano shrieks and the 200 men and a bottle of pop and sausage-roll that went to mow a meadow. I learnt as much as they did – to tell a cockle from a limpet, spot a sea-anemone and what is kept in a mermaid's purse. Once they were in bed, I'd sneak off to the Keats Inn for a Guinness and chat up the barmaid.

Our days began with Room Inspection. Miss Parsons went first and I followed like Prince Philip, hands clasped behind back, smiling and winking to mitigate her relentless scorn.

'Bit of fluff on the floor,' she'd rasp, 'and these counterpanes could be straighter. Still you've made some sort of effort. Seven out of ten. Now do not. Move!'

This way of pausing for emphasis came from a lifetime of waiting for silence.

'Stay. In your rooms. Until I send a Round Robin – probably Mister Nichawls.'

The turn I did afterwards at the Twins' soirée included my lanky attempt to resemble this spherical bird. I may not have known a buttercup from a lesser celandine but at least I knew a Round Robin wasn't a messenger. I never let on.

The royal progress done, we gathered in the lounge for prayers and another pep-talk.

'I've noticed – in fact, Mister Nichawls has noticed too, haven't you, Mister Nichawls? – that someone. Has been tearing flowers from peopawl's gardens and strewing them. On the paths. It's not. Necessary. The poet Keats apparently said "A thing of beauty is a joy forever". A Joy Forever, Glynis Rutt, busy talking! And around the island you will see on rubbish bins:

> Let it not be said unto your shame
> That all was beauty here until you came.

Until you came, Allan Dye, blankly staring. At the ceiling. The reputations of Sudbury is in your hands. What does that mean, Linda Glasspool, not listening! Tell her, anyone? Stephanie. Baum? . . . Yes and don't you forget it. Perhaps you can find other messages written about . . . not only on rubbish-bins, no, Linda, but everywhere. We'll have a littawl prize for the one who finds the best. Mister Nichawls can be the judge. There's the gong for breakfast. Do not. Charge like wild elephants. Not. Necessary. Try to be a littawl more gentawl.'

But as the days drag by, I learn that she too has a kind of life and is enjoying this journey as little as I am. 'This evening', she confided, as we sat exhausted after another day, 'I should like to be at a nice mystery with a nice cup of coffee, not this muck, and a nice Marie biscuit in the intervawl.'

One morning Room Inspection discovered a wet bed. Gloria Hazell stood beside it, hiding her face. 'What do you call this, Gloria? Look up, girl, don't hang your head. What do you call it? . . . Don't know? I know what I call it. Dirty. Disgusting. What do you call it, Mister Nichawls?'

'It's not the sort of thing you can control,' I told her.

She tried to kill me with a look. 'Not. Good enough. Nought out of ten, this room.'

After prayers that same morning she asked: 'Now what is this in my lap? ... Yes, Stephanie, letters and parcawls. And what is the collective word for letters and parcawls? ... Well, Joyce Waby? ... Post, yes. And this morning in your prayers you used another collective word – sin. With no ess on the end, Edward Glazebrook, one of the worst offenders. No. Ess. I always say this word especially clear. Sin. Collective word, meaning all evawls, malefactions, triawls and troubawls. Don't. Forget it.'

Wight goes in for the picturesque – hand-weaving, old stocks, smugglers' coves – but on the summit of Boniface Down, like an undetected Martian landing, several early-warning radar devices revolve incessantly.

'Today we are going to Alum Bay. You will not. Take your shoes off. Why? Anthony Ruddawl? ... Because of the glass, yes. Alum Bay is riddawled with littawl pieces of glass. So if you want a test-tube of coloured sand, where will you get it, Alan? ... Yes, buy it in the locawl shop.'

Alum Bay has a pebble beach and sandy cliffs as brightly coloured as a layer cake from which the sea has bitten a helping. To the left, the white, razor-edged Needles lead to a barber's-pole lighthouse. Miss Parsons's locawl shops were chalets selling glass vessels to be filled with strata of coloured sand – in every form from test-tube to dog and motor-car. Some are already filled; several shops have bins of the stuff to save you scrambling about; others offer the laziest-but-one group cellophane packets of the twenty-one different shades – Alum Bay Takeaways. Miss Parsons and I were laziest of all, sitting on the beach while the children clambered on the rocks with nail-files and coins, scraping and filling. Some rashly brought their finished work for approval.

'Well, Barry, if you must. Spend your money and time on it, I can't. Stop you. But may I ask what you're going to do with it now you've got it? A littawl glass lighthouse full of sand ... give it to your auntie? She won't thank you. She'll bless you for it. And I speak from experience. I've got one on my mantelpiece now and I'm only waiting for my nephew to forget it before it goes where it belongs – out with the rubbish. What is it, after all? Waste stuff from the seashore. Not. Necessary. You could describe it with one word with a capital R. What's that, anyone? ... Quite right, Gloria. Rubbish!'

Waiting for the ferry at Ryde the last day, we ate packed lunches and watched the *Queen Elizabeth* and *United States* go by on high tide. Miss Parsons had allotted this time to shop for presents but it was early closing

191

day. One boy, feeling I deserved a gift, brought me a paper-bag full of ladybirds he'd gathered from the lawn.

That was not the end of teaching. I stayed at Brixton for a year, then taught illiterates in Islington part-time. Some years later, back in Bristol I had to eke out my television earnings with a few days a week at the secondary modern where my brother worked full-time. We looked alike and the children hardly knew of my existence till the end of term when Geoffrey and I did the mirror-sketch from *Duck Soup*, two identical Grouchos. Geoffrey worked hard, got a second-class degree, rose to adult education but finally gave up and is happier keeping a music-shop.

I dread schools. Both as pupil and teacher, I was grit in the machine. Perhaps at Oxbridge I might have found earlier encouragement. My twenties seem so bleak and lonely that, though the outcome might have been the same, sooner must have been better. I was what they call in staff-rooms 'a late developer'.

Diary of the time approvingly quotes some lines from Jane Austen's unfinished novel *The Watsons*. I still approve:

'I would rather be a teacher at a school (and I can think of nothing worse) than marry a man I did not like.'

'I would rather do anything than be a teacher at a school,' said her sister, 'I have been at school, Emma, and know what a life they lead. . . .'

Part Three Father

Joe Egg is a fool,
He tied his stocking to a stool.
When the stool begins to crack,
All the beetles run up his back.

Children's chant from Market Rasen,
quoted by the Opies in
The Lore and Language of Schoolchildren

9 Mixed Blessings

Garry Thorne decided he would never make an actor and applied to Granada to be a television director, asking to use my completed play *Walk on the Grass* as an example of the sort of work he'd like to do, if they gave him the chance.

A few days later they summoned me to Golden Square (the sun clear and warm for a change, Regent Street crammed with shoppers, pretty girls in swarms), told me they'd enjoyed the script and wanted to produce it. I had to say I'd already entered it for the BBC West Region Contest but that I was working on another. They asked to see a completed first draft and to do the first if the BBC passed, so I worked on the new one all summer, turning out, says Diary, 'twenty pages of rambling and expository dialogue with no sign of a plot'. Started again at school with a new class (half of them unable to read the word 'Alfred') and, coming home to what promised to be a lonely and industrious evening with mutton-chops and a ninepenny peach, I found Miss Daunt answering a phone call from my mother. The BBC wanted me to show up there the next day. I bunked off, took the train and at the Bristol Broadcasting House, where I'd once collected autographs, they told me my play had won the £200 prize. Several Amis-like cub-reporters interviewed me and laughed immoderately till I told them the play was a domestic drama. The other prizewinner, a marine biologist, demanded to know if I was 'one of those angry chaps'. On the way for a drink, we met the girl whose breasts I'd kissed in the china-shop. She was married now and a mother but had been in my first play at drama-school. Loose threads were being tied. Dad would have called it a remarkable coincidence. In fact, the Palatine Pair, Woodbine Winnie and Richard the First, had thought the prize was for £1,000 and reckoned I'd been short-changed. They were right, of course – for what they called a 'prize' the BBC were getting a play dirt cheap. Not that I cared – I put the money in the bank and still had most of it a year later. Anyway, Granada bought the next play for £300 and I gave notice at Sudbury Road.

Garry became a restaurant manager and ran a modest place behind Knightsbridge with all the flair of a *maître d'* at the Savoy Grill. 'The Stockpot' became the new evening refuge for the Twins' old circle. The waitresses were honey to bachelor drones like me and I willed myself into love with an English resting actress and slobbered over a Nordic blonde, getting as far as her bedroom but not her bed. The actress had been married and divorced and was more cautious than I.

'You seem to think yourself pretty lonely.'

'Yes, I do.'

'And this makes you hurry to find someone. I know how you feel. I was so lonely at one time and then I thought marriage would answer everything. It doesn't. You could make a terrible mistake. It could put you off the track.'

'Off what track? Self-glorification? I don't care.'

'You'd find you did.'

I was certainly in a hurry to find a wife. My resolve for the year before had been to write and sell a play and that had come about. This year I'd decided to marry. Now that my first shot had misfired, I looked elsewhere. I found no one available in the cast of *Walk on the Grass*, which was transmitted – live, of course – on Maundy Thursday, or as *Diary* put it 'was given away to the poor'. The Bristol *Evening Post* wished it had been 'a case of local boy makes good but . . . .' The *Sunday Times* liked it, the *Listener* didn't. None noticed that the play was tinged with Chekhov, Turgenev, Ibsen and Paddy Chayevsky; none knew that its characters were my family and my sister-in-law's. It makes dull reading now but was a step in the right direction – towards reality.

The second, *Promenade*, was already in production. It described a weekend spent in Brighton with Bernie and Gordon. The cast were all in their teens and twenties and I wondered if the infant Susannah York was old enough to consider marriage, then found she had a husband already.

Now that my chances of a woman had improved, I saw my basement room with Miss Daunt as a handicap. I studied the style of other men. A tall anglicized Australian actor scored with a beautiful brigadier's daughter who waited on tables. His approach seemed heavy-handed but he succeeded so I sought his advice. In bed, he told me, she was unbelievable. I described my domestic problem, sharing a flat with an elderly lecturer in Middle English. He was about to leave his room for some months, he said, half a first-floor flat in Chelsea. He was playing middle-range parts in the new Stratford-on-Avon season and would like someone to take the room and pay the rent, so I gave Miss Daunt notice and moved my stuff to Michael Blakemore's room. The house, a few yards off King's

Road, was the slum of the square. 'The tenants are an ageing Battle of Britain pilot and his loving wife, a Yugoslav merchant-seaman and a frumpish woman of uncertain age who shares our party-line. My flat-mate overheard the start of a call she received last night.

'"Am I speaking to the young lady who's prepared to do anything?" said a man's voice.

'"Well, not quite anything," replied Miss Hessian. She appeared on our stairs some minutes later to say she'd put a card in a local shop offering part-time work in the evenings – anything accepted. "And now *this* is happening! Men ringing up all day. I've had *one* terrible experience with a man. It's not at all what I meant."'

Osbert Sitwell lived next door and was sometimes to be seen being helped up the steps. Apart from this, there was something in the papers at the time called the Chelsea Set though we saw nothing of it. Three mornings a week I joined the bus-queue for the 19 or 22 to take me to my class in Islington. Otherwise I stayed home working on my third play.

A sudden attack of mysterious chest-pains kept me from school for some days, though not from rehearsals of *Promenade*. Walking with the cast from drill-hall to pub for a lunchtime drink, I'd cry out as the pain struck me, a sudden vicious jab in the ribs. An Earl's Court doctor diagnosed wind and prescribed Milk of Magnesia. Some days later and no improvement, he said it might be rheumatism and ordered hot baths and liniment, which I rubbed forcefully into my aching ribs. Finally, a hospital consultant put a stethoscope to my chest and, after a few seconds, told me my lung had collapsed and admitted me to the Princess Beatrice with a spontaneous pneumothorax. My diary cursed and said 'the play has every chance of success but they need me there as a gadfly to remind them of the words.' Friends gathered with grapes and irises and early roses which died like fever victims in the fetid air of Earl's Court. I was in a private ward, sharing with one other patient at a time. The first, as I was shown in, seemed to be sitting or kneeling behind his bed. He wore glasses and a deaf-aid and was there for removal of a cyst. He emerged from behind the bed to shake hands and I saw that he'd been standing at his full height of four-foot ten. He was a Polish violinist who'd studied under Brahms's Joachim in his latter days.

'No good at all,' he said, 'too deaf to hear if I was off-key. But excellent on the interpreting.'

He was replaced by a tramp with a beautiful head of skin the colour of burnished wood, who slept for a few hours, asked me the time, said 'Ah, breakfast', and discharged himself, leaving a mattress full of fleas that the nurses had to de-louse by baking.

I was moved into the main ward as company for a boy from UCLA who had tried to get back into his hostel after hours, fallen twenty feet into an area and broken both ankles. There was a television set, high above the floor, on which I'd watch *Promenade*. Granada offered to provide a monitor for me to view in comfort but the sister refused. No reason. Just refused. It meant the other inmates would have to see my esoteric play instead of the soccer match they'd all prefer. Also, I'd had to alter the most colourful character from Jew to Gentile so as not to offend Mr Bernstein, the managing director.

'Heatwave ever since I came in. What a place to spend a glorious summer! Last night an old man died. He has a short journey – the windows overlook a cemetery. Life goes on. His bed is taken by another old man, expected soon to die. He climbs out of bed the whole time, stands naked and smiling, complaining of wet sheets and asking for his clothes.'

The American, finding his request for a bedpan went unanswered, first complained of anti-semitism, then threatened sister with demotion: 'I got strings, Sis. I can break you.'

My lung made no progress and after a week they took me to theatre, cut a hole in my chest to admit a rubber tube, the other end of which was in a water-bottle acting as a valve to reinflate the right lung. The American's jokes turned on me as he threatened to cut the tube or roll my bottle along the floor.

The other patients knew the play was mine by photographers who came to take me and by my own apologies. The whole ward watched the transmission. The flavour had been caught but you couldn't hear the words. The press next day said the same, though *The Times* thought 'the theme lingered in the imagination, enriching what had gone before', the *Spectator* talked of 'ambitious, water-colour Osborne' and the *Sketch* headline was 'Gangsters? What a boring bunch!' My own feeling was that I would have switched it off.

After some weeks, my lung was reinflated and I left hospital. 'Everyone moving so fast,' said Diary, 'carrying incredible burdens, making superhuman leaps from passing buses, dashing in the face of traffic.' Some days' convalescence in Bristol, then a sudden relapse. Now I was in the hospital where my brother had transfused blood. Patiently I kept my journal, noting the sick, the nursing staff and visitors who'd finally reach the Old Vic stage as the twenty-odd characters in *The National Health*.

My parents, visiting, brought mail, some of it from viewers about *Promenade*. 'What a play! That such talented artists should lower their prestige by appearing in what can only be described as "rubbish"!' This was not, as you may think, from Miss Parsons, but five girls and a boy in Edinburgh. Others liked it and a girl in Weymouth thought I'd modelled Rhonda on her similar experience (an unwanted pregnancy). I wrote back saying I hoped everything was all right now. In fact, I'd based the girl on a memory of Thelma and now – out of the blue – came a letter from her too, from Cheltenham where she taught art in a huge comprehensive, asking what I was doing these days and inviting me to stay in her flat whenever I'd a mind. My reply from hospital brought a visit from her the next weekend, 'twenty-seven now, with negroid features and a plump attractive figure'. She seemed mellowed and even sad and a letter two days after that lamented the bad time she'd had with men and her failure to find a husband. Her last words – a quotation from W.C.Fields – became the last words of *The National Health*: 'It's a funny old world we live in and you're lucky to get out of it alive.'

Well-timed. I watched men dying all around – one old one with a cup of tea in his hand, a young one during Visitors. My lung hadn't responded and they put in another tube. During an even hotter spell, I lay hoping for the best.

Thelma came three Sundays running. We could only hold hands but I'd like to have dragged her into bed and my guess was she'd like to have been dragged. With her reappearance, this long race, slowly run, can make its spring for the finish. My lung dilated once more, I told them at Palatine that I was going to stay with Thelma. Brother Bert from Stratford was staying and asked:

'That the young woman with the broad knees?'

'That's her, Bert,' Dad said. 'A bit free with her favours, they say, but always enjoys the Old Man's stories. Which is more than I can say for Buzfuz.'

As I stood with others waiting for the bus to Cheltenham, he appeared opposite and shouted across the Gloucester Road: 'If you're going to spend the weekend with your young Bella, you'll want your dressing-gown.' He crossed over, waving it and when I took it, turned to the queue. 'She won't want to see him walking about with nothing to hide his loins. Well, Buzfuz, enjoy yourself!'

It was a bad start, having to sit with the other passengers for forty miles but we *did* enjoy ourselves and I never unpacked the dressing-gown.

Thelma was still uncertain about me. 'Do you want to sleep with me on the double mattress or shall I make up the divan?'

Friday evening was the last day of her school term. We walked through the elegant streets in the glorious summer sun, beside the Promenade, overhung with chestnut blossom, the white terraces rising among the great trees like Gainsborough ladies in a landscape. Beyond the Imperial Gardens, butter-coloured caryatids held up the pediments of antique-shops. Well-dressed layabouts chatted in sports-cars beside a fountain. 'Impressive – but it rubbed me up the wrong way,' said Diary. This was hindsight, a priggish footnote. The truth was more to do with lager, Scotch and finally the cool wine we drank with fine French salad she'd made, and bed, which wasn't end but beginning, not only of the weekend but the radiant summer. I might have stayed and we might have gone away together but old habits die hard and I had a television revue to work on in London.

Monday afternoon broke into a thunderstorm and I caught a coach to Stratford, where I was visiting Michael Blakemore. Easy now to see I should have taken Thelma and spent my playwright's earnings on an hotel room but I had more than thirty years of bad thinking to put right before I could commit to the life I longed for that was now being granted. It was a special Stratford season, an all-star centenary. Olivier, Edith Evans, Charles Laughton, Paul Robeson, Albert Finney, Vanessa Redgrave were all appearing. But Diary tells the truth: 'a depressed crowd of actors. Michael only gets through it all by desperate gagging.' Tony Richardson's production of *Othello* included a couple of dogs. ' "They had a very good notice in the *Kennel Weekly*," he told me. "The headline was 'Great Danes in Shakespeare' and it said how 'Battleship and Cruiser, out of Primrose, blue ribbon winners at Crufts, are in *Othello*, others in the cast being Paul Robeson and Sam Wanamaker.' " '

Peter Hall was the director of the company and of *A Midsummer Night's Dream*, in which Albert Finney and Vanessa Redgrave were among the lovers and Michael played Snout the Tinker.

I enjoyed myself, going to dinner on the first floor of Vanessa's half-timbered digs or sharing Albert's cakes in the 'As You Like It' tea-shoppe.

The sun had come out at last as though it meant to shine forever. We went to stay with Thelma's friend, the playwright Peter Draper, at his cottage in Brixham, South Devon. I was more used to describing pain than pleasure and my notes babble incoherently, hoping lists will do.

'. . . a whitewashed cottage, cool inside, with low ceilings on a timber frame . . . a garden walled round with stone . . . tea on a lawn with slabs of fruit-cake . . . Thelma's old lover John with his pregnant wife and baby . . . Peter's wife and three daughters . . . a Border collie, a bored cat . . . picked apples and plums from the trees around . . . slept in the nursery . . . from the window a view through trees of hills and cattle and the vanishing sun . . . in the morning one of us would at last leave the bed to pick ripe plums, the tree so close that, when one of the windows fell from its frame, we found it later held safely in the upper boughs . . . a remote cove to a beach of slatey stone . . . sunned, swam, ate and drank. . . .

'Swimming one day was like a miracle, the breakers throwing us towards the shore, shouting and singing for joy. The wait seems to have been worthwhile.'

We visited Dartmouth from Brixham and decided we so liked the place that we might do worse than rent a flat and set up house there. The town is small enough to take in at a glance from Kingswear across the Dart, its few streets rising steeply behind the quay and the ferry-station. The nearest bridge is twelve miles upstream and the only way from Brixham is still by the ferry-boats that cross all day, the last at eleven, an innocent fact that later proved malign, a fatal motif unheard at the time.

The year wore on between London, Cheltenham, Bristol and Devon. I started at a new school, helping with more non-readers. No work Fridays, so I got away early for weekends with Thelma, hungry for love and sure of finding it. One entry reads: 'Entirely uneventful weekend, except that I asked her if she'd marry me and she said yes, of course.' Not quite true apparently. She's reminded me since that she asked if we shouldn't live together first. 'Oh, no,' she tells me I said, 'nothing like that.' I doubt if I added that I'd vowed to marry by the year's end. We gave notice to our schools and fixed it with the registrar for the day after Boxing Day.

My brother and her sister had both been married in church with Prayer Book, Mendelssohn and reception so we could do without all that. We'd have to, in fact, as her father couldn't run to another. We walked on Leckhampton Hill, wondering whom to invite to a frugal do afterwards. We discussed money (my fees from the plays), our lack of furniture, the risk, our parents' reactions, the unavoidability of Dad's speech and the threat of the story of the Silvertown Explosion.

She had a lively circle – writers, artists, photographers, the sculptor Lynn Chadwick. One morning I was reading in her sitting-room, she was making lunch in the kitchen, when the door opened and a famous face peered round it.

'Ah, hullo! Bronowksi. Pud in?'

She was Pud, he was Bruno, another of her friends. I asked him polite questions on his recent journey to the States and he answered (a), (b) and (c), marking them off on his fingers. I felt it might have been more proper to submit my questions on slips of paper.

'Our love-making improves every time,' I wrote, 'and when we meet after a few days away, the relief is a godsend. Still, the old male obsession with passing women is not the least impaired. Straight from being with her, I can't ignore girls in street or train. Yet she never seems to glance at passing men. Are women able to interest themselves in one man at a time? Or are they more sly?'

Thelma had missed *Walk on the Grass* and one afternoon, both of us visiting home, I tried to read it to her in the tiny back garden amid the remaining apple trees. It may have been a way of warning her that life with me would never be private but always open to be plundered for plays. More likely I wanted praise. Dick put paid to this by walking about in the avenue and back lane chucking fallen apples over the wall at us, which must have been more fun than the play, though Thelma tried not to laugh, especially when she saw me snarl between clenched jaws, 'I'll kill him, the mad old bastard!'

Thelma and Mary, my sister-in-law, talked of the strangeness of their marrying the Nichols brothers but Mary also had a warning. She felt it her duty to tell Thelma that I had gone to Italy some years ago to forget a boy-friend of mine who'd joined the Merchant Navy. Thelma said, if that was true, the cure had been effective.

The quiet wedding took its course from 'a few friends' to a thirsty mob who had to be fed and watered at our expense. Her dowry was a double mattress, single divan, pressure-cooker, nylon carpet and – for the future – £200 in teacher's superannuation. I brought less – a cast-iron frying-pan, one unsold play and some cash. The formalities went well, in a dull room with token chrysanthemums and – visible beyond the registrar – an oil-painting of a bride in white. Thelma was candid in dark green but nervously put on her posh voice for the promises. Bernie had arrived the night before and I could feel his smile in the small of my back. The party was in my brother's flat. Garry brought the Twins and a case of wine. Thelma had made more canapés than the forty guests could eat. Stoning a pound of prunes the day before, I'd wondered whether this was the right step, after all. The best present came from a TV producer who'd read the latest play and was telling the BBC to buy.

For the first months we lived in the rented ground floor of an old vicarage above Brixham. Our windows looked on an orchard and beyond to the graveyard and church, where on Thursday nights we could see the bell-ringers in braces and rolled-up sleeves pulling ropes in sequence. A short cut through that way was protected by three geese who honked when anyone came near. We put a deposit on a flat in Dartmouth, one of a number being made from a Victorian mansion near the Naval College, surmounting a grand botanical garden that straggled down the hill, with palm-trees and pine-scented copses. We started buying furniture for it and, in April, Thelma told me she was pregnant.

'Oh, no!'

'Are you saying you don't want children?'

'Well, not yet. We haven't had any time together, just the two of us.'

'Too late to think of that. We've done nothing to prevent it. Did you think that once we were married it would be a matter of choice? You still have to take precautions.'

'I know.'

She had asked me, it seems, in the first place and I'd rejected all thought of such unattractive measures. In those days, before pill, coil, intra-uterine devices and vasectomy, the only available methods might have been devised by conjurers. The aesthetic appeal of Catholicism had much to do with the squalor of sheaths. 'You're lucky, sir,' a Bristol barber used to say, 'they're fresh in today.'

'One advantage of *being* pregnant,' says a wife in one of my television plays, 'you don't have to fret about *getting* pregnant', which was a great consolation in a difficult year. We left the vicarage and abused the hospitality of friends until our flat was ready in September. On the Gower coast near her home village, we learnt the pleasures of making love on the sands and in the sea. In London we stayed in Michael Blakemore's new flat (till he married an actress called Shirley), with Robert Bolt and his wife at Richmond and again at Michael's, where one morning a dull chest pain told me my lung was down again. Into the old Royal Free this time, a hospital a century old, built to deal with an epidemic of cholera. My notes of the time are worth comparing to those I made in my last hospital, a year before. The same clinically recorded speech and accurate account of events in ward and theatre, they are now less selfish. My parents visited. 'Dad larked outrageously in the ward, dear old man, and laughed till the tears came, a born clown overtaken by caution and respectability. I spoke hastily to Thelma and she had a cry; one has to be so careful – it's a strain for her living in someone else's home now she's four months gone. The warmth of her love for me is sometimes scaring. Can I equal it? I've certainly learnt how much I miss her by being parted from her here. A cold sort of man, I must try harder than most.'

In the crowded tube-station where she met my parents, Dad called across: 'Hullo, Stella – breasts as big as ever, I see.'

'It's a comfort', I wrote, 'to know she's waiting and that next year – if all goes well – we'll be bringing up baby.'

This time they drained my pleural cavity and blew in talcum-powder to stimulate an effusion so that my lung adhered to the chest wall. It sounds primitive but has held ever since.

Our new flat was ready that autumn. We furnished it from local sales, never paying more than £5 for any piece. My new agent Peggy Ramsay was unable to raise my fee: for my two new plays – *Ben Spray*, based on Bernie Cooper, and *The Big Boys* on my teaching at Brixton – I got £300 apiece. A bulldozer and tree-saw began destroying the field next to our flat, where earlier we'd fed on blackberries. Our landlord, a Cockney vandal, was going to cover it with bungalows.

We went on making love – though with difficulty – till one Sunday morning Thelma woke at four with labour pains and the show was on the sheets. I rang the midwife, who said she'd meet us at the Drapers' house in Brixham, where the birth was planned to happen. No ferries ran till morning and we had no car so I knocked up a neighbour, who drove us via the nearest bridge at Totnes, about an hour's journey. We all expected the baby soon. Her contractions came more often, then mysteriously slowed. They were still regular enough to keep her in bed most of the time. Doctor and midwife tranquillized her while I got stoned on Scotch and cigarettes. Sunday and Monday passed. The children, back at school, lost interest, bringing home their Christmas presents and Wise Men made from bottletops. The baby was a treat too long delayed. I remember very little and Thelma says she wanted above all to stop them dosing her with pills and oxygen, to give her a chance to achieve the natural birth she'd rehearsed. Tuesday passed and on Wednesday Peter Draper returned from London and we started going to local pubs festooned with paper-chains. Thursday went the same way and on Friday, the doctor woke from what now seems an inexplicable stupor and decided he must deliver the child with forceps. Something prevented the natural birth, he said – she had a narrow pelvic opening, perhaps the first long car-ride? I wondered: could it have been all those drugs? But by this time I was too tired to care and had begun to fear for Thelma – and of course for myself. How could I live without her now?

At the hospital they told us they would ring in two hours. After five, I rang them, by this time prepared for all manner of monsters. There'd been some mistake – the doctor was supposed to ring me but must have forgotten. It was a lovely girl, eight pounds six ounces, mother and baby both doing well. I saw her that evening – lovely was a matter of opinion. To me, she looked like all the other new arrivals in the nursery with her – bald, tiny, her only singularity the forceps scars on her jaundiced face.

We stayed there for Christmas – 'an even greater misery than usual' – and brought her home soon after. When we told our parents that her name was Abigail, they thought it sounded rather Jewish, but in the Bible, we said, she was described as 'a woman of good understanding and a beautiful countenance'. Jewish or not, my mother came to help us over the early days and gave me time to finish my new play, based on our wedding reception. The new year had started well and even Diary was looking on the bright side:

'1961 should be better for us – at least two plays will be seen, I'm up for an Arts Council bursary, we have our own home and a child to check our selfishness. We long for spring, windows open to our balcony, sandy afternoons, beery nights. Fingers crossed! No birds on the sinister side yet, no lions whelping in the streets.'

It was on a trade visit to London (the showing of *Ben Spray*, work on a film with John Boulting, rehearsals for *The Reception*) that we first noticed Abigail's fits. Michael Blakemore was playing Me in the farce about our wedding and we stayed in his Hampstead flat. One evening Abigail lay on a bed beside their baby Conrad, born at about the same time. One of us remarked that she lacked his vigour and hadn't as strong a finger-grip but we were all novice parents and could only guess why – boys were more active or maybe she had colic. Did that account for the faces she made, the eye-blinking, working her mouth and tongue, shaking her hand? None of us knew. We visited Robert Bolt and Jo at Richmond, taking Abigail in a carry-cot on the train. They were experienced parents and Bob too thought the funny turns were colic or wind. Jo wouldn't commit herself, saying parents weren't the best people to ask, one should always go to a doctor.

'Funny turns, you say?' asks the doctor in *Joe Egg*, 'how would you describe them?'

'Frightening,' says the mother.

'No, I meant: what form do they take?'

'Blinking with her eyes, working with her tongue, shaking her head, then going all limp.'

'Funny turns indeed at your age! Saucy beggar. We are not amused.'

'But what d'you think it is?'

'Wind.'

'That's what our friends said.'

'Always wise to get a second opinion.'

This play, written a long time after the events, was of course an elaborate construction, perhaps more an exercise in style and humour than a true account of the way it was. The act of writing cicatrized the scar and I have no wish to pick at it, so the best way may be to set down here what my diary recorded at the time. Because it was only an occasional book, scrappily kept at long intervals, these entries are lost among my other concerns: my career, lust for women, visits from our parents and friends, Great Events, book-lists, and above all the physical life around us – the moors, towns and coast of Devon. I do not pretend these notes contain the whole truth – in that respect the artificial play may be closer – but it was by reading them over in context that I found the theme for the fiction: that the rest of life goes on, disaster or no. During the massacre of the innocents, Breughel had a man piss against a wall. It's in the earthquake you forget to put your teeth in.

'After these fits, she would go limp. Began to react less to stimulus, was constipated, fed erratically. Doctor prescribed phenobarbitone. This soothed the fits but she looked no better.

'Soon as we got to Dartmouth, I rang our new GP. (Not the one who bungled the delivery. He was in Brixham and we never saw or heard from him again.) This one seemed to hear the symptoms calmly, which reassured us, though the fits were an ugly sight – especially on the train. She'd stopped feeding altogether and hadn't dirtied a nappie for days, neither cried nor moved, just lay still between spasms. As soon as he saw her, though, he was alarmed and arranged at once for Thelma to take her into Exeter hospital. He spoke aside to me of "danger lists" and was frank about his fears. There was no mention of an ambulance so we asked our neighbour to take us. She and Abigail have been there five days, undergoing clinical tests. So far they've ruled out meningitis and cerebral haemorrhage. Surely it was the birth? Five days? Sedatives are keeping down the spasms but nothing's been done to cure her yet, though she has started feeding and crying again. I've never been so dead with worry as I was when our kind neighbour drove us in – and me back alone. As we left the house, Thelma said, "I don't think we shall be bringing her back, do you?" but now my worry's worse – *how* shall we bring her back? With a sound brain? Is it curable? One gets saturated with anxiety then goes beyond.

'How can I start another play in this state? . . .

'Well into May: we've been to London again to see the baby at Great Ormond Street. She's incurable and won't reach adult years. Her brain's defective in several places and tomorrow they're doing a biopsy to confirm that it's not hereditary. Thelma suffers more than I – in her case, positive concern; in mine, mostly negative – we've no child after all. At nearly thirty-four I begin to want a family. If it's anything inherited, we'll adopt.'

(Odd that I didn't note the paediatrician's name: Dr Schlesinger, father of the John who had welcomed me to Nee Soon and was now a film director.)

'Halfway through June: it's dull today and we've been to Exeter to make final decisions about Abo. Consultant there can't tell us how long she'll live but suggests we let her go into a nursery, so that Thelma will be able to clear her mind and start another child, which of course we want to do at once. Until this has been arranged, she is with us – fat and strange, her dark eyes rolling, head shaking as though in a slow, persistent "no". She cries only under great strain, never smiles or reacts and cannot order her perceptions. Hard to know whether she suffers or only dwells in a stupor. Unless she improves dramatically, she's no use to herself or anyone and it's only medicine that's kept her alive this long. It's a mysterious accident, says the specialist, perhaps a virus infection, but there's no reason to think it's hereditary. I find it odd that Thelma and I have come closer together over all this. If we'd been the kind who live for children, it may have been catastrophic . . . .

'Abigail is still with us. She does nothing but is lovable. Funny to feel the bio-chemistry working and long to caress and squeeze her. Babies are so pure physically.

'Great deal to do, apart from writing: gardening, trying tennis, swimming off the beaches here, taking pictures. Thelma gives me painting lessons. We listen to two LPs on the portable player we bought the day they told us Abo couldn't be cured. So far Bach, Stravinsky and Ravel chime all through the flat. . . .

'During my parents' visit, Dad and Thelma got on well together – he likes cuddling her and making her laugh. She says he has nothing of the bum-patter, only a lonely man, keen for physical contact, a man brought up in a Puritanical home who's always craved the tactile warmth of a large family and which he finds now with children. He was so moved to see that at first glance Abo is a normal and healthy child that he went off to the bathroom to cry. He told Mum secretly he'd gladly give his life to make her well. . . .

'Abigail's improvement slow. She makes experimental sounds now and tries to raise herself. A physiotherapist came yesterday, pushed her about for an hour or so and showed us how to exercise and relax her rigid shoulder-girdle. Promised to see her again in a couple of months, which might mean she can see hope and after all it's she who's helped the boy who lives nearby and was like Abo a year ago. I wish we could start another. They say the trick is to stop trying. I know the poor baby's sickness has affected Thelma more than she showed at the time. You must control these feelings but my mental paralysis of the moment may be due to anxiety I repressed earlier.

'Now that ATV have bought *The Mouse Race*, my comedy about small-town life, we're faced with a local embarrassment. One of the characters is based on Christopher Robin Milne, our closest neighbour – or rather (since we've never met) on the *idea* of being a public child. I've bought books from his shop, of course, and seen him autographing copies of *Pooh* but we've not spoken. Now it so happens that he and his wife Lesley also have a handicapped child, as do the Vickers just up the hill, whence we're all invited to dinner on Thursday – a chance to see what sort of man Milne is and whether I should tell him about the play or make some changes in it . . . .

'A dull evening it turned out. The Vickers are a bit too good to be true, which I guessed when I heard they'd been telling Thelma that life's impossible without faith and other lies of that sort. They are Good People, though, and he left after dinner to drive handicapped people home from some cultural event. We've entered a world where everyone is crippled in some way but bearing up bravely. In fact, we hear from the doctor that Mrs Vickers took the news of her child less well than Thelma. The Milnes seemed constrained by the almost accursed gathering. That three couples with damaged children should be living cheek by jowl!'

(No more mention of the Milnes but we grew to like them and to realize that their girl was only slightly damaged compared to Abo. He was showing me his runner beans and raspberries when I plucked up courage to mention the character I'd based on him. He laughed excitedly. 'You rotter!' he said but didn't otherwise object. The play was finally shown as *The Heart of the Country*, the most ambitious so far, ruined by its performance.)

'To Bristol by train. Took Abigail, of course, nursing her in our arms. Other passengers showed usual enthusiasm for a baby (aaah!) but this cooled rather when she didn't respond. This kind of thing's more awkward for them than us. We wonder whether to say "She's epileptic" straight away but would that be even worse? Or showing off? . . .

'Pretty grim seeing Abigail beside Tom, my brother's son. His noise and energy upset her and we had to step up the anti-convulsant drugs to control her fits. Tom would stand by her cot and scream and she'd be off, her right eye and that corner of her mouth twisting and clenching, winking and dribbling, while she made weird snorting sounds and her head turned slowly on her neck. . . .

'Back in Dartmouth, the first fancy-dress ball of Christmas was all we had feared. Left the house in a fine drizzle, dressed and made up as clowns, pushing Abo in a folding pram. The bus-queue outside Woolworths so intent on their own misery no one gave us a glance. At the

Bamboozle Bar, met by Nigger Minstrel and by Don and Megan Sutton, half-naked savages or troglodytes. Her déshabillé shocked the local bigotry but made dancing with her all the more enjoyable. When we staggered from the floor, her face and hair were covered with my lipstick. More drink afterwards at their place then had to push baby up the hill. I seem to remember leaning on the pram and lurching forward. . . .

'My parents had sent some coloured plastic bricks and one day I was with her in what used to be the billiard-room where I now write each day. I piled four bricks on a rug near her head and went to my desk. A sound made me turn and I saw she'd pushed them over so I built the tower again and this time watched. First her eyes, roving aimlessly, glanced once or twice in passing at this brightly coloured object a foot away, then her arm began to show signs of intention and her fist to clench and spread with effort. The other arm, stiff and bent at shoulder level, stayed where it was. She was using, for the first time, one arm instead of both as a result of what she'd seen. Not only had she seen it but intended altering it! So the bent arm began to twitch along the arc of her reach towards the four piled bricks. Her legs, always active and busy, kicked and circled in sympathy and she sighed and grunted with the struggle. It took some minutes' hard labour to reach the bricks with her fingers and push till the pile collapsed. Several times the hand actually or almost touched them before being jerked away by spasm and she cried with rage – yet settled for another try. Amazing her determination to see it through despite the risk of bringing on another *grand mal*, signalled by the blue irises moving down to the left and one arm making a grand rhetorical gesture as though to exhort a crowd. . . .

'The demolition games joined the evening rituals. We've been trying to coax some reaction from her and the bricks were our first sure-fire success. We built towers at every point within the radius of her reach, even sometimes beyond, which made her stretch and strain till we relented and moved them closer. It's too slow for visitors – they haven't the patience to watch long enough to see whether there's truth in our story. We can see them trying to be kind. Anyway their voices distract her and she never does well with an audience. It's bloody little to wait for but it's all we've got. Not infallible either. Often the struggle wearies her and she falls asleep or is more interested in the firelight or the new tooth she's cutting that won't ever be used because she cannot chew. . . .

'Christmas brought more plastic toys. Today she pushed a lorry off the table. She still can't sit up but has to be strapped in her chair. When she falls forward she often bumps her nose on the tray, then protests mildly till one of us props her back, one arm hanging, face lop-sided on her fat trunk. This makes her sound ugly but she's a far prettier baby than most we see – fair hair, sunburnt skin, blue eyes, well-formed body. In fact, sound as a bell. . . .

'While I was in London, an educational psychologist came to test Abo's intelligence (*sic*) but she was in a stupor and he grumbled at the wasted visit. Very tactful. Thelma was so depressed when I rang that it occurred to me we should save her spirit by putting Abigail away. People in London were dimly aware and Toby Rowland offered to get her a place in the Actors' Orphanage. Not sure he realizes how bad she is! Gloomy day, though somehow when I got home nothing seemed so bad. She's no trouble really and never answers back. Tragedies are worse when you're away or they're someone else's. We have our own flood, famine, plague, martyrdom and charity lying on the rug but I seldom see it in that light down here. In London for a day it was abstract, like the air-crashes and far-off wars we agonize over on TV. . . .

'You don't expect cosmic events in the diary of a nobody but today, while trying to breathe life into some coals in the grate, I listened to the broadcasts of John Glenn's orbital flight. Tried to explain it all to Abo as she lay there pushing her tower down, but coronations and royal weddings are more up her street. In this steep valley our reception's none too good and we get a macabre overtone of flamenco music while Glenn's saying, "Everything's go up here and – boy! – that's Australia one more time, roger and out." Felt relativity as reality when he talked about flying into Tuesday night again from Wednesday morning. Had to blow on the fire several times before it burnt . . . felt closer to the Ice Age than the twentieth century.

'Spurred by Glenn's example, I passed my driving test. We now go off in our mini-van for a breath of moorland air, exploring the deep lanes closed to bus or too far off to trundle Abo. She lies in her carry-cot in the back, saying "ah" the whole time – but we read a lot into it. . . .

'The doctor has confirmed that Thelma's pregnant. . . .

'In London I heard that no one liked *Continuity Man*, the stage-play about my father. Too mild, everyone said. Peggy Ramsay told me: "Your trouble, Peter, is you're not wicked enough. There's not enough vice in you. That's why your lung collapses all the time. There's plenty of wickedness in me – and vulgarity. I don't care!" She pours out her advice in such a torrent you can't be heard without shouting so I said nothing. That there's truth in her comments is all the more upsetting – but how do you start being wicked all of a sudden? Buy the *Illustrated Home Abortionist*? Or is Abo a more pathetic victim? Perhaps go after other women or get drunk? I drink and flirt averagely. I was averagely ungrateful to my parents. I'm not generous and was till a year ago selfish and ambitious. When I lost my ambition I began to grow up. Probably it was only Peggy's way of saying the play stank. . . .

'Tall Ships Week. For five days a thousand sailors, cadets and officers brought the local girls a taste of the pleasures of war. Every lane was full of fumbling couples and, pushing Abo about, we were often nearly bowled over by pelting girls, delirious not to miss a minute. Thelma wanted to dance with someone off the *Amerigo Vespucci*. The first to ask was Scottish. The second was a midget who, despite her evident pregnancy, was all hands. . . .

'Left Dartmouth and returned to Bristol two weeks ago. So far, mixed feelings. . . .

'Thelma's nearing her time again and the doctors have decided, in view of her history, not to risk a home confinement. This upset her, for she doesn't, as she puts it, Believe In Doctors. No wonder. But I'm glad – despite *accouchement sans douleur* and shallow breathing and all the rituals of natural delivery. *She's* more important than some principle. Abigail's going into hospital for a month to give us a good start with the new one. She's no better. Her progress in Devon was checked by a relapse and she's never recovered. Dr Grace Wood, whom we thought of for weeks as Grace Moore in the hope she'd *sing* her diagnoses, said she'll never amount to much. When she's got another baby, Thelma may accept this. I have already – nearly two years old now, she can do nothing more than swallow food we place on her tongue and say "ah"; she's smiled occasionally but still can't focus her eyes and, though neither blind nor deaf, can't order her sensations as well as a bird or cat. So why keep her alive? Easy to cope with her now but what if she lives to be twenty, like some we've seen? As usual, I dare say the people with moral objections to killing them don't have to give it another thought after they've said what they believe. Why do they value damaged lives so highly and shrug off eight thousand a year killed in road accidents? Some such reflection jutted through the thin flesh of fiction in my last play (*The End Beds*) but I funked a clear stand so it finished like my others – what a friend called "Knocking on doors and running away". . . .

'Took Abigail to the Spastics Centre, where they'll look after her every day, once she's out of hospital. It's run by charity and football pools and seems at first glance a cheery place. One teen-age girl sang snatches of old songs and new – hymns, rock 'n' roll, anthems, ballads, but incompletely, the women attendants rounding them off for her. That's all she can do – she has this isolated aptitude, nothing else. A boy crippled by meningitis lay groaning and would not be touched. Thelma saw two men in their twenties in a separate room, sitting in bed making Christmas decorations. The supervisors hoped to take Abo that morning and were sorry when we said this was only a visit. One of the women spoke frankly – "She'll get *spoilt* here" – (*sic*) "she's so bonny. Well, it's not so good when they get the withered limbs." This place was comforting though, with the air of a birthday party where the kids have got at the whisky.

'Hortham Hospital was different, approached through the green belt to the east, where Friesian herds still graze in parks before ornamental lakes, though the great manors with Palladian fronts now house only the officially mad. Purdown, Glenside, Manor Park, Meadowsweet, Stoke Park, where troupes of mongols haunted my boyhood. Hortham, on the other hand, has the look of a transit camp. If only it were! For most of the inmates, it's journey's end. As we entered the room Abo would be lodged in, an adult idiot was hitting a spastic who wouldn't eat. Some others sat or lay about – a boy with a head so large he could not lift it from the pillow, with the usual human features disposed at random about his vast face; a girl twisted into a crouch, quite still, as though intent on catching an invisible frog; another spent her life banging her head against the frame of her cot. Beyond them a bright celebrity jabbered on a screen.

'Later in the week we visited and took her for a walk in the pram. She'd had more fits than usual and was suffering from the change. In the grounds we learnt to tell patients from staff – they were the ones who waved. One stood facing a wall, dead still. God knows how long he'd been there. Another solitary was playing cowboys, peering from behind a shelter, raising his fist like a gun and – instead of making an explosion – roaring like a lion. One suddenly emerged, playing with his cock.

'Thelma wept in the van going back and wished we'd left her in the Spastics Centre. In a village a boy ran from behind a bus and I nearly killed him. Women gossiping didn't turn their heads as my brakes squealed. The whole region smells of death. . . .

'We've been following the trial of Mrs Van de Put in Belgium, who killed her thalidomide son. When she was first shown the deformed boy four days after his birth, she said "Kill him." They assured her the problem would be easily solved by putting him in a home. "*My* problem," she said, "but not my baby's." No one should express an opinion until they've been to Hortham. At the Centre, one of the women was indignant that some parents never visit their children, but I find it easy to understand. In the natural way, Abo would have died at birth, perhaps killing Thelma. Nothing's easy. We must be guided by kindness. Who's the least kind – Mrs Van de Put or those who never visit? . . .

'The verdict was: not guilty. A bewildered jury feared that any other would have put her in jail. She admitted killing the child and the right verdict was guilty of murder but they were right to acquit her. And what does such a precedent do for Law? We should have the courage to change laws that are cruel. . . .

'I've just read back the entry that describes Abo's birth but I failed to convey how terrible that week was. Five days! Perhaps luckily I had no idea how bad a birth and how mismanaged! Thelma's now in hospital. Monday night I visited her, Tuesday morning went to school – my brother's, where I've started teaching. Phoned midday and labour hadn't started. Walked Clifton, thinking of plots and plays, looking at girls. Nothing's so important I lose interest in women's bodies. A cold, sunless November day, the thirteenth. Good job I'm not superstitious! Went in later and was stopped by a nurse in the corridor.

' "She's in the labour room –"

' "Not still?"

' "She won't be long. A little girl."

'Thelma told me it hadn't been easy but she'd controlled the labour with her breathing and relaxing so the nurses didn't realize and other women in the ward had to tell Sister she was near. She'd refused to take gas or air but swallowed a tranquillizer. Another sister, beside her when she was being wheeled from ward to labour room, said "Put your knees down."

' "I'm in pain," said Thelma, "this helps."

' "Put them down. It looks bad." And she forced them down. The stuff of which camp commandants are made!'

Louise spent her first year or so with an elder sister who couldn't play. They were joined in time by a brother and then we needed no persuasion to let Abo go into hospital for good. Another girl came quickly and after that we took more care. For me, except for rare visits, the episode was closed, though while it lasted everyone was kind – or tried to be. Early on many tried to assure us we should feel no personal reproach. Garry's mother, Lenore, told Thelma so at a party.

'Please allow me to TELL you something. I know you're not in motion PICTURES nor even in THEATRE but you may know who I mean when I mention the FINE ACTOR Spencer TRACY. Very Butch man, like a ROCK. HE had a child like yours. And that fine and ELEGANT actor Walter Abel ALSO had a child like yours. MANY OTHERS I could mention – only their names escape me NOW – all proving you and PETER have NOTHING of which to be ASHAMED!'

Talking it over with Bob Bolt later, I said: 'As far as playwriting goes, this kind of accident's useless. There's nothing to be done with it.'

10 We Go to the Ball

In the early and middle 1960s, several unknown writers and directors happened to be living in Bristol – Charles Wood, Tom Stoppard, John Hale, John Boorman – and journalists later tried to suggest we had formed a group. In fact, as with the Chelsea Set, if there was one, we never knew where it went for a drink. Charles and Tom were on the *Evening Post*, Charles laying out classified adverts, Tom reporting on funerals and gymkhanas; Hale had directed the Bristol Old Vic and was now writing. Boorman was making quasi-documentaries at the BBC and I was teaching. I was also the only native, though Charles had married the third member of Thelma's schoolgirl trio – the actress Valerie Newman. They lived near us in a rented flat with their son and daughter. Charles's early television plays had dazzled and depressed me. Wherever I went, there seemed to be talents finer than my own. Much later, in two popular TV series, he depicted me as an elegant star writer, handsome, courteous and sated with success. A sample of his cruel humour. In fact my best play *The End Beds* had been turned down by every script editor in Britain, including those at the BBC, who at once offered to buy the rights when it reappeared as *The National Health*. The stage-play, *Continuity Man*, rejected for the live theatre, was bought by the BBC, and became the first of six happy partnerships with Christopher Morahan. In this one 'Thelma' was played by Susan Maryott, whom I found – with a feeling not unlike vertigo – to be John Schlesinger's sister, a fine actress giving a radiant performance, among her last, for she killed herself some weeks later, unable to face life without the playwright John Whiting, who had died of cancer.

Roger Livesey had a good shot at Richard the First and Foremost. 'When you see Mister Livesey,' Dad told me the morning after it was shown, 'be sure to convey my congratulations but also tell him he missed out one or two of the Olde Man's most characteristic actions. For example, when I do the charring for Cork-tipped Katey, I usually run the vacuum along the inside of my trouser turn-ups. Gets rid of any scurf, debris, nail-parings, orange-peel or general gubbins.'

Livesey was one of three actors – all of whom had played Dad – I'd one day notice sitting together at a canteen table. *The Hooded Terror* was a modish thriller set in Dartmouth, again directed by Morahan, and I wrongly felt the plot was strong enough to bear stretching to a full-length stage-play, which was put on in a token season of local plays at the Old Vic's second house. I had a small reputation by now, not large enough to earn me a decent living though, and by 1965 we were deep in debt to Charles and my agent. His star was shooting out of sight. He'd bought a mini-*car* – not a van like ours but a car with seats *in the back* – and kept it, as in the regular army he'd kept his bedspace, immaculate. Afraid for its safety in the city where he worked, he left it every day outside our house, so that we could keep an eye on it, for despite our debts, we qualified for a council mortgage and had a terrace house. Each morning he rang our bell to alert us and every evening to dismiss the guard and to tell us his latest news – of his play running in London, 'Orson Welles was in last night, love – loved it!'; of the many others that poured from his study in a torrent – 'Osborne's doing it at the Court, oh and Tynan wants the Mutiny one for the National, and I told you Codron's optioned the latest'; finally of his films – 'They're cheering us in Cannes, love – we're getting the big prize.'

My journal is raw with the open sores of envy, a new vexation for now that I had clambered up a few steps I saw how far there was to go. I'd started on the snakes-and-ladders game that's given me far more pain than pleasure over the years and no one has goaded and hurt me more than Wood and Stoppard. Tom, of course, was always A Star – even walking up Blackboy Hill, before he'd been canonized by critics, public and New Year's Honours' List.

An unlikely godmother, John Boorman – knowing of my debts and despair – asked me to write his first feature. The producer, David Deutsch, had given him the chance to make a film exploiting the current success of the group who'd replaced the Beatles at Number One – the Dave Clark Five. None of us had ever heard them so I bought one of their best-known singles and listened to most of one side, then most of the other.

'Sorry, John, I don't believe I can, though Christ knows we need the money.'

'Listen, Peter,' he said in the boyish Cockney voice we found so disarming (and still do, even in the mansion he owns in Co. Wicklow), 'this is your chance to earn enough to clear your debts and gain the time to write that bloody stage-play.'

'And what will *you* get out of it?'

'A Hollywood contract.'

I knew he was right but he and Deutsch still had to twist my arm. The three of us went to Cockfosters – melodies of Mahler and tweet of budgerigar! – to meet the star in the posh house he'd bought his mother. He showed us round, we admired his Golden Disc and watched a craftsman thatching the roof of the cocktail-bar. He outlined the film he had always wanted to make about smugglers – with a leading part for his dog and a lot of 'way-out photography'. Afterwards I told John I was the wrong man for the job.

'Listen, don't pay any attention to what he wants. I'm the director. You and I are going to make the film *we* want to make.'

David Deutsch had doubts about me and came to a showing of my latest television play *When the Wind Blows*, a domestic quartet describing a visit Thelma and I might have made to Palatine Lodge, very well played by Eileen Atkins, Alison Leggatt, Alec McCowen and Ralph Michael. David was usually a buoyant shouter but this sobered him.

'Yes, interesting,' he said, grim-faced and *sotto voce*, 'though let me beg you to remember that our film will be aimed at the American bobby-soxer petting in a drive-in theatre in Kansas.'

He and I were of one mind – this was not a job for me – and I expected to be told next day that they'd found someone more suitable. But John won through – and our need for cash. We wrote the script from scratch in a month, a pretentious odyssey about middle-aged entrepreneurs exploiting young talent, crammed with irony, philosophic overtones and three-syllable words. David protested that our stars weren't actors and couldn't manage such dialogue, so Michael Blakemore was engaged to coach them. Only a few lines of mine survived to the finished film, which had a mixed reception, much admired by Brian Forbes and thought by its star to be ahead of its time.

In the race Charles had entered me for, I had put on some speed and could just see him, still streaking away but not out of sight. He'd given up his old job and had more writing work than hours of the day. While I was on the film script, he rang me with a list of his latest credits.

'Oh and by the way, love, I'm doing a pop film too.'

'Are you?'

'Yes. Film for a pop group.'

'Which one?' I asked, though I'd guessed already.

'The Beatles.' And there was a chuckle in his voice.

'That's nice.'

Working on *Catch Us If You Can* was important for me in several ways, mostly personal, though it confirmed my intuition – that narrative film can be a supremely exciting dramatic form, provided writer and director work as one and know where they're going and aren't put off the track by hucksters and wholesalers. It is only when one complements the other that enduring successes are made – *Citizen Kane*, *Some Like It Hot*, *The Maltese Falcon*, *The Third Man*, *Woman of the Year* and *Great Expectations*. Cinema's inherent handicap is Money; theatre's advantage has been that it was cheap – 'was' and 'has been' because now it's become a suburb of cinema and is cheap no longer. Cinema has raped theatre and passed on the money taint like a dose of clap. The promise of movie rights, and TV, video and cable subsidiaries, means that soon no one will put on plays for love and money-lenders will take the temple, as they have in New York. John made this film entirely on location, starting in London and finishing off the coast of Devon. We had set the action in places we liked – Salisbury Plain, Bath, the Mendips, Bigbury-on-Sea.

I saw very little of the London shooting as for two weeks I was on my back with 'flu in the Blakemores' flat. Now that they'd had my lung, Abo's fits and my 'flu, they surely felt they were running a Nichols family clinic. As soon as I could walk, I preceded the unit to Bristol and the rest stayed in Bath. One night Michael came over to catch his old friend Albert Finney in the National Theatre week at the Bristol Hippodrome. My mother was baby-sitting for us so I went to collect her at Palatine. Dad told me he didn't envy me, he couldn't hear in theatres any more.

'It's not so much that I can't hear, Bert, Robb, Geoffrey – whosit? – Peter! Yes, it's more that they gabble. D'you remember *Hedda Gabler* at the Bristol Old Vic? Very well named, I thought. When I was young, actors spoke clearly. You've possibly noticed that when enjoying the Story of the Silvertown Explosion? Or Jeremiah in the Turkish Bath?'

Then that pose like Kean with the dagger – 'Finish me awff? I'm darned near finished awff already!'

'Yes, all right, I've heard it. Are you fit to go now, Mum?'

'Nearly.'

'Capstan Connie's making sure she's got her packet of fags. Beyond my comprehension why – for the sake of a gasper – anyone should go out of their way to shorten the natural span granted to them by the kindly fates above, Boy! Who said that? I'll give 'im a kick in the pants – boom!'

'For goodness' sake leave off a minute, Dick, I can't hear myself think.'

He came with us into the street. 'Very good of Old Mother Hubbard to go and look after your nippers –'

'I need a change, I must say, from you going on morning, noon and night.'

'Frankly, Buzfuz, I prefer to sit here quietly and listen to Brahms or Mozart.'

217

'Quietly?'

'Hold your tongue, Vi. You're not offended, Peter?'

'Not at all.'

'Doesn't make the slightest difference if you are! I don't give tuppence. I won't creep. Unlike Friend Graves of Electrical Goods taking the oaths of allegiance to the jolly old Masonic Guild. Put your feet in properly, Vi, and I'll shut the door. Now, if I were you, son, as you're facing this way, I should go down York Avenue, turn right at the bottom, right again up Station Road and back to the main road that way. Or you could do a three-point turn here....'

But I had already driven off. In the near-side wing-mirror I watched him picking up something from the gutter by Palatine's front gate.

The Hippodrome was packed for Finney and Maggie Smith and Robert Stephens in *Much Ado*. With Blakemore, we went backstage and met Albert and Bob in their room. I picked up Mum and drove her home, dropping her opposite.

'Are you coming in for a cup of something?'

'Better not. Thelma's making coffee. Thanks for sitting.'

Michael was worried that he'd left the unit early and someone might have needed him to give Dave Clark an inflection. He was – and is – compulsively concerned about dropping bricks and has a way of going absent while someone is speaking, fretting away inside at some black eye or old slight. The only way to hold his attention at such times is to spice your talk with sex.

I'd hardly got back when Mum rang to say Dad hadn't heard the doorbell and she'd had to let herself in with her key, gone through the house calling him, right out to the back where the milk had boiled over and finally found him lying on the greenhouse floor. He'd collapsed and was unconscious. She'd called the doctor and he was on his way.

Lying there by the step in the light spilling from the dining-room, he looked more solemn than when he slept and that at once convinced me he was dead. Waiting for the doctor, I noticed that the grandiose radiogram (converted to long-playing by a Proper Man) was still warm and humming, the tone-arm resting at the end of a Mozart symphony. Mum made the drink I'd earlier refused. I listened to Dad's chest and tried to feel a pulse and the doctor borrowed a mirror to make sure and finally said, 'I'm afraid he's gone.' He later spoke very properly of a good innings and a good way to go and we all said far the best and better than hanging on for weeks.

'Funny thing,' says Amy in *Forget-me-not Lane*, 'a few days earlier he'd asked for a drop of Scotch where before he wouldn't even eat a trifle if he detected sherry.'

We 'made him comfortable' and I rang Thelma. She said later that she went to tell Michael.

'Peter's father's dead.'

Michael stared at her intently.

'Listen, Thelma, I'm afraid I may have put up a black with David Deutsch. Would it be all right if I rang the location office to apologize?'

After he'd phoned, she and Michael walked the few hundred yards to my brother's house. A teacher's not being on the phone was nothing unusual at the time, though even Blakemore jibbed when I made the climax of *Joe Egg* depend on it. He and Thelma had to knock some time before Geoffrey appeared in pyjamas, shamefaced, saying they'd certainly picked their moment. They told him the news, he nodded, said he'd better get over to Palatine and went to dress. Mary came down, decently upset but rather more embarrassed to be found doing *that* at such a moment. Death always brings appropriate images and this one prompted the first scene of *Hearts and Flowers*, a later television play that told the story of Dad's funeral. I'd got stuck on the father's death in *Forget-me-not Lane* and wrote the other to clear my block.

During the few days before the funeral, while Dad lay in state in the front room like some saint or tyrant, a crowd of us cleared the house. Mum never slept there again. She'd hated the place for years and could hardly wait to go. With her widowed friend, Mrs Graves, Cliff's aunt, an antiseptic woman described in *Joe Egg* as a walking sheath, she purged downstairs while Geoff and I did the attics. We day-dreamt our way through the old man's rubbish and some relics of our own childhood – magic, music, photography, early passions – and failed to notice at the time that Cliff's aunt was picking clean his papers like a vulture at the burning ghat. Only later I came to see that nothing was left – no cards or letters, no Silvertown Explosion, no diatribes against the Masons, not even a sheet of his old notepaper, 'Humorous Entertainer and Monologues', with its wide margin of quotes from his notices in the *Grocer* and *Walthamstow Gazette*: 'If laughing ensures growing fat, each of the audience must bulk considerably as a result of Mr Nichols's sketches of London low-life.'

The debris in the attic was source material for Magritte – a paper-bag of solidified cement, some cast-off teeth, a huge parcel that contained only an unused suitcase, and a window-display for Fixolene – a 1930s man with patent-leather hair and an arm brushing it that swung to and fro by electro-magnet. Our Draconian policy – scrap what had no value – sometimes faltered as one would say 'Perhaps we could keep this box of golf-balls?' and then the other would have to ask 'Falling beneath the spell?'

In his last years he'd taken to lifting rubbish off other people's dustbins, buying any bargain, however useless – a quantity of combs, a dozen boaters ('Cheaper by the dozen, boy' – 'Only if you *want* a dozen') and, above all, long-playing records. He'd sneak them in under his coat, knowing by 'The Rustle of Spring' that Vi was busy with a pupil, and slip them into the pile. Sharing his Puritanical temper, I know that when he played those later he'd have the extra pleasure of deception, as braver men might savour adultery or secret drinking. His wardrobe too was crammed with dead men's clothes – Brother Bert's suits, Monty Graves's jackets, odd galoshes and golfing caps from Co-op colleagues, daps (Bristol for plimsolls) from neighbours, and from Vi's Canadian relatives several Florida beach shirts and a bundle of garish ties, all of which had been worn by Dad in bizarre combinations but were now cast off for the last time in Mrs Graves's purification of the house.

After a few days, it was done. What we hadn't thrown out or claimed was left to the funeral guests. Bert and Hattie came from London, as they had for his wedding. Where once had stood the only car in the avenue, students crammed the kerb with theirs and a colleague in Domestic Appliances had thoughtfully warned the police to keep clear a space for the cortège. The hearse preceded the family limousine into Ashley Down Road but before we could join it, a red open sports-car roared into second place. The middle-aged trendy at the wheel saw too late what he'd done but now had to cruise along, part of our train, till the way was clear for him to escape. I dared not meet my brother's eye, as we sat with our mother, aunt, uncle and cousin looking ahead at the Big Cheese's coffin. An early heatwave had begun and we sweated in our suits. From the pouch in Bert's pocket came the smell of tobacco. Down Ashley Hill, along Sussex Place, right past the Metropole-de-luxe and on towards City Road we went in the silent Daimler.

'Lot of coloureds along here, Vi,' said Bert at last.

'Oh, it's gone down terribly, St Paul's.'

'And Violet –'

'What, Hats?'

'Isn't that the church you were married in?'

'That's right. He never let us forget, did he, boys?'

Geoffrey and I told each other afterwards that we'd both been trying to resist the same mental image – of the coffin-lid opening and Dad sitting up and raising his tit-fer.

'Always pay your respects to those who've entered the jolly old vale of tears, boy.'

There was a long, slow drive to the crematorium, a perfunctory service and then a quick return journey, the limo rolling as it cornered. I saw one of the Co-op undertakers check a list, cross us off and fold it to the next. Back at Palatine, we gave the guests a cold buffet but Hats wouldn't take any ginger cake in case it didn't agree. After they'd caught their train, Thelma and I collected the flowers and drove them in our van to Hortham where the nurses welcomed them to brighten Abo's ward. Driving to pick up the other children from the Woods' house where they'd been all day, we used a stretch of motorway and there, overtaking a truck, I suddenly felt the motor fail and realized we were out of petrol. By now sweltering in suit and woollen dress with fur, we hitched to a garage in the cab of a long-distance truck. The driver was amazed at our attire, but we funked explaining – the dead father, the spastic daughter, the flowers....

There was a postscript. In moments when he played Lear rather than the Fool, Dad had threatened to cut us from his will. He was forever changing it. Vi and Cliff's aunt, going through his effects like a dose of roughage, had not come across it. Some days later we found it hanging in an old school satchel in the cupboard under the stairs. After the house and contents had gone to Mum, he divided the rest of his estate between Geoffrey and me. In fact, there was nothing left but a few debts, which I settled out of my film earnings. I could imagine the last laugh.

'Ever been had, Buzfuz?'

With the money from the film I wrote the first version of a play about Abigail. I remember it as savage, sentimental and overdone. The parents were based on us but reduced to bitter stereotypes. Peggy Ramsay was shocked to learn how bad our daughter was but said she couldn't ask anyone to stage such a play. I drew up a list of producers who might think otherwise – Michael Codron, Tony Garnett, Ken Tynan (now with Olivier at the National), James Roose-Evans at Hampstead, Brian Forbes (well, he'd liked the film!).

'Really, darling, I can't waste these people's time with something so personal. They're terribly busy.'

Still she tried one or two. Roose-Evans wrote: 'But oh dear! When will these young authors learn to *construct*?' – and by now I was nearly forty. Privately I sought opinions from Chris Morahan (C-minus) and John Hale (the most helpful, though worried by its uniform black). The BBC declined it and the RSC mislaid it. The Royal Court offered me one night without scenery. I lost heart and re-drew the list to include the fringe and provincial rep. Thelma had had our third daughter, Catherine, and I was doing hack-work to keep them all – some weeks on a film called *Georgy Girl*, adaptations of Waugh and Fitzgerald stories for television – but something told me the play *A Day in the Death of Joe Egg* was not as bad as all that.

Michael Blakemore was now at Glasgow Citizens' Theatre, playing leads and sharing direction. He asked if I would let him do it there and, lacking a better offer, I said he could try. He warned me he may not be able to push it through the board, a group of local traders with cultural pretensions, but would do what he could. He convinced an adventurous businessman that here was a play to repair the Citizens' tarnished reputation and asked me up to Glasgow to work on a new draft. The city that had spurned my Dracula was getting another chance. It is now of no more than academic interest how the play changed through its various drafts – not even that, in fact, as my stuff has never been a university favourite, perhaps because it lacks the crossword-puzzle element – those ambiguous clues, arcane quotes and deliberately misleading allusions that are meat and drink to the scholarly mind. 'I am thinking of doing another version fast,' says Diary in September 1966, 'in a couple of weeks, say, opening it out entirely, having the actors speak to the audience and discuss their characters with each other. The subject needs ventilation more than hypnosis and I think my fundamental mistake was in trying to bully the audience into a spooky mood of sick comedy when they should retain their judgement and look at it from all sides. Exciting thought that, if the actors step out of character, the girl playing Joe could do so too. What would she have to say about imitating a spastic? How would it seem after she had gone *back into* character?'

This was the thought that cracked the problem for me, gave me the right distance, though many of the friends I tried it on said it was a bad idea. Chris Morahan, John Hale and Michael himself encouraged me to try. 'A looser, freer structure', wrote Mike, 'is promised so explicitly in the first scene that I think it a pity not to make the most of it later on.'

'But most people', continued Diary, 'don't even think it's worth working on. When I tell them I think my best writing's in it, they look stunned.'

By early 1967, I had a new draft ready – but this was still a year before the abolition of stage censorship. The Lord Chamberlain's Office had to license all material for professional production and sent Michael a list of required changes.

Page 3: vicious sod . . .

Page 4: your legs thrashing about . . .

Page 5: my tongue halfway down your throat . . .

Page 6: wondering if we could get our guinea-pig fitted with a coil . . .

And so on. Every playwright from this period had a similar inventory. I resented the interference but didn't see it as a serious obstacle until they baulked at the presentation of the spastic child. We applied for an interview and, one day, after taking our leads Joe Melia and Zena Walker to lunch in Soho, we caught a cab to St James's Palace, where we met the Assistant Comptroller of the Queen's Household and his assistant, a wing-commander. A guardsman in a bearskin tramped up and down outside. Michael, the only child of an eminent Sydney oculist and a woman who had since married a soap peer, had none of my hostility to the upper-middle class and asked me to let him speak for us both. One glimpse of the grace-and-favour houses made my non-commissioned hackles rise and I was back on the troopship with the condescending ritual of Christmas dinner served by second-lieutenants with drawling voices. The atmosphere was friendly, almost apologetic, with Nelson cigarettes on offer and tea promised soon. Michael praised the buildings. 'Aren't they agreeable?' said the Comptroller. 'As you know, the gateway is the only survival from Henry VIII's original palace which was built on the site of a mediaeval leper hospital. Many of your colleagues think it a very appropriate place to house the official censor.'

We all laughed.

'As you know,' said the wing-commander, 'it's not a job we particularly enjoy. Indeed, we support those among you who advocate its abolition. However, until that happy day, we are duty-bound to protect people from gratuitous unpleasantness.'

Which brought us to my play. For some time we fumigated the early scenes, horse-trading a 'sod off' here for a 'piss yourself' there, while prim women brought tea on a trolley, even providing the slice of lemon Michael preferred to milk.

'Now,' said the Comptroller at one point, 'how do we feel about "has he flashed it lately"? Ah, thank you, ladies. . . .'

It's an easy step from prude to philistine and they took it in their stride. To protect the feelings of spastics' parents and spastics themselves, they would prefer that the handicapped daughter should not be seen. Michael explained that I was myself such a parent or could not have written the play, and that, if the child was kept offstage, we should be back in Victorian melodrama, with something nasty locked up in the west wing, when our aim was to present the case as part of the everyday life of those who live it. This they understood, quite so, point taken. In that case, they would suggest the child be played not by an actress but a dummy. Till that I had been buttoning my lip but now my mouth fell open. A sort of life-size doll, they went on. Perhaps it might be workable – a marionette or puppet – or one of those things ventriloquists use. Archie Andrews sort of thing. Michael soon showed how this would be a crueller joke than any in the play and the principle of a visible actress was at last conceded *but* that now raised the matter of what a ten-year-old girl could be allowed to hear. For instance, the scene where the father suggested to the mother that they go to bed could not be done in the child's presence.

I pointed out that she was so mentally handicapped that she would not follow anything anyone said.

'The character, yes,' said the Comptroller, 'but not the child actress. The audience will know she's not really handicapped.'

'But she won't be a child either. She'll be at least fourteen,' said Michael, 'that's the youngest age the GLC allows.'

'But the audience won't know that.'

'Even though they'll know she's not a spastic?' I asked.

'We could not license a scene in which an ostensible child apparently heard one adult proposing sex to another.'

'I wonder would it be possible', suggested the wing-co., 'for the child to be pushed off in her wheelchair just before this conversation and brought back on again afterwards?'

'But', said Michael, 'she'd be sitting in the wings behind a canvas flat. She'd hear every word.'

'Yes, but she wouldn't be *seen* to!'

This solution to their moral dilemma became a condition of the licence and was written in. I added stage directions and Michael staged it that way in Glasgow and, I believe, London. The first published edition of the script included it and companies across the world have done that business ever since without knowing why.

Something was still troubling the Comptroller.

'This scene when they're describing the baby's birth,' he said. 'And the father uses the words "Down, Rover!"'

We waited. 'Yes?'

'Is it accompanied by a gesture?'

'Gesture?'

'Yes. An obscene gesture. We couldn't allow that.'

'I'm sorry,' said Michael, 'I'm not with you.'

'Would there be a gesture showing that he's discouraging a tumescent penis?'

'There seems to be some misunderstanding,' I said, 'the words refer to the mother's shallow breathing in natural childbirth sounding like the panting of a dog. Down, Rover – you see? Not perhaps a very brilliant joke but nothing to do with –'

'Ah! I *do* beg your pardon! Forget I spoke.'

'Working here', said his friend, 'gives you a dirty mind. We read filth into anything.'

'Well,' said the censor, 'we *have* to. One theatre in London, if they send in a script saying "She walks across the stage", we have to ask if she's got any clothes on!'

Again we all roared. I was given another Nelson.

There was no other business. We all relaxed and they told us their favourite show was *Salad Days* and why weren't there more like that?

Back in Bristol, I signed a contract full of wild contingencies – a West End transfer, a feature film and 'a presentation in a first-class theatre in the evening bill on Broadway in the city of New York'. I was busy with two more television plays and Thelma had some obstetric disorder caused by her last delivery. We left Michael to rehearse it in Glasgow and report by telephone. Towards the end of the third week, he called me to come and see a run. Thelma needed hospital treatment and for the first time ever we paid for a bed in the posh Chesterfield Nursing Home, locally known as the Mint, where Cary Grant's mother lived in style.

'Where are you taking that telly?' Thelma heard a sister ask a young nurse.

'Missis Leach wants to see Cliff Richard.'

On his last visit to see her, Grant had come on the same ship as *my* mother, who was returning from a year in Vancouver. Vi had only seen him once, when – as part of his travel deal – he'd spent an hour with the steerage.

By now we had a mother's help so I was able to leave the children and fly to Glasgow. Nothing I had heard so far – from Michael, Joe or anyone – had prepared me for the first act run they showed me in the empty Victorian theatre under a working-light one afternoon in early May. The cool tone of the finished script had been matched by Michael's direction, Andy Park's incidental jazz and unbeatable performances by Zena and Joe. None of it curried favour. Our aesthetic principle had been to present the facts, get the jokes right and leave feeling to the audience. By a little miracle, this had all been done, with the result that, when Michael heard the act's last line and said 'Lights down – and – curtain, thank you, very nice, relax,' he turned to find me in tears. He was justified in rushing me backstage to show the actors what they were achieving but my reaction was atypical for what I had heard was not someone else's story but my own and, more important, not an echo of other writers or imitations of friends and family but my own voice, a tone and rhythm that told me that at nearly forty I'd cleared my throat at last and was saying what I meant. Having knocked on the door, I hadn't run away but stayed to speak. To make an audience cry or laugh is easy – they *want* to. In reviews of *Joe Egg*, it became a critical truism to speak of its capacity to do both at the same time yet this is only worth doing if one thereby catches a whiff of life, a true tang of the bitter mixture we all have to drink. I might have been less happy that May afternoon in Glasgow if some prescience could have shown me a long line of comedies about death and dying, the blind, deaf-mutes, monstrous birth, sterility, vasectomy and mastectomy, old age and cancer. Every handicap now has its hilarious smash hit, each with its hard jokes and soft centre, sucking up to its public in the approved style of funny-boohoo.

Stanley Baxter and I had tea again in Fuller's, Glasgow's Ivy or Sardi's. He seemed friendlier, relieved that at last I'd given up acting for writing. Citizens' was, of course, where he'd had his first success. He wanted, he said, to play legit in the West End but no one had asked him.

Thelma's latest post-natal operation was the Sunday before Tuesday's first night but nothing would stop her coming. I went out to meet her at midday and watched the old Dakota taxi to the long glass finger. The same one that had brought me home from Singapore? Certainly it was the same model, now named Pionair in an effort at reassurance. I watched some businessmen and families and a party of nuns cross the tarmac and was about to turn away, thinking she hadn't been well enough after all, when she appeared at the head of the stairs – a hesitant figure in a wide purple coat. Slowly, unaided, she started down the steps. I ran the length of the corridor and found her approaching, one hand on the wall and tears in her eyes.

'It's longer than I thought,' she said.

We stayed with the Blakemores overnight. Conrad, exactly Abigail's age, was now a demanding boy infatuated with Scotland who wore a kilt and called himself Hunting McIntyre. With our wives, Michael and I were circumspect, trying not to read too much promise in the favourable omens for the play but sharing a secret optimism.

While Thelma rested, I appeared in a television puff, cut down to a minute to make room for a set-to between a vicar and a councillor. I wish this first taste of publicity had induced me never to give another interview but the fact is that I still sometimes agree to meet journalists – an example of what Doctor Johnson called 'the triumph of hope over experience'.

Thelma and I had aisle seats in the dress circle and behind us two ladies from Kelvinside read their programmes aloud.

'She's good, Zena Walker. I've seen her on television. I don't recognize this one –'

'Who's that?'

'Peter Nichols. Says he's married to an art teacher and they have four wee ones and a cat.'

'Bless his heart. Would you like one of these Mintoes?'

Joe was exhilarated by the house and raised his performance to over-drive, which threw Zena for awhile till she shifted gear as well. Joe had predicted good laughs for the first ten minutes until the child came on in her chair and that would be the last. He took the teaching sketch too fast but he and Zena won them over with the saucy exchange we'd rescued from the censor. The laughs were building well, the house enjoying the easy banter with no hint of what was coming. Then Joe went to answer the doorbell and Zena took off the tray to the kitchen. Pause. Joe returned pushing the stage Abo slumped in her chair. The ladies behind stopped rustling their sweet wrappings, the house fell silent. He began his monologue, broken only by her apparently random 'aahs'. Thelma was hearing this for the first time, this stylized version of our home life. Zena, playing her, came back and joined in the husband's jokes. For some time there was the same awkward silence that we'd sometimes met from visitors when we had done our 'act' for them, a reaction which had first hinted at the possibility of a comic approach. Then someone broke the ice and soon the laughter came free and full. We uncrossed our fingers. A microscopic moment of history had passed, a taboo had been broken. The ladies chewed their Mintoes again and in the interval they checked their programmes.

'That one with the cat hasn't been on yet.'

At the final curtain there was strong applause. We had won and we knew it. Peggy Ramsay thought they'd done it terribly well but she hadn't changed her mind, it was still too painful.

'Do say a word of thanks to Michael Codron, dear. He's come a long way.'

Codron was doing his well-known imitation of an Easter Island Statue.

'Thank you for making the effort,' I said.

'Wouldn't have missed it for the world,' he said but the deathly composure hardly flickered. He didn't mention the play but Peggy told me he'd found it facetious.

'Did the people come from the Royal Court?'

'Yes, but they've already run for their plane back to Town. Seems they've rather gone off the idea of a Sunday night without scenery.'

'Nothing doing?' said Michael Blakemore. 'I thought not. I watched their faces. All like death.'

Next day the Glasgow reviews, though confused, were mostly good. We

227

bought more at the airport and I looked down as the city disappeared below. I would always be grateful to Glasgow for giving me one of the happiest and most decisive weeks of my life. The children watched us land in Bristol, not knowing Thelma had been further than the nursing-home a mile from home. Louise was old enough to wonder why she came by plane and how she'd found their presents in Clifton – a tartan beret, toy bagpipes and a plaid bib.

The day after, Michael rang to ask if we'd read the rave review in the *Guardian*. We told him there'd been nothing but a notice of some student Shakespeare. He rang the national editor and told him his Scottish critic had given a new play a startling welcome and would he please reprint it in the British edition. The fact that he did so changed all our lives. The review in turn brought others to see the play, including Ronald Bryden, whose notice in the *Observer* the second Sunday sent London managers commuting to the Clyde to see for themselves.

We were busy with a family move to a friend's farm near Bristol, where we were to stay that summer while he was abroad. Thelma was so weak she could only supervise the arrangements. I'd resigned myself to a three-weeks' run at Glasgow and felt the year had been worthwhile when – one morning at nine – Peggy rang.

'Well, dear, Memorial want to transfer the production to London – as it is. Bernard Delfont's man's got his cheque-book out but would want to make some changes. And Ken Tynan's got hold of a copy somehow and wants it for the National. All you have to tell me, dear, is which you'd like.'

'What's Memorial?'

'That's Albert Finney's company, run by Michael Medwin. Based on Albert Memorial, yes? Ha-ha. Think about it, dear, and ring me.'

There was nothing to discuss. The National would do a new production with another cast – Maggie and Robert perhaps – and their system would keep it in the repertoire till public taste accepted the play. It would be given a chance to germinate and weather several seasons. But Memorial's transfer meant Michael Blakemore, the actors and the Citizens' theatre would profit from their loyalty to the play. In any case, I could not imagine it being better done. So we signed with them.

We went on with our family life, Thelma recovering and all of us enjoying the phoney farm, with its chickens and ducks and wild rabbits on the hill, its sties let to a neighbouring farmer, whose pigs squealed for swill all day, and its two cows, one of them barren. A village woman came twice daily to milk the Jersey and talked to me of her handicapped son.

'He's really a mongrel,' she said – and if Codron found my play facetious what would he have made of *that*? – 'but he's very kindly, you know – good-hearted.'

In her innocently related chronicle, the cruelty of rural life reared up like some episode from Flaubert.

'There's this lad who was hurt by a motorbike and lost the use of his legs. Well, you know what fellows are, they like a laugh, they like to take away his crutches. And my boy – you ought to see him go for them if they try it when he's around. And then there was this wedding and the men bumped the bride up and down on the ground but my boy stopped them, he got quite savage with the groom, said he shouldn't ever let them do that to her.'

They had formed a society but called it a school. 'Four thousand pounds we collected door-to-door. Wonderful place we've got, over Glastonbury. They've all gone to the circus today. One of them's fifty-three years old. Just started at the school. You should have seen how bucked he was when he came home the first day with his school-tie on.'

Which echoed the line in the play: 'We know one, a man of seventy-six, just joined the boy-scouts. They said they wouldn't have him any longer in the cubs.'

On the last night I rang Joe in Glasgow. Thelma had relapsed and was rushed to hospital for blood transfusions so it hadn't been possible to see the play again.

'It's been marvellous this week,' Joe said. 'It'll never be better. Albert's just been up. He told Zena and me we seemed to be enjoying ourselves. David Merrick came.'

'That the Broadway producer?'

'Yeah.'

'What did he say?'

'He thought you weren't doing your work properly because the characters spoke to the audience. It was the same in *Hamlet* – all those soliloquies, very sloppy. Anyway in the second act he was stunned.'

'Too stunned to make an offer though.'

'You don't need him.'

The play came to the Comedy just before my fortieth birthday. Irving Wardle wrote in *The Times* that 'this is one of the rare occasions on which audiences can feel the earth moving under their feet.' Charles and Valerie Wood, filming in Turkey, opened their paper in the Ankara Hilton and, as they read this, the hotel shook and an earthquake started.

The opening night was a meeting of family and friends – John Hale, Boorman's wife (John – sure enough – was in Hollywood!), Bernie Cooper, my mother, brother and Mary, Edgar Williams and his wife, Chris

Morahan, Peter Jeffrey. Only Dad was missing but he would have spoilt it somehow – by shouting at the actors to speak up or grumbling about filthy language. It has struck me since that I didn't write a decent stage play until after his death.

In the interval, we were given drinks in an ante-room, where several American producers had got Albert Finney in a corner and were baying at him like hounds with a nice plump stag. When Medwin introduced 'Mister and Missis Author', they turned like Daleks and advanced on us, hands outstretched, chanting 'Wonderful, moving, my Guard! What a play!'

The play's posthumous fame has led to a general belief that it had a long West End run. In fact, it ran for about four months, had only one full house and has never been seen in London since. Properly handled, it should have survived but by the time it had got the *Evening Standard* Best Play Award, we had already closed. Publicity was butter-fingered. I had no experience of journalists and agreed to do an interview on *Twenty-four Hours*, a generally respected television programme. No one on the team had seen or read the play and my chat with the presenter was preceded by a film-clip of an autistic child screaming in a bathroom. Kenneth Allsop's line of questioning assumed that I believed in the murder of spastic children and massed ranks of parents had been gathered to tell me I was wrong. Again none had seen or read the play and the whole misguided mess must have lost, not gained, us an audience.

On the whole, the various journalists who dealt with us over the next year or so did not bother with the play. They preferred to read what other journalists wrote, depicting Thelma as 'mini-skirted' or bravely Smiling Through or me as a sober-sides who smoked Gauloises and gave bleak smiles. *Life* photographed us in typical English pubs that took us all day to find. The *Daily Mirror* gave us a whole page. I spoke on 'Woman's Hour'. All of them were decent and had nothing to do with the play, in which the inane Pam had said: 'There was a fabulous article in *Nova* about it.'

Over the next few years we kept hearing from people who'd read about the play and on occasion even from someone who'd *seen* it. There were, of course, a few mad letters – such as this one from a woman who called herself A Research Psychologist: 'No child is ever born with a damaged brain – God would never be so cruel. All damage is caused by the parents. Your wife is an art student. If she does any work in this line at all, it will be abstract. Abstract is the result of a crime committed. It is God's punishment. Picasso strangled his baby brother when he was seven, Moore told lies and his mother said he would turn to stone (Lot's wife),

Dali was promiscuous and caught out by a priest. Do not condemn your wife. Possibly you had said "No children" when you first married. God, however, gives life, you only provide the means. He alone can judge.'

A more Jungian view was given much later by the anthropologist-psychologist John Layard, whom we met through Francis Hewlett. Francis and Thelma had studied art together at the West of England Academy but lost touch until he reappeared the day of our youngest daughter's birth, by which time he was Head of Painting at Falmouth College of Art and his house on the harbour was a permanent show of his drawings and paintings from over twenty years of intense application. As soon as we could afford to, we began buying his work and now our home houses a second Hewlett retrospective – landscapes, portraits, ceramic jokes. His fraught childhood in Eastville left him with such hidden wounds that – in his forties – he became critically ill with the intestinal syndrome called Crohn's Disease. Medical treatment having failed, Francis faced the prospect of recurrent surgery and a friend said that, sooner than surrender to the knife, he should talk to an old witch-doctor who – as cranks do – had fetched up in Cornwall and was living nearby. Francis's first reaction was like Bri's in the play – 'I'd rather have nothing than a lot of lies' – but his condition was critical and he agreed to meet the man who was then, in 1969, nearly eighty but who'd been W. H. Auden's mentor in Berlin when the poet was twenty and Layard nearly twice that age. Earlier Layard had done field work in the New Hebrides and published his findings in *Stone Men of Malekula*. Back in Europe he had been cured of psychosomatic paralysis by Homer Lane and became his disciple. Auden was very taken with Layard's views, which seem to have been a goulash of Lane, D. H. Lawrence and Georg Groddeck, arguing that all illness was brought about by mental humbug or, as Auden's line had it, 'We are lived by powers we pretend to understand.' We should act on impulse, give way to the moment, be ourselves.

The bisexual Layard fell for Auden, but Auden only fell for Layard's views. Layard threatened suicide and Auden told him he should go ahead, if that was how he felt. He was living on impulse and being himself with the boy tarts of Berlin's bars and alleys, practising what Layard preached. Layard shot himself in the head, the bullet lodging near his brain. That he survived was a miracle, that he outlived the poet stranger still. Not long after this, Auden referred to him in 'The Orators' as Loony Layard, a second-rate healer, which is said to have hurt the older man a lot, not least because Auden had trotted out his notions shamelessly in his recent verse. But how much did Layard ask for it? He made the crucial mistake of not liking Auden's writing, though he liked his mind and his youth. Also he enjoyed lighting fuses but couldn't always take the explosion. Even in his eighties much of what he said was only to annoy because he knew it teased us.

'But he's no use at all until you get him to the point,' said Francis, who spent many hours with him over a period of years talking out the tensions that had led to his inflamed gut. 'He makes such sense of my dreams and links them so sensibly with the other cultures he either knows or knows about and you begin to feel a wonderful unity about human experience.'

Elizabeth, Francis's wife, was more sceptical. She said perhaps it was only mumbo-jumbo, but anything that helped was welcome – in other words, she would rather have a lot of lies than nothing. One morning she, Thelma and I were in the kitchen when John, 'a crumbling Edwardian with few teeth and a posh voice', came from his morning session with the bed-ridden Francis. He demanded soup, but when Liz served it complained of the vegetables floating in it.

'That's vegetable soup,' she said.

'I only like clear soup.'

'Shall I spoon them out for you then?'

'It's all right.'

While he slurped, I stared from the window across the water towards Flushing and St Mawes. Francis had just been telling him about us for he soon took issue with my atheism.

'You're brain-washed,' he said, after I'd parried his first few thrusts, 'one of the most bigoted men I've ever met.'

'Because he doesn't believe in God?' said Thelma, her voice shaking.

'And you shut up! You're worse! Bullying your way around, telling everyone what to do and think. That's probably why you had a spastic child. You need a good hiding.'

Thelma left the room soon after and I should perhaps have told him to mind his own bloody business and not attack her with the most emotional tool he could lay hands on. She later said she had run upstairs and cried in the bedroom because he'd touched on a truth she'd never admitted to herself – that her independence as a single woman was threatened by pregnancy and she behaved as though all life could be controlled, pain could be overcome by strength of will. But the birth pangs had been intense and she'd resented them and refused to let the baby go. There was some truth in Layard's assault.

I found our several meetings lively, this voice from another time and place with his therapeutic bludgeon always at the ready. Even more I enjoyed Francis's brilliant imitation of him, for he is the best mimic I know. He believes that Layard saved his life and, since the old man's death, has found no one to replace him.

A few weeks later I was surprised to receive a thirteen-page letter in Layard's spidery scrawl about *Joe Egg*, which he had read since our meeting. The first five pages were a rant against that 'huge baby Jung – swelled-headed and terrified of death – ' and Pauline Christianity, with a lot of interesting word-play on Psyche – moth or butterfly – 'the spirit moveth where it listeth among the flowers – fleurs, fleurettes, flirts visited by bees, spiders – or web-spinners, spinsters, man-eaters, etc., etc., bla-bla-bla ...', but finally he settled on the play which he found 'splendid but bewildering. By page 86 I had begun to think: this is all a nightmare and misinterpreted at that. And then – lo and behold – the dream is actually told and – my God – misinterpreted!'

I suppose it was natural that he should pick on this recounted dream of a failed suicide, but I was struck by what Layard could not know – that the speech had never been done on the stage. It was printed only in the early Faber edition and left out of all reprints. For London, on Michael's advice, I rewrote the last scene to bring Joe back from hospital and leave her alone onstage at the curtain, the last person we see, the last image we remember. In this, the dream speech was cut.

'I had a dream in hospital,' says Sheila to the father Bri, the morning after he's tried to let the girl die. 'You were lying in bed beside me, smiling as though you had a secret. I said "What's the matter?" and you said "It's all right now" and I said "why?" and you turned to show the bullet-hole in your temple. But I knew, the way you do in dreams, that you hadn't killed yourself, only damaged your brain and now I'd have to look after both of you.'

Of which Layard wrote, 'I've little doubt this is a real dream, dreamt by "Sheila" (but who is she? is it your dream or hers?). Here lies the mystery, the revelation – that bullet in the head – which is subsequently turned round to mean the precise opposite of its real meaning. This is a secret, an arcanum, only to be talked about, not written of. Bri half understands it but only half, for at least he clears out, though we're not told why. He half knows the deeper meaning, which concerns Joe's fits. These are taken throughout as being bad, the doctors are rightly laughed at for trying to cure them and Joe's whole condition with their drugs and other mechanized means. I know I'm treading on tender, dangerous ground because of personal feelings but I've gone too far to turn back now. The point is that the whole play is without a glimmer of hope so very rightly it's a great success in this abysmal-clever age. Though you rightly ridicule the doctors, you make the same mistake as they. You (Bri) think

233

the fits are bad. In fact they're the only positive things, the only life-saving element, the child's one despairing cry to live, to be *understood*, but they're squashed every time and regarded as disease. In fact they convey dis-*ease* – the only method of revolt, an appeal for attention and understanding – not the "mothering" or rather "smothering" or being sorry for. The fit half-frightens the very people who have caused the fit so that they try to suppress it again.'

Then follows a tirade against Hippocrates and in the end the anti-climactic message, The Cure Is Removal Of Guilt, which comes as a pop after the big guns. I didn't find much connection between this and our (just) living daughter, but still no other comment on the play has raised so many interesting questions or showed such insights. 'This letter calls for no reply,' he assured me so I sent none, but within a few weeks he wrote asking if I'd got it. Then I told him of our daughter's condition in detail and that the dream had, in fact, been Thelma's.

'Of course I knew it had been hers,' he wrote, though there's no sign of it in the first letter.

'He wasn't a good writer,' Francis said, 'and he knew it, which is why he wanted to help you understand what you'd written. He wanted those with ability to know more. For me, it was his presence that made him a healer. And that was odd because he was never the same twice. When his patients discuss him, each one knew a different Layard. I mean, all that derision of conventional medicine, but he took all the drugs the doctors could give him!' At the time of his letter, I knew nothing of the bullet that had lodged in his own head until Auden and his other friends took him to the hospital and had it removed. In his journal Auden wrote: 'He appears to be one of those who "have seen the light" once, after which is darkness. To me illumination is a progressive process.'

John's letter, in fact, got a good deal wrong – not least in believing that the play was a great success, which he blamed on the mad confusion of our abysmal ignorance, but by the standards of a Neil Simon or Alan Ayckbourn, it never was – in London or New York anyway – and few people saw it in performance. Some who afterwards caught it in rep or amateur productions found the experience helpful. One woman who had seen the Bristol Old Vic do it wrote: 'I kept hoping Joe would die quickly of pneumonia. When, a few years later I had my first child, she was grossly handicapped and screamed non-stop. At three, she had pneumonia and because we had seen your play, my husband and I decided we would not call a doctor quickly. Luckily she died soon and without pain. I may sound cold but I felt her life was a living death and she certainly wasn't happy.'

Joe Egg is not my best play, though it is generally thought to be. Seeing Richard Dreyfuss and Stockard Channing give a good account of it in New Haven two years ago, I was struck by how funny it was. The jokes come over as irrepressible, the motor of the play is the shared humour of the man and wife. It has never been judged as a comedy, perhaps because of its impurity. Critics prefer the Mandarin pose of Joe Orton to the muddle of *Joe Egg*. 'Charcoal grey', sneered an American review, 'to the Hades black of Mister Sloane.'

It has done far better in Europe and the States than in this country. Easy and cheap to mount, enjoyed everywhere but in London, yet left on the shelf for sixteen years – why should that be? Perhaps the bad start. In some ways, the transfer from Glasgow was mishandled. We knew nothing. Like Charles Wood, we believed the *Evening Standard* Award was a cash prize and were disappointed to find it was only a statuette. I didn't go to collect it and so missed my chance to 'make an entrance'. In any case, the play was already off by then. It should have been nursed till the prizes brought the houses the play deserved, but Albert Finney decided to play the lead on Broadway to help publicize the New York opening of his film *Charlie Bubbles*. Anyway Joe Melia wasn't keen to go – his wife was ill and he thought America a Fascist country – so we were glad Albert wanted to play it. Everyone from New York said he was A Great Store and people there would pay to hear him read the phone-book. What we failed to grasp at the time was that he only intended reading this particular phone-book for eleven weeks. The London run was wrapped up so that Zena, Joan Hickson and John Carson could support Albert in New York.

Thelma decided we should take our three toddlers and German au-pair for the opening, while the company re-rehearsed with Albert. What's more, she had never flown and was scared of planes. Joan Hickson, who played the hero's mother in the play, felt the same and only agreed to go on condition we accompanied her by sea. She was let off rehearsals early and met us on board SS *Bremen* with her friend, Mary Norton, author of *The Borrowers*, who was going to see the Walt Disney people about a film. Before we were out of the Solent, Thelma was seasick. She never left her cabin during the rest of a nine-day crossing, much of which was spent hiding from Atlantic storms. She emerged as we entered the New York waterways and we all watched the Statue of Liberty go by, knowing well what the inscription meant about huddled masses yearning to be free. Immigration officers came aboard and sat behind desks in the ballroom.

'Gimme that,' said one, snapping his fingers, not looking up from his table.

'Give you what?' said Thelma, i/c Documents for our party of six.

'Papers.'

'Which papers would you like?'

It was not the last time we should anger an American by using the conditional tense.

'Gimme your passports,' he growled, glaring at her through his shades.

He flicked over the pages, pausing to look closely at a name, age or distinguishing mark, then yawned towards the gold watch among his wrist-hair.

'You a rider?' he finally asked me.

'Yes.'

'Technical rider?'

'No. Playwright.'

'Yeah? Doing a play in Noo York?'

'That's right.'

'Any messages in your play?'

It was as though he were asking if we had any organic foodstuffs, small arms, narcotics or rabid dogs about us.

'Well, you could say so.'

'Forgeddid. Turn ridearound and go back home. Let me tell you something – on Broadway they don't want mental rearmament. They want physical disrobement. Naked girls. Any thoughts in your play, any messages, forgeddid – okay? But good luck anyway. I hope you make a buck. There's nothing else here.'

We lined up in a freezing shed with Mary under N, waving across at Joan and our au-pair under their letters, had our codeine impounded, were robbed by a cab-driver and a luggage-transporter and finally reached our hotel, where for two weeks we lived in a twilight world. Manhattan is no place for children, especially in the depths of its glacial winter. Thelma and the German trudged the streets with our toddlers while I rehearsed. They bought groceries in supermarts and we ate mostly in our suites, except when Albert or some frightening hit-men took us to 21 or Sardi's or the 8th Avenue Deli.

'You wanna drink?' the waiter asked one night.

'Yes. I should like a beer.'

'How's that?'

'Could I have a beer?'

'You old enough? You *look* old enough. So sure you can have a beer.'

'Sorry?'

'You wanna beer?'

'Yes. I wanna beer.'

'Okay.'

It was the conditional again. I couldn't tell whether Thelma enjoyed herself. I can't say it was what they had led us to believe. Peggy Ramsay had laughed when she heard my wife was coming.

'You authors are such funny men. It's like taking a ham sandwich to a banquet!'

Tom Stoppard had been lionized there so I sought his advice.

'Will it be like I imagine?'

'What do you imagine?'

'Will we meet Fredric March?'

'Not *the* Fredric March.'

He advised us to take life easy before the first night because of the round of parties and sex-crazed homage we should enjoy afterwards. It was easy to take life easy before the first night because no one but the company knew we were there or why and for the most part we visited museums and the ice-rink in Central Park, where 'Georgy Girl' was always being played on the electric organ, and the carousel we knew from *Catcher in the Rye*. Once our skin crept as an air-raid siren sounded from some nearby rooftop.

'No, it's not an air-raid,' a cop told me, solemnly, 'they practise every day at noon.'

On the German girl's day off, Thelma took Louise, Daniel and Catherine to shop for food and then to the free zoo, where they fed the rank but vigorous beasts, some wild ones caged, some tame and wandering free. At last they were driven by an Arctic breeze into the free cinema to watch a programme of wildlife shorts. Thelma sat on the aisle and was dozing in the unaccustomed comfort when she felt her paper-bag of that day's groceries being gently pulled away. All the warnings of our friends came back but none of their advice. She was being mugged but would not submit; some instinct made her grab the bag and hold on, tugging and struggling to keep the food she'd bought her family. After some time she saw, by light reflected from the screen, that she was fighting a goat. New York, in its vanity, offers the world many colourful symbols of itself but – for me – none better than the Buñuelesque image of being mugged by a goat in the pictures.

The first preview was a matinée and I walked Louise down Broadway to see the second act. There was a full house and queues at the box-office, so we stood at the back.

'Is that lady pretending to be Mummy?' Louise asked.

'Sort of, yes.'

'And Albert Finnegan pretending to be you?'

'That's right.'

'Then where am I?'

'Not born yet.'

'Is Abigail coming on?'

She was delighted by her sister's appearance, carried on by Zena, and joined in loudly when they sang the carol, a family ritual. People looked round and I had to shush her.

'Look!' she said. 'That's Joan.'

'Pretending to be little Nana.'

Afterwards I took her up on stage. The great empty auditorium didn't disturb her absorption in this scenic version of our home.

'We never had a goldfish,' she complained. 'Or a budgie.'

Rehearsals and previews continued. The child playing Joe was Jewish and had a showbiz momma who one night approached me and told me how truly wonderful the play was but she begged me to think again about the jokes against black people. They could harm the show. Minority groups might picket the theatre.

'But they *are* meant to be ironic, those lines,' I said.

'Oh sure and listen, I agree with you – they should all go back where they came from – but they have such power here now, I beg you. . . .'

There were no cuts and no pickets.

The first night was successful, the reviews good. I agreed with the critics that Albert, though miscast, gave a fine performance. It was not his fault that he alone was advertised and that New Yorkers were led to believe he not only wrote the play but directed it. My name did not appear once in a full-page spread in *The Times*.

Albert was as good as his word and stayed eleven weeks. After that, of course, few people wanted to see a less-known actor reading a phone-book. I was required to waive my royalty and after a four months' run the play closed. According to *Variety*, Albert got ten per cent, his company two per cent of the gross plus twenty per cent of the net, the balance split between the American partners and Albert. Oh, yes, and a third of repertory and stock and the film . . . and, despite all that and the weeks when I got nothing, we still made enough to buy our Blackheath house cash down. As the immigration officer had said, there's nothing else.

My many visits in the years between have not changed my original view of New York all that much. I still see it more as a nineteenth-century city than the modern marvel I expected. The glass, the steel, the dazzling forest of light, do not alter its moral centre. The values are Victorian, its mores Dickensian, its faith in *laissez-faire* only an extra-polation of Disraeli. The same massive novels, brilliant operettas, deified artists, revered pundits, opulent plutocracy and the same ghettoes where a brutalized and criminal poor waits its turn. Is it their hot breath that drifts in clouds from holes in the streets? True, the religion of Victorian London was unified under an established church and New York's takes many forms, but they still share one central tenet: success exonerates. America is a deeply religious nation and believes – as Britain did – that our lives are a progress towards Utopia and that this consummation depends on the success of heroes. In New York this has become a cult and the heroes are, like Albert, Great Stores. From time to time they go into an arena for some gladiatorial combat that will affirm their Storedom.

Storedom somehow eluded us. After a week of waiting for the parties and orgies we had been promised, we took the train west to visit friends and relations in another country called America.

On the first night, the producer's wife had given him a pyramid of golden eggs from Tiffany's. She showed them to us, wanting our admiration, but we could only think of the hospital ward near Bristol and the goose that had laid them.

Postscript

Three years later she was still there in the same ward, while Thelma and I had moved with our other children to a Victorian villa near Greenwich Park, bought with our share of the profits from *Joe Egg* in New York.

8 May 1971 was a glorious Saturday, the sort of spring day when England seems the most agreeable place on earth. Later a friend and his son – Liverpool supporters – were coming to watch the Cup Final on our television and I gave up the morning to suburban pleasures, playing tennis with a neighbour at Ranger's House then with daughter Louise in the back garden. Arsenal beat Liverpool 2-1, which elated my son Dan but depressed our visitors. The boy cried and we consoled him with tea and cakes. They were just leaving when the matron of Abigail's hospital rang from Bristol to tell us that her lungs had finally got the better of her heart and she'd died an hour ago. We exchanged the necessary platitudes and I thanked her for her care. Thelma and Louise were both upset but I shed no tears over what we all knew was a happy event. In fact, the only time I'd cried over Abigail had been at the first run-through of *Joe Egg*. Thelma soon occupied herself by making a few decisions – we should tell our parents, of course, then Charles and Valerie Wood, our new friends Michael and Gill Frayn, and post a notice in *The Times*. I asked what for, reminding her that only we had known Abo in any sense that could be called 'knowing' and most of what we knew had been invented, features drawn on a blank canvas. But Thelma's instinct was right, as usual. The occasion had to be marked in some way.

Without our help, events during the following week arranged themselves in strange patterns. At a starry garden party on Sunday, our two remaining daughters nearly drowned in the pool and had to be saved (a) by the host and (b) by a well-known actor plunging in fully dressed.

'To lose one daughter', says my diary, 'may be regarded as a misfortune, to lose two more looks like carelessness. To stand about while Proper Men save them seems emblematic of my trance-like incompetence.'

Joe Melia rang on Monday to invite us to a drama school performance of *Joe Egg* and we told him the news but agreed to go with him anyway. It was still a troubling play for us to watch and now the lines about whether the child would outlive her parents had a new poignancy. The people in Hampstead that night were as moved by Abo's story as others had been, from Finland to New Zealand, and there were moments when I felt an urge to stand and say, 'She's dead, it's over, don't be upset, there's a happy ending', which would have made a moment of audience participation not easy to forget.

On Friday we went by train to Bristol for the funeral – family flowers only – and the Co-op's limousine took us by Clifton College and the zoo across Durdham Down to Canford, where the hearse was waiting with its child-size coffin.

'There she is, Mum,' I murmured to Thelma, using for about the last time the manner of speech we'd invented to give her a voice. As we arrived at the chapel, an undertaker whispered, 'Give me a nod when you've stood long enough and the coffin will go down.'

Faced with the small and silent group of mourners – my mother, Thelma's parents, my brother and his wife, two nurses from the hospital – I doubted whether I'd been right to insist on a secular funeral. We followed her in, a light burden for the four bearers, and sat in the front pew, our relatives behind us. There was to be no minister, no music, no liturgy of any kind. Nowadays we should know better and sing and read from the King James Bible and enjoy the rituals of a faith we don't share and praise a God who could allow such a life as hers. Then we were more austere, more moral, and stood wondering 'Must no more be done?' and 'What ceremony else?'. But Thelma's feelings saved the day. As the box was set in position on the lift, she knelt and closed her eyes. We followed her lead and, for all I know, one or two of us even prayed. I dare say everyone tried to remember Abo and to make some excuse for her eleven empty years. Anything I felt for her was in *Joe Egg* so now my thoughts were all of Thelma as she knelt beside me, gripping my hand and trying not to cry. Unlike Sheila in the play, she had never let herself be consumed by her damaged daughter. Even on one occasion she had tried to end the child's existence, denying the medicine that suppressed her fits. She'd watched her struggle for some hours and in the end relented and spooned in the drugs that allowed her torpor to continue. Now she stood, I gave a nod and the coffin sank. It was only then she gave way to tears.

Once we were back in the limousine, she said to me, 'It was the size of the box.'

The next funeral was waiting and the few of us were soon away. At the junction with Falcondale Road, our driver had to halt at traffic lights and while we waited gave a stealthy wave to a mate of his in a car in the opposite street, bringing other mourners of another death. On our right was the public library and, with the kind of pleasant shock that comes with the recurrence of a running joke, I saw that the facing house was the one we'd visited on far-off Sundays to persuade my father we'd be better off there than at Ashley Down. I pictured him now in the empty bedroom looking out, calling 'Look here, Vi, come and look out here! You want me to move in here? Well, what can you see? Yet another blooming funeral.'

MORE ABOUT PENGUINS, PELICANS AND PUFFINS

For further information about books available from Penguins please write to Dept EP, Penguin Books Ltd, Harmondsworth, Middlesex UB7 0DA.

In the U.S.A.: For a complete list of books available from Penguins in the United States write to Dept DG, Penguin Books, 299 Murray Hill Parkway, East Rutherford, New Jersey 07073.

In Canada: For a complete list of books available from Penguins in Canada write to Penguin Books Canada Ltd, 2801 John Street, Markham, Ontario L3R 1B4.

In Australia: For a complete list of books available from Penguins in Australia write to the Marketing Department, Penguin Books Australia Ltd, P.O. Box 257, Ringwood, Victoria 3134.

In New Zealand: For a complete list of books available from Penguins in New Zealand write to the Marketing Department, Penguin Books (N.Z.) Ltd, Private Bag, Takapuna, Auckland 9.

In India: For a complete list of books available from Penguins in India write to Penguin Overseas Ltd, 706 Eros Apartments, 56 Nehru Place, New Delhi 110019.

A CHOICE OF PENGUINS

☐ **_Small World_ David Lodge** £2.50

A jet-propelled academic romance, sequel to _Changing Places._ 'A new comic débâcle on every page' – _The Times._ 'Here is everything one expects from Lodge but three times as entertaining as anything he has written before' – _Sunday Telegraph_

☐ **_The Neverending Story_ Michael Ende** £3.50

The international bestseller, now a major film: 'A tale of magical adventure, pursuit and delay, danger, suspense, triumph' – _The Times Literary Supplement_

☐ **_The Sword of Honour Trilogy_ Evelyn Waugh** £3.95

Containing _Men at Arms, Officers and Gentlemen_ and _Unconditional Surrender_, the trilogy described by Cyril Connolly as 'unquestionably the finest novels to have come out of the war'.

☐ **_The Honorary Consul_ Graham Greene** £1.95

In a provincial Argentinian town, a group of revolutionaries kidnap the wrong man . . . 'The tension never relaxes and one reads hungrily from page to page, dreading the moment it will all end' – Auberon Waugh in the _Evening Standard_

☐ **_The First Rumpole Omnibus_ John Mortimer** £4.95

Containing _Rumpole of the Bailey, The Trials of Rumpole_ and _Rumpole's Return._ 'A fruity, foxy masterpiece, defender of our wilting faith in mankind' – _Sunday Times_

☐ **_Scandal_ A. N. Wilson** £2.25

Sexual peccadillos, treason and blackmail are all ingredients on the boil in A. N. Wilson's new, _cordon noir_ comedy. 'Drily witty, deliciously nasty' – _Sunday Telegraph_

A CHOICE OF PENGUINS

☐ *Stanley and the Women* **Kingsley Amis**   £2.50

'Very good, very powerful . . . beautifully written . . . This is Amis *père* at his best' – Anthony Burgess in the *Observer*. 'Everybody should read it' – *Daily Mail*

☐ *The Mysterious Mr Ripley* **Patricia Highsmith**   £4.95

Containing *The Talented Mr Ripley*, *Ripley Underground* and *Ripley's Game*. 'Patricia Highsmith is the poet of apprehension' – Graham Greene. 'The Ripley books are marvellously, insanely readable' – *The Times*

☐ *Earthly Powers* **Anthony Burgess**   £4.95

'Crowded, crammed, bursting with manic erudition, garlicky puns, omnilingual jokes . . . (a novel) which meshes the real and personalized history of the twentieth century' – Martin Amis

☐ *Life & Times of Michael K* **J. M. Coetzee**   £2.95

The Booker Prize-winning novel: 'It is hard to convey . . . just what Coetzee's special quality is. His writing gives off whiffs of Conrad, of Nabokov, of Golding, of the Paul Theroux of *The Mosquito Coast*. But he is none of these, he is a harsh, compelling new voice' – Victoria Glendinning

☐ *The Stories of William Trevor*   £5.95

'Trevor packs into each separate five or six thousand words more richness, more laughter, more ache, more multifarious human-ness than many good writers manage to get into a whole novel' – *Punch*

☐ *The Book of Laughter and Forgetting*
   Milan Kundera   £3.95

'A whirling dance of a book . . . a masterpiece full of angels, terror, ostriches and love . . . No question about it. The most important novel published in Britain this year' – Salman Rushdie

A CHOICE OF PENGUINS

☐ *The Philosopher's Pupil* **Iris Murdoch** £2.95

'We are back, of course, with great delight, in the land of Iris Murdoch, which is like no other but Prospero's . . .' – *Sunday Telegraph*. And, as expected, her latest masterpiece is 'marvellous . . . compulsive reading, hugely funny' – *Spectator*

☐ *A Good Man in Africa* **William Boyd** £2.50

Boyd's brilliant, award-winning frolic featuring Morgan Leafy, over-weight, oversexed representative of Her Britannic Majesty in tropical Kinjanja. 'Wickedly funny' – *The Times*

These books should be available at all good bookshops or news-agents, but if you live in the UK or the Republic of Ireland and have difficulty in getting to a bookshop, they can be ordered by post. Please indicate the titles required and fill in the form below.

NAME _____ BLOCK CAPITALS

ADDRESS _____

_____

_____

Enclose a cheque or postal order payable to The Penguin Bookshop to cover the total price of books ordered, plus 50p for postage. Readers in the Republic of Ireland should send £1R equivalent to the sterling prices, plus 67p for postage. Send to: The Penguin Bookshop, 54/56 Bridlesmith Gate, Nottingham, NG1 2GP.

You can also order by phoning (0602) 599295, and quoting your Barclaycard or Access number.

Every effort is made to ensure the accuracy of the price and availability of books at the time of going to press, but it is sometimes necessary to increase prices and in these circumstances retail prices may be shown on the covers of books which may differ from the prices shown in this list or elsewhere. This list is not an offer to supply any book.

This order service is only available to residents in the UK and the Republic of Ireland.

● ● ●